Finding Jonah

A True Story of Love, Hope, and Survival

LINDA D. TWERSKY

Published by
LINDA TWERSKY
FORT LAUDERDALE, FLORIDA
www.findingjonah.com

ISBN: Print: 979-8-9897936-0-0
     E-book: 979-8-9897936-1-7

Cover and Interior: Gary A. Rosenberg • www.thebookcouple.com

Printed in the United States of America

This book is dedicated to the memory of my beloved grandparents, Sylvia and Jonah Kaufman, and my beloved mother, Helen Kaufman Twersky. Their love and guidance is in every word of this book and in all my endeavors.

It is also dedicated to the memory of my beloved father, Israel Robert Twersky, whose passion for knowledge, books and history gave my earthbound existence wings.

There are stars whose radiance is visible on Earth though they have long been extinct. There are people whose brilliance continues to light the world though they are no longer among the living. These lights are particularly bright when the night is dark. They light the way for humankind.

~Hannah Senesh

Write what must not be forgotten.

~Isabel Allende

Contents

Prologue

When you listen to a witness, you become a witness.

~Elie Wiesel

It remains a confounding mystery to many why some people survive accidents and catastrophes while others perish. Often it can be the slightest, most imperceptible shift in a position in time and space caused by a look in a different direction, a decision to be somewhere else, or a gust of wind that determines an outcome as significant as life or death.

This is a true story of catastrophic events that some survived, but most did not. Like many stories of survival, the complex events of history, the capricious nature of human behavior, the cunning and sheer grit of the participants all conspired to make it nothing less than miraculous. I was told the story by my grandmother and mother. It was their experience. It is their story. Like many human survival stories, it is one that is both surrounded by and peppered with tragedy and loss, heartbreak and horror. Since they are no longer here to tell their story, what follows is my attempt to tell it as it was told to me. My hope is that this telling of their story accurately captures a breathtaking and extraordinary time in their lives as well as a moment in the history of humankind when the world went mad.

If you only read or listen to the news daily to understand what is happening in the world, you may still be missing a great deal. Certainly, being present and living life fully in the moment with minimal time spent ruminating about the past or worrying about the possibilities of the future may be very good for mental health, but history provides a different perspective on current events. To have a deeper and wider understanding of the world beyond your doorstep, it is important to have knowledge of the continuum of history and where you fit on that continuum. For that, you need the stories of the past. Those stories, those histories, are essential for a thorough understanding of what is happening in the world at this very moment.

My grandmother, Sylvia (Shayna) Ozdoba Kaufman lived one of those stories. She was born in 1910 in a part of the world that would, in the next three decades be ravaged by not one, but two world wars. When she was two-years-old, the Titanic set sail on its ill-fated maiden voyage across the Atlantic ocean. When she was twenty-nine, Judy Garland followed the yellow brick road into the hearts of American filmgoers. But Shayna was far from those events. She lived in a tiny Polish village in Eastern Europe, called Zbojna. You would likely only have heard of it if you lived there or nearby, knew someone else who lived there, or were passing through on your way somewhere else.

She also lived in a country that Gerard Silvain and Henri Minczeles called Yiddishland in their book by the same name. It was not labelled Yiddishland on traditional maps nor did it have an army, but if a country can be defined by its language and culture, it was as real as any nation ever was. When she came into the world, she joined the over eight million people who, even though they lived in a nation known to the world as Poland or Roumania, Lithuania or Russia and spoke the language of that country, they also spoke Yiddish. After their home in the Middle East was destroyed, her ancestors combined Hebrew, their ancient tongue, with the languages of the places they moved to create Yiddish. This became their *Mame-loshn* (mother tongue). These Eastern European Yiddish speakers not only created a language, they also created a vibrant world that they baked and cured, honed and sculpted for almost a millenium. That world is now gone. Yiddishland no longer exists. My grandmother lived in that world. She was also a witness to its end.

Thanks to my beautiful *bubbe* (grandmother) and the other adults around me, my early years were embued with the world of Yiddish in stories and folklore, language and cooking, laughter and tears. It was a world whose ancient religious beliefs, flavors, songs, wisdom and zest for living she and the other Yiddish speakers brought with them to America. If that world was a magical one, and it seemed that way to me, my *bubbe* was a sorceress. She could create anything in the kitchen from the most delicious five-course meal to a three-tiered wedding cake. She could take fabric and a piece of thread and turn them into anything from a sparkling evening gown to a quilted bedspread with matching curtains. In her hands, silk became flowers and wounds were instantly healed. Nothing was beyond her capabilities.

One might think I am biased because I am her granddaughter, however, I am not alone in believing Shayna was an extraordinary woman. Everyone who knew her believed that she was. She would say that she was just an ordinary woman who had lived through extraordinary times. Yet even she recognized that not everyone had the courage, the wisdom, or the *chutzpah* (nerve) to make the choices she made and follow the path she took. Many of those people perished. Their collective stories are written in history books, shown on films and documentaries, and recorded by scholars. Their souls live on in the hearts and minds of those who know they existed. We keep the flame burning out of love and respect for those whose lives were brutally cut short and because we are aware of the dangers of forgetting history and not carrying its lessons with us into the future.

I had the supreme blessing of having my *bubbe* in my life well into my adulthood. I can still see her eyes as they gazed into mine one of the last times. She was sitting in the chair beside her bed, looking troubled as she labored to breathe. My mother had just called 911 and we were sitting with her, trying to comfort her or perhaps ourselves, as we waited for an ambulance to come. We looked at each other. We held hands. Even being unable to catch her breath, my dear *bubbe* fixed her radiant brown eyes on mine and softly said, "*shayne eygelekh* (beautiful eyes)."

She was holding on to life by a thread, but her overriding thought was of her granddaughter's beautiful eyes. That was my grandmother. What I saw in her eyes, though, was beyond beauty. Deep and brown, sad yet loving, they had borne witness to almost a century of events—many of which she did not choose to see, would never have wanted to see. Before they closed a final time, I gazed into them and was overwhelmed by my feelings of love for her and an awareness that this was a significant juncture in time. She was my link between the past and the future. Her life story, her very existence, was a doorway to my past as well as an important part of world history. I felt the pain of that doorway closing, leaving behind it all the knowledge, the lessons, the richness of her life. I did not want it to close. This book is an effort to keep that door open, even the merest crack. It is a way of bringing what I believe is an amazing and important story into the future for all who come after her. Let it be a lesson. Let her memory be a blessing.

I am Shayna's messenger. This is her story.

CHAPTER 1

1918
Zbojna, Poland

In the midst of war and crisis nothing is as clear
or as certain as it appears in hindsight.

~Barbara W. Tuchman, *The Guns of August*

In a tiny farming village in Poland whose fertile, green fields were nestled in the shadows of primeval forests of towering and ancient oaks, a woman poured whiskey for tired soldiers. The young men lifted their glasses with one hand and with the other arm lifted dusty sleeves to wipe moisture from their brows before it dripped into their eyes. Their boots as well as their clothes wore the dirt of many long and unpaved roads. She was tired, too, but soldiers were plentiful these days and selling them drinks was a good way to supplement the family's income. She also knew that being allowed to serve alcoholic beverages was a privilege bestowed upon very few establishments. Most of the Polish population was prohibited from selling spirits for religious reasons. That job was left to enterprising minorities who were able to get a license from the government. Her bakery was, in fact, the only one in their *shtetl* (village) Zbojna that offered this treat, and the soldiers knew this. They had known it throughout the war they were fighting for the last three years. It was a devastating war that would one day be known as World War I.

The woman, Sarah-Miriam, and her husband Moshe Ozdoba built their modest wooden home on the main street of Zbojna roughly ten years after their first one, which they inherited from Moshe's father who inherited it from his father, had been destroyed in a fire. As in their first home, the front room served as a bakery with a counter for completing business transactions and a café with four square, wooden tables where they served sweet and savory baked goods to all and spirits to anyone who was of age. The back part of the house, the family living area, was slightly bigger than the one in their previous home with a kitchen and three tiny bedrooms behind that. Their home was in the Jewish part of town where approximately 100 people, roughly twenty families, settled. These families, the Jewish citizens of Zbojna, earned a living as merchants, bakers, shoemakers, tailors, watchmakers and other similar professions. Not being able to own land, the Jewish people of Poland were forced for centuries to find professions other than farming which was how the rest of Zbojna's inhabitants, the Polish farmers—also numbering roughly 100 people—earned their living.

Since Poland was not an independent nation during World War I, but rather was split between warring factions—the German and Austro-Hungarian empires—its countryside and larger cities often played unwitting host to terrible battle scenes and other war operations. But this *shtetl*, and especially its bakery café on the main street, had a reputation of being a neutral spot where soldiers on any side were able to safely stop for rest and refreshment, much like a watering hole in the jungle where lions and gazelles can have a drink and share a peaceful moment. This fact helped to keep the family safe during the war and meant that it was unusual to hear gunfire in this area.

Sarah-Miriam brought drinks on a tray to a table in the corner of the bakery near the window that faced the front. The four young soldiers, her only customers at the moment, thanked her politely. Then they lifted their glasses, clinked them gently together, cried out their *saluts* and poured the burning liquid down their parched throats. The men shook their heads and laughed. They appreciated the spirits and this respite from the battlefield. They also received news that the war might be over soon. They were ready to lay down their arms and return to their families. They were also ready for another drink, but Sarah-Miriam had disappeared back into the kitchen. They lowered their shot glasses down to the table surface with four bangs. Strangely, those were followed by more loud bangs. They looked at each other. These sounds were coming from outside and they knew immediately what they were. The soldiers wasted no time and dropped to the floor.

One brave soldier slid on elbows and knees over to the window to see what was happening. The others watched him lift his head to peer out the window. They remained silent as they waited for him to report back, but were ready to grab their guns and spring into action, if necessary. The soldier dropped down as more shots were fired. He turned around to his companions and said quietly, "It looks like Haller's men and there are a half a dozen or more of them coming down the main road!" *Hallerczykis*, as many Jewish and some Polish people called them, were a group of mercenary soldiers formed in France by a Polish general, Józef Haller de Hallenburg, to fight alongside the Allies in World War I. Sometimes called the Blue army for the color of their uniforms, Haller's men were also known for indiscriminate killing and tormenting Jewish people.

"Those idiots!" cried another soldier. The soldiers in the café were German and, although fighting on a different side than the soldiers outside, were not eager to join an impromptu battle with them unless they were forced to do so. In any case, the lookout soldier was unable to determine whether there was some kind of skirmish between sides or if these soldiers were harrassing Jewish civilians, so he shook his head and said, "I can't see who they are fighting with."

Just at that moment, Sarah-Miriam came out of the kitchen with more drink and fresh slices of bread. She was shocked to see the soldiers on the floor and then she heard the shots coming from outside which had been covered up by the cooking noises and chatter in the kitchen. Her instinct made her start to run to the window to see what was happening. Before she could, the soldier nearest to her jumped up and gently, but hurriedly guided her down to the ground beside him. "There are guns firing outside, ma'am" he told her, "we have to keep down."

She dutifully obeyed. With her face closer to the wood floor than even when she was scrubbing it, her mind raced. She tried to comprehend what was happening. People are firing guns? Why here in Zbojna? Where are the children? Her mind went immediately to her two youngest,

Shayna who was seven-years-old and Hershel who was six. Sarah-Miriam panicked. They had gone outside to play. Outside. Her heart leapt in her chest like an Olympic pole-vaulter performing a record-breaking jump.

"My children are out there," she cried out, "I have to go!" She tried to get up, but the soldier's strong arms kept her from leaving the floor.

Sarah-Miriam's body jerked involuntarily as more shots were fired and one uninvited bullet entered her home by first shattering the curtained window, then lodging in the back wall of the café. "Everybody, stay down," one of the soldiers yelled. "Don't try to be a hero."

The worried mother tried to calm herself as she turned her mind to her other children. Her eldest children, sons Yehuda (called Yudke) and Shmulke, both in their twenties, were married and in their own homes. Next in line was the handsome Sholem who was fifteen and spending the day helping his father with the family wholesale business. They had left early in the morning to buy corn, wheat, and possibly livestock from farmers that Moshe would then resell to shopkeepers and other merchants. Her two older girls, Edke, thirteen, and Mirzsa, ten, were back in the kitchen baking bread.

"Edke! Mirzsa! Don't come out of the kitchen!" she cried out to her girls, tears filling her eyes as she thought about her two youngest children.

◆ ◆ ◆

Earlier that afternoon, before the arrival of the soldiers, Shayna and Hershel had returned home after completing the day's lessons at the schoolhouse down the street. They greeted their mother who was standing in the doorway, her flour-dusted hands held high in the air to keep the powdery substance off her children's hair and clothing. One by one, she kissed them as they came in the door and asked them how school was today. "Same as always, nothing new, mama" was the typical reply, although occasionally there was a juicy story they had to tell her about a classmate's older sibling getting married or a family planning a move to America.

"Do you need my help in the kitchen, mama?" Shayna asked her mother. She learned to bake almost as soon as she learned to walk and now was always eager to help in the kitchen. Sarah-Miriam smiled to herself. Her youngest daughter with her serious nature and willingness to take on adult responsibilities never failed to impress her. She seemed to be growing up so fast. "No, *mayn zis kind* (my sweet child), Edke and Mirzsa are baking today. You can go out and play, but stay close to the house." They were accustomed to hearing her add that last comment. She had no premonition of the events to come. She was, in general, a protective mother especially now that a war raged around them.

Shayna looked at her brother. Although she was a year older and a bit taller and he much more rough and tumble, the similarities in their sweet faces with their finely-chiseled noses and cupid's bow lips made most people believe they were twins. Shayna thought about what to do. Since it was a beautiful spring day, it did not take long for her to decide they should go out and pick wildflowers. Just across the street from their home lay a vast expanse of fields with an endless variety of wild-growing flowers and flowering shrubs, grasses and reeds. And mama liked to put flowers on the tables in the café.

She shared her idea with her brother who nodded eagerly and immediately the two disappeared into the back of the house, giggling as they went. They each quickly changed out of their school garments and into something more suitable for play. Shayna also grabbed a woven basket with slightly curved edges that she had made in art class. It would be perfect for holding the flowers they gathered.

On their way out, the two children stopped in the kitchen where their older sisters were helping with the day's baking. Their mother's kitchen was one of the wonders of their childhood. It was always filled with the delicious aroma of warm breads, pastries and cookies fresh from the oven. Just walking into the room made their mouths water. Shayna reached for a piece of *mandel-broyt* (almond cookie) that her sister Mirzsa had just carefully sliced into thick, even wedges, perfect for holding and dipping into hot tea. The older girl gently slapped her sister's hand. "That's for the customers," Mirzsa said, but she was smiling as she gave a piece to her brother.

The two youngsters finished their cookies before they reached the front door. Once outside, they squinted their eyes and smiled up at the bright mid-afternoon sky. A soft, but sturdy spring breeze caught Hershel's full head of dark curls and made them dance this way and that like so many marionettes on a string. Shayna's brown braids stayed neatly in place as they ran down the cobblestone path in front of their house, and across the dirt road. They always held hands, as mama taught them, when they crossed the street. Although there was not much traffic at the moment, the road was sometimes busy, mostly with horse-drawn carts and wagons, especially on weekday afternoons. On the other side of the road, Shayna let go of her brother's hand to allow him to run freely through the flowers and tall grasses. As he approached the first colorful flower he saw, he proclaimed loudly, "I'm going to pick this one for mama." His small hand grasped the base of a yellow crocus in full bloom, yanked it from its home and took it with him as he ran off in search of more.

"Wait for me," Shayna cried out, laughing, as she tried to keep up with her energetic brother running with exuberance through the grassy carpet of pink amaryllis, red poppies, white stellaria longpipes, and purple clover. Shayna skipped merrily behind him, enjoying the beauty around her as she filled her basket with colorful flowers and kept an eye out to make sure Hershel did not wander into the nearby woods. Shayna did not know if it was true, but she heard stories of children disappearing in those woods. In any case, her parents strictly forbade them from entering the woods unless in the presence of an older sibling or adult.

The two children continued this way, enjoying their wild garden, pausing only to pick flowers or point out a butterfly winging by or a bird nesting in a nearby tree, until the moment they heard gunfire. They both heard that before, but not this close. They stopped and looked in the direction of the noise. The loud bangs were followed by the sound of men shouting. Hershel looked at his older sister. They were both surprised. They understood that there was a war going on, but soldiers typically used the main road in Zbojna to go somewhere else or to stop in the café for bread and drink. They did not fight here in this village.

"Let's go home," Shayna said, sounding calmer than she was feeling. Hershel nodded in agreement and with a fistful of wild flowers, he turned to follow his sister back in the direction of their home. They walked quickly at first, but as they heard the sound of gunfire getting louder, they instinctively began to run. When they got to the main road, Shayna took her brother's hand. As she did, out of the corner of her eye, she became aware of a flurry of activity on the right. Her head automatically turned toward the direction of the commotion. That was when Shayna saw the soldiers in the blue uniforms coming their way.

◆ ◆ ◆

Inside the café it was quiet except for the muffled sound of Sarah-Miriam crying. Outside, the sound of the firing rifles was becoming more distant. The scout soldier crawled back to the window to look out and see if the threat was over. As he looked to the right, he saw the back of a horde of soldiers in blue uniforms tramping down the main street, lifting their rifles and shooting as they went. He looked to the left and saw that no more were coming their way.

"We can get up now, but let's be careful," the soldier called out, "they seem to be heading westward on the main road, and they are clearly still shooting." Before he was able to complete the sentence, Sarah-Miriam flew up and out the front door which banged loudly as it hit the outside of the wooden house. She began yelling, "Shaynaleh! Hersheleh! Where are you?"

The cobblestone pathway that leads from the front door through the front yard to the main street was neatly lined with bright, yellow crocuses that Sarah-Miriam tended carefully. But the rest of the yard was filled with all manner of tools, an old wagon and some garden supplies. It was easy to trip over something if one was not careful. The frightened mother ran through the yard, circling around the trees and shrubs that cast dancing shadows in the late afternoon sun. She first checked the east side of the yard where the shooting began and the window was hit. No children were there, just some rusting tools, a shovel, some heavy rope, and a broken wheel laying in the grass. Then she raced to the west side of the yard where an old, wooden wagon, in serious need of repair, stood horseless and missing its right front wheel. With nothing to hold up that corner, it was listing in the direction of the missing wheel which served to hide its contents from anyone standing in the yard.

"Shaynaleh! Hersheleh!" she continued to cry out.

"We're here, mama," the wagon seemed to say.

Sarah-Miriam ran to the wooden structure just as a child's hand reached out from behind it and the rest of Shayna followed. "We're in here," Shayna called out as her brother rose up beside her.

"Oh my God!" Sarah-Miriam cried as she ran to them and reached into the wagon to lift her son out. She hugged him ferociously to her as she helped Shayna climb out of the crooked wagon.

"Are you alright? Are you both alright?" their mother asked, breathlessly, scrutinizing Shayna's slender body, looking for any injuries as she gently set Hershel down and checked over his small body.

"Yes, we're fine, mama," Shayna reported as her mother, her cheeks wet with tears, looked them up and down again. At this point, Mirzsa and Edke and the soldiers joined them outside, all of them staring at the children.

"We're okay . . . Are all of you alright?" Shayna wanted to know as she looked at her sisters and noticed the soldiers.

"Yes, yes," Sarah-Miriam looked at her two older daughters for the first time since the shooting began, "yes, thank God, we are all fine . . . now, tell us what happened. What did you see?"

Shayna took a deep breath and began, "We were picking flowers in the field over there." She pointed across the main street. "Suddenly, we heard guns firing. We started to run home and, as we crossed the street, I could see they were *Hallerczykis* and they were coming toward us and they were shooting." She paused.

"Oh my God," Sarah-Miriam cried as her hands involuntarily hugged her face.

"I didn't think we had time to get away, so when I saw the wagon I grabbed Hershel and we jumped in and put our heads down," she swallowed hard, took a breath and continued. "Then we stayed very quiet and waited . . . until we heard you call our names."

Sarah-Miriam stared at her daughter in shock and disbelief, muttering something under her breath about *farshtunkene* (stinking) *Hallerczykis,* but aloud she cried, "Oy, *mayne kinder* (my children). That was so smart, Shayna! Thank God, you are both alright!" The grateful mother pulled her two youngest children to her apron and held them tightly.

The sisters, too, were in shock. They feared a very different outcome. They moved closer and wrapped their arms around their mother and younger siblings. Even the soldiers joined in, creating one large group hug. Everyone was caught up in this emotional moment except the young boy toward the center who was becoming uncomfortable with all this human contact. Hershel squirmed his way out of the jumble of people and shook himself off like a wet retriever after a long swim. He then turned back to his mother who was still attached to her daughters. She had not realized that her son escaped from the group hug. He grabbed a piece of her apron and tugged on it a few times. She did not feel it immediately, so he tugged, again, harder this time.

Sarah-Miriam finally sensed the pull on her dress and turned around. Her eyes were wide with surprise as she looked down to see her son behind her. "What is it, *tateleh* (little father)? Are you hungry maybe?" she asked. He shook his head from side to side. He was not hungry. He slipped his right arm, which was behind him, out in front. In his hand was a bouquet of crumpled, but brightly-colored wildflowers that no one noticed he was holding. He stretched out his arm and offered them to his mother.

"I picked these for you, mama," he said sweetly smiling.

CHAPTER 2

1928
Shayna

A story has no beginning or end: arbitrarily one
chooses that moment of experience from which
to look back or from which to look ahead.

~Graham Greene, *The End of the Affair*

Four months shy of her eighteenth birthday, Shayna walked down the street with the light step of the young and the hopeful, carrying a worn leather suitcase that was as old as she. The sun was the tiniest speck of yellow-gold on the horizon, and everyone in her house was still asleep when she quietly closed the door behind her. The road under her worn, but polished, leather shoes—the main street of her *shtetl*—was a dirt road that would lead her away from the place she was born. Except for trips to neighboring towns like Lomza and Ostroleka and several visits to the city of Warsaw, it was the only world she ever knew. Each step kicked up clouds of dust that had known the hooves of many horses, the wheels of many carts and wagons. She took a deep breath to steady her slender form as the hem of her long, beige cotton dress danced in the morning breeze. She was not afraid. She was sure that leaving home now was the right decision. This confidence served to quell any nerves she might have about the journey that lay ahead. Nevertheless, it was a big step and one she was taking alone.

She saw the wagon that she ordered a few days prior to take her on the first leg of her journey. It was being pulled by two old horses. The wagon stopped for her as one of the horses stamped its feet and snorted. The driver called out, "do you need some help getting on?"

She said, "No, thank you, I am fine." She put her foot in the iron step and pulled herself up into the wagon as her eyes fell on the man holding the reins. He turned to smile at her. She smiled back and noticed that the shape of his bald head matched his round, pudgy body.

"You are the young lady going to Ostrow Mazowiecki?" he asked with a deep, gruff voice that startled her slightly.

"Yes," she answered.

"Good, have a seat. Make yourself comfortable," he said, clearing his throat and sounding like he was chewing on something.

That would not be easy, she thought to herself as she looked for a spot on the hard, wooden benches. Growing up, she received more than a few splinters riding in these wooden wagons. She must have a high threshold for pain because she never cried when mama took a needle, gently dug it into her soft flesh and removed the sliver. It was not ideal transportation, but it was her only option for getting to a town or city that was large enough to have a train station. Cars were seldom seen on these rural roads in Poland and were too expensive for her anyway. She sat down carefully now, placing her suitcase on the floor in front of her and her handbag on her lap. The bag contained the *zlotys* she needed for her journey along with a chicken sandwich wrapped neatly in a cloth napkin and a few apples in case she got hungry on the road.

Patting her bag, she took a deep breath, looked up and greeted the other two people already seated in the wagon with a nod and a Mona Lisa smile. One was a bearded man with a pipe who lowered his paper briefly to nod in her direction and grunt a greeting of sorts. The other was an older lady with a brightly-colored kerchief over her shoulders and a head full of thick, grey curls that bobbed constantly in the warm morning breeze like dancing snakes. Shayna noticed that she had many suitcases and bags around her. The lady smiled at her warmly. "Such a *shayne maidel* (pretty girl)," she purred almost proudly as if she were responsible for Shayna's appealing countenance.

"Thank you," Shayna said, lowering her eyes and touching her shoulder-length wavy brown hair that was held together by a jeweled barrette at the back of her graceful neck. It was not that she was shy about getting attention for how she looked or that she did not understand that good looks were a highly valued commodity in the world. It was just that in her home a good mind and a strong back were more important than how one looked. Their attention was diverted for a moment as the driver looked back quickly to make sure all his passengers were seated, then clicked his tongue and snapped the reins to signal his horses to begin trotting.

"And where are you going by yourself, young lady?" the older woman cooed.

Shayna paused for a moment. She did not mind spending time in light banter with strangers or anyone for that matter. Most people, in fact, found her to be a very charming and articulate conversation partner. It was just that right now her mind was on other things. "I'm going to Warsaw to visit my cousins," Shayna answered, lying in an effort to shorten the conversation.

"Oh, the big city," the older lady clucked. "I'm on my way to stay with my daughter who lives in Nowogrod. She is going to have . . ." Just then the right front wheel of the wagon dipped into a hole in the road and lurched the wagon suddenly to the right, turning over several of the woman's bags and letting loose a cascade of parcels across the wagon floor.

"Oy," the woman cried out, "all the presents!"

Shayna quickly put her handbag down on the bench, jumped up and began to collect some of the runaway items. Even the paper reader put his pipe and paper down to lend a hand. The woman was very distressed, but so grateful to have two rescuers. Finally, when all the items were back beside her on the bench, she thanked Shayna and the man profusely and began fussing over her bags, carefully putting everything back and checking and double-checking to make sure all items were secure. This gave Shayna a welcome opportunity to sit back, take a deep breath, and get lost in her thoughts. She noticed for the first time that the air smelled sweet. Maybe because she was leaving home and going farther away than she had ever gone, her senses were sharply tuned in to everything around her. She watched as the scenery outside the wagon drifted by, changing from the modest wooden homes of her *shtetl* to lush green farmland, grassy fields, and beyond that, the tall trees of the deep forest. She sighed and settled herself as best she could for the long ride on the hard bench.

◆ ◆ ◆

The night before, Hershel sat on the edge of her bed watching his older sister fold clothes neatly into an open leather suitcase that lay near him. The suitcase was an old one that had been around since she was a baby, but it was just the right size and weight for a young woman who was about to *shlep* around the world even though it certainly did not hold all the clothes she owned. She spent the summer she turned fifteen attending a sewing school in nearby Nowogrod where she quickly established herself as a talented seamstress with deft fingers and a creative style. She learned to make everything from elaborate wedding dresses to curtains, quilts and holiday clothes for men and women. Since then there had not been a moment when she did not have at least four sewing projects underway   a skirt, dress or blouse for herself, an item of clothing for a friend or someone in the family, and items for customers who were eager to pay for her beautiful, high-quality work. She loved creating and being productive and she enjoyed the independent feeling that earning money gave her. She folded the *zloty* she received carefully into a hand-sized satchel that had a metal clasp to open and close it. Her parents gave it to her when she started working. The satchel was crocheted with brightly-colored orange and yellow flowers on one side and she kept it in the top drawer of her dresser. She opened the drawer, lifted it out and moved it to a leather handbag that she was taking with her tomorrow on her journey.

At sixteen, Hershel was developing masculine edges to the fine, almost delicate features of his face that would ultimately serve to distinguish him from his lookalike older sister. The two of them were inseparable as children and continued to stay close, especially as their older siblings began to make their way in the adult world. Although he had plenty of friends and cousins to play with, the more grown-up and feminine interests that recently began to distance her from him over the last few years had been difficult for him. He just started getting used to that when, overhearing an argument between Shayna and her parents earlier that day, he discovered that she was going away.

"Mama and *tati* are not happy that you're leaving," he said as if those words would have the power to change her mind.

She looked at him with affection mixed with some big-sister impatience and asked, "Remember, I told you why I had to go?"

She had explained everything to him very carefully after he heard part of the discussion she had with her parents. There was an old, established custom in Poland that a girl must not get married until her older sisters are married. Shayna's oldest sister, Edke, married several years ago, when she was eighteen, but her next oldest sister, Mirzsa, was almost twenty and still had no prospects. Their father, Moshe Ozdoba, a very religious and serious man, thought it of vital importance to respect the custom. He approved wholeheartedly of the proud and handsome Jonah Kaufman for his beautiful and headstrong Shayna—even felt it was *bashert* (meant to be)—but believing it would be bad luck for Mirzsa if her younger sister were to marry before her, he strictly forbid Shayna from doing so.

"And mama and *tati* understand why I am going," she continued. "They even gave me some money for the trip."

"OK, but why do you have to go so far away . . . all the way to Mon-te . . . ?" his tongue faltered on the strange sounding name.

"Montevideo, Uraguay," Shayna filled in the blanks, and continued, "It's a beautiful place in South America and we have cousins there. I have to go away because, well, I've always wanted to see the world. Besides, I don't want to stay here and watch Jonah marry someone else. It is very possible that he will not wait for me. Why should he? He is too good. Someone else will steal him away."

Either because she loved him so much or because it was true or both, Shayna genuinely believed that Jonah Kaufman was too eligible, too desirable a bachelor to wait for her older sister to marry first. It was not that she did not have faith in the strength of their love. They had virtually been together constantly since he and his family first moved to

Zbojna when the two were children and began playing together. Childhood affection blossomed into much more and now even as young adults they were rarely apart. It was just that romantic notions about love were concepts that did not make sense to her. In her practical and realistic mind, she did not imagine Jonah would wait for her. Certainly not if other women were tempting him not to wait. What if one of them was too convincing? She also had no idea when her sister was going to marry. She knew Jonah was an ambitious man. Why would he wait? No, she could not stay here and watch her Jonah get grabbed by another woman. The mere thought was unbearable. Let her be halfway across the world if that were to happen.

Hershel got quiet for a few minutes letting his sister's passionate words sink in. Shayna resumed packing, and then she added, "You might want to think about leaving, too, when you have an opportunity. There is a better, more modern world out there with new and wonderful things to discover, far away from our tiny *shtetl.*" Shayna knew this because she loved to read, was, in fact, reading by the age of four. She would visit the lending library down the street and open many a magical book, written in Yiddish, to satisfy her thirst for knowledge, take her to faraway places and fill her head with stories of historic events and fascinating people. The library was in a charming wooden building that functioned as a synagogue during *Shabbes* (Sabbath) and the other Jewish holidays, but was also a schoolhouse and a library on Sundays and weekdays.

Shayna looked up from her packing and reminded her brother of their many cousins and other people they knew who left Poland and now live in New York City. He thought about this and countered with, "Well, *tati* went to America before we were born to check it out, but he decided he didn't want to live there." It was true. Their father followed two of his brothers to America in 1909, the year before Shayna was born, to see for himself if it was a suitable place, that is, Yiddish enough to raise his growing family. He did not.

Shayna shrugged, "Maybe he felt New York City was too big for him. Who knows? But it's not just about living in a big, modern city versus a tiny, backwards village, it's also about leaving a country where we are clearly not wanted and we don't have the same opportunities that others have." She reminded him of the *Hallerczyki* incident in which they almost died, that did, in fact, kill one of their neighbors. She also reminded him that their father and other Jewish people pay higher taxes to the government than do non-Jewish Polish citizens.

He frowned, at a loss for a good reply. "But you'll be on a big ship . . . all by yourself," he mused out loud.

Shayna was lost in thought for a moment. Her decision to leave her home had not been made lightly. And for a seventeen-year-old girl to travel from her *shtetl* in Poland to Montevideo, Uraguay half a world away took very careful planning. Long before the idea to leave home started to take shape, she had been exchanging letters with her cousin Mindy who was a few years older than she and whose parents, seeking a better life, had moved from Poland to Montevideo in 1922. Mindy's letters, filled with stories about parties and social events, theaters and museums, made life in that city sound idyllic. Still, her decision to move there was based solely on her circumstances here in Zbojna, that is, her inability to marry the man she loved. If she was able to marry him, as they both wished, she would not be leaving. Or, better still, maybe they would be going to the faraway place together.

"I won't be by myself, silly," she answered as she carefully tucked one of her favorite cotton dresses into the suitcase. "There will be lots of other people there."

"Yes, but they will all be strangers," he said moodily, correcting her.

"Yes, I know," she responded as she lifted her head and looked out the window. Two courting bluebirds air danced out of a tree and disappeared into a red-gold sunset. *How lucky they are to have each other*, she thought to herself. *I'm not concerned about the strangers, only that Jonah will not be with me.*

At that moment, their mama, Sarah-Miriam, appeared in the doorway, drying her hands on her apron. She frowned and pursed her lips when she saw what her daughter was doing.

"Hersheleh, dinner is almost ready. Shayna, I could use some help in the kitchen. Your sister is not feeling well," she said. Hershel could already smell the wonderful aroma of her chicken soup with its juicy logs of sweet carrots and fluffy matzoh balls bobbing in the savory broth. He wasted no time in jumping off the bed and heading for the kitchen, eager to fill his belly with his mama's delicious cooking.

"Of course, mama, I'll be right there," she responded as she stopped what she was doing to go and help her mother. She had time to finish packing after dinner. The suitcase was almost full anyway, so she needed to leave many of her clothes behind. Maybe Mirzsa could use them. The two willowy, raven-haired sisters were about the same size. The sun was disappearing from the horizon as she lit the kerosene lamp beside her bed and looked at the darkening, shadowy world outside her window. The weight of knowing that by doing what she believed she needed to do, she was causing her mother so much pain bore down on her like a thousand sacks of potatoes. She took one quick look at her opened suitcase, then stepped out of her room to help her mother and eat one last meal with her family before she left.

◆　◆　◆

The wagon slowed to accommodate traffic on the bridge over the Narew river. Shayna knew this river well. She had crossed it many times and, on occasion, played nearby when her family spread a blanket to relax and picnic on its grassy banks. The wide river meandered south from Northeastern Poland and separated Shayna's immediate family on the west side, in Zbojna, from aunts, uncles and cousins who lived east of the river in towns like Nowogrod and Lomza.

It was her wagon's turn to cross the bridge and Shayna watched as the horses stepped gingerly off the dirt road and onto the cobblestone surface of the bridge, making a hollow clop-clop-clop sound with their hooves. She looked over at the woman who, in an attempt to secure her packages, placed her bags on the bench, laid herself out over them and seemed to have fallen asleep with her head on her outstretched arm. Shayna smiled to herself and enjoyed the quiet. A V-shaped flock of Greylag geese soared high overhead framed by a bright, blue sky dotted with big, cotton clouds. *Where were they going,* she wondered, *and how far had they already traveled? Was it as far as she was about to travel?* The first leg of her trip, the road to Warsaw, was just over ninety miles, but she would not go that entire distance in this wagon. That would have taken the better part of a day—at least twenty hours—maybe even longer with stops for people and animals to take rest and refreshment. Rather, later this afternoon, the wagon was going to deliver her forty miles south of here, to a town called Ostrow Mazowiecki, where she would step off the wagon with her suitcase and handbag, brush off her skirt, pay the driver, and board a train to Warsaw.

Her town and many of the towns she passed on this first part of her trip were too small to have a train station. These and the myriad other villages of Poland lagged behind much of the rest of Europe in twentieth-century development and modernization. *At the moment my train leaves the station in Warsaw,* she thought to herself, *I will be farther away from Zbojna than I have ever been and much closer to the modern world.* In Zbojna, the train passed through on the other side of the main street where she lived, but it did not stop there. Many times in her childhood, she lifted her head and thrilled to the sight and the sound of the great black locomotive approaching. As it passed her at lightning speed, it made her breath catch in her throat and made her think of the exciting stories she often read of faraway places.

She smiled to herself as she realized that she would soon be boarding one of those trains. In the meantime, as the wagon approached its next stop, the *shtetl* Nowogrod, she had plenty of time to let her mind review her plans. She needed to be meticulous in that planning both for her well-being and to convince her dubious parents that she was capable of this undertaking. From Warsaw, she explained to them, she planned to travel by train to the port city of Hamburg. From there, she would embark on her greatest adventure yet—traveling half-way around the world to South America aboard a ship. Originally, she planned to sail from the port city of Danzig which was a shorter distance from Warsaw than was Hamburg.

She thought better of it when she realized that although Danzig was not a Polish city, Poland had special rights there and she heard the authorities might not allow an underage girl to board a ship by herself. That was not the case in Germany. When she wrote to her distant cousins in Hamburg and their responding letters were so warm and welcoming, the decision was easy. She would go to Hamburg and stay with her cousins until she booked passage to Montevideo.

Shayna felt good that everything was carefully and neatly planned. Except for Jonah. She hated keeping the truth from him, but she knew that she could not tell him of her plans. He would never have let her go and Shayna believed that she had to do this. Can she allow herself to hope, even a little, that he will follow her there? Jonah was a good son and the youngest son—the only one still at home. He was devoted to his mother and father. On the one hand, she could not imagine him leaving them. On the other hand, she knew that he loved her. She looked at her watch. Jonah would be waking up soon. She wondered when her sisters were going to tell him that she left. It will probably happen sometime later today, but by then she will be far away—far from his eyes, those eyes she loved, and his beautiful mouth that would have spoken the words that might have kept her from leaving.

CHAPTER 3

1928
Jonah

*It is so much darker when a light goes out
than if it had never shone.*

~John Steinbeck

The smallest sliver of early morning sunlight broke through a tiny opening in the otherwise closed curtains hanging over the window on the wall beside Jonah's bed and fell across his handsome face. The square-jawed twenty-year-old squinted and gently rubbed his sleepy, warm-brown eyes with two strong fists. He looked at his watch on the nightstand beside his bed. It was almost eight o'clock in the morning. His parents must have let him sleep late. The last few days, he had been working long hours with his father in the older man's international lumber export business, and in the evening spending time with friends until the morning hours. They were probably worried that their youngest son was not getting enough rest.

He stood up and stretched, wincing slightly as he pulled the tight, sore muscles in his neck and upper arms. It was clearly a case of overuse since he spent the better part of yesterday wielding a heavy axe to chop down very thick and tall coniferous trees. It was business as usual deep in the forest with his father, Hershel, who was still known far and wide as Hershel *the Royte* (the Red) for his full red beard, even though it now contained as much grey as flaming red woven into its glorious strands. They received several orders from customers who needed wood. Hershel usually hired laborers to do this back-breaking work. At fifty-six, he was no longer able to do it himself and even though his son was willing and strong enough to help, he wanted Jonah to focus on the business aspects of the operation. "The business needs you for your clever mind and salesmanship. Save your back, my son," he said when Jonah grabbed an axe to help the men. Nevertheless, he was proud of his muscular son, and Jonah enjoyed the physical exertion. It was breathtaking to be the cause of one of these mighty pine, spruce, fir, or cedar trees—some over a hundred years old and standing as tall as ninety feet—trembling, then swaying and eventually toppling down to earth with a great thud. He learned how to control the speed and the direction of that fall by carefully directing each blow of the axe to just the right spot and depth in the tree.

The downed tree would then be stripped of its leaves and branches. Sometimes, if a customer requested, the bark was removed, revealing the smooth wood beneath. This process brought out the distinctive fragrance of each different kind of tree. The logs were then tied together with heavy twine, usually four at a time, creating a raft-like structure that floated down the river. Boatmen were hired to guide the logs and ensure that they were delivered into the right hands. Children playing along the river bank shouted and waved as they watched the giant logs floating downstream.

Today, though, Jonah would not be accompanying his father to the forest. Instead, he was going to take his mother to the thermal spring waters just northeast of their town for her weekly spa treatment. The poor woman had been ailing for the past year and while nothing seemed to cure the pain and stiffness, these baths gave her some relief. The doctor called it rheumatism, but he and his father worried that it might be something worse as they watched the slight, but robust Chaya-Raisa wither and grow frail.

◆ ◆ ◆

Like Shayna, Jonah was the sixth of seven children with three older brothers and two older sisters. One difference, though, was that his younger sibling was a sister while Shayna's was a brother. The other difference was that most of Jonah's older siblings moved to America. Village life in Poland did not please them as they grew into young men so much so that the many stories of life in America, the *Goldene Medinah* (Golden

Land), beckoned with a powerful lure. Shlemke who at thirty-five was the oldest brother, married Sarah-Gitta when they were both just eighteen and was the first sibling to move to New York six years ago. They already had three children, Abraham (Little Abe), Raye, and Edith. Srolke, thirty-three, followed them two years later, took the name Irving and married Nettie. The next in line, Abe, born Avram, now twenty-five, married Rose in 1923 and followed his older brothers to America just last year. Back in Poland was Esther, twenty-two, who just married Izzy Finkelstein, her second cousin on her mother's side. They were getting ready to move to America. And Rachel, twenty, married Mayer Nissky and moved to Nowogrod. Living at home with their parents, Chaya-Raisa and Hershel, were Jonah and sister Rivka, fourteen.

Jonah missed his older brothers, but the large gap in their ages ensured that he was accustomed to their being out of the house. Besides, it was exciting getting their letters and hearing how they were building new lives in such an amazing place. It sounded so promising, so full of opportunities. He hoped to follow them . . . someday. In the meantime, as the only son left at home, certain expectations and responsibilities landed directly on him, filling his schedule to the brim. He did not mind that he needed to put off more long-term ambitions for the familial responsibilities that his brothers, by default, passed onto him. For one thing, Jonah had a heart as big as the Carpathian mountains. He was quick to act on behalf of people he loved in whatever capacity he was able. It was just his way. Then, of course, there was Shayna.

He smiled when he thought of her. He could not help himself. She was . . . well, she was everything. They met eight years ago when his family moved to Zbojna from Ostroleka, a town situated just South of Zbojna and across the river. She was eight-years-old and he was eleven. From that very first moment he saw her, he was smitten by her charm and her no-nonsense intelligence. She was the only girl in the village who said exactly what she was thinking, and even when it was not pleasant, people never seemed to mind. There was just something about her. He always wanted to be near her . . . was happy, as long as he was near her. He did not think about why. What did it matter? He was a practical man. All he knew was that every cell in his body danced to the music of her voice and his soul basked in the light of her eyes. Shayna. His Shayna. Everyone in the village knew they were meant to be together. They saw it. It was impossible to miss.

◆　◆　◆

Ignoring his sore muscles, Jonah washed, shaved, and dressed quickly. Instead of one of his lumberjack work shirts, today he put on a nice, crisp cotton shirt that his mother ironed for him. He swept a black comb covered with just a bit of hair crème a few times through the thick, dark waves atop his head that his mother loved to remind him were magnificent. After taking a quick look in the mirror to be sure his hair was in place, he strode into the kitchen and took a deep breath filled with the delicious smells of breakfast—frying eggs, slices of freshly-baked challah, smoked white fish, pot cheese, and cherry preserves. At the kitchen table, his father sat reading one of his favorite Yiddish dailies while drinking black coffee that he loved to sip with a sugar cube in his mouth. Rivka sat on the left side of her father, her chin leaning into her left hand and spinning a hard-boiled egg on her plate with her right.

"Rivka, dear, please stop playing with your egg—it will get cold," Chaya-Raisa pleaded as she glanced over at her daughter." She immediately turned to her son, smiled and said, "Good morning, *tatele* (little father), two eggs over easy this morning?" She never wore the pain that he knew she was experiencing. Nevertheless, he saw the telltale signs of it in the tight lines of her face and the rigid way she held her body. He wanted to tell her that he would just have some fish this morning, but she looked so eager to please him.

"Yes, please, mama," he said as he placed his hands on her thin shoulders and kissed her gently on the cheek. Then he walked over to the table and tousled his sister's still uncombed mass of dark curls. Rivka jerked her head away, groaned and gave her brother a half-annoyed smirk as she continued to play with her egg. He pulled out a chair and sat down on the right side of his father as he smiled and winked at his sister whom their parents fondly call the *bandit* (troublemaker). She earned the name by faithfully demonstrating that she could always be counted on to do precisely what her parents did not want her to do.

"Good morning, *tati*," Jonah said to his father as he tucked a corner of a napkin into his collar and patted the rest of it down to protect his shirt.

"Son, it is a good morning," Hershel emphasized the 'is' as he leaned back in his chair, slapped his hands to his chest, looked at his son and continued, "We have each other, we have fresh air to breathe, good food to eat, and a successful business. God is good to us."

Rivka mumbled something and rolled her eyes.

"What was that, young lady?" Hershel asked his daughter.

"Nothing," was all she said in response.

Hershel turned back to his youngest son and announced with a twinkle in his eye, "you look well rested, my boy."

Jonah smiled back at his father, "Yes, I am . . . thanks for letting me sleep in today."

Hershel took another sip of coffee and cleared his throat, "You have been working very hard helping me with the business, which I appreciate. In fact, I am expecting a slow day today because we filled two big orders yesterday. As we discussed, today will be a good day to bring your mother to the mineral baths."

"Of course . . . God-willing, it will help her," Jonah agreed, smiling at his mother.

Hershel responded with, "*Alevai* (may it be so)."

Chaya-Raisa brought Jonah his eggs, then sat down at the table opposite her husband. She had no food in front of her and just sipped her coffee. Even though they did not approve, Jonah and his father did not protest the lack of food on her plate. They knew it would do no good. Jonah thanked his mother, then eagerly took a thick slice of challah, covered it with some cheese and egg and began eating. With a mouth full of his breakfast, he turned to Hershel who was back to reading his paper and asked, "So, what is happening in the world, *tati*?"

"What is happening in the world?" Hershel repeated the question. "That is a good question," he continued with his eyes on the newspaper. Hershel received three of the thirty Yiddish daily newspapers that circulated in Poland since 1918—one in the morning and two in the late afternoon—except on *Shabbes*.

"Let's see . . . America is continuing to lower the number of immigrants they will allow in. Your brother, Avram, and his wife just made it there by a hair's breadth," Hershel said with a sigh. He was momentarily overcome with the sadness of missing his sons and their families, but he understood why they wanted to leave.

"And our president," he continued, "God bless him—is trying to transform Poland into a modern, multi-cultural nation. If only that would happen, then we Jews might hope to be treated like real Polish citizens." Poland had, once again, become an independent nation after the end of World War I. President Josef Pilsudski and his centrist government was attempting to move the country in a more liberal and open-minded direction. This would bode well for the minorities in Poland of which the Jewish people—at 10% of the population—constituted the largest group. Unfortunately, other political entities espoused a more antisemitic agenda and were fighting against the president. They saw themselves as true patriots and had a vision of their country as one with a purely Polish national character with no room for minorities.

The family's discussion about the state of affairs of the Jewish people in Poland was interrupted suddenly by a knock at the door. They all looked at each other. They were not expecting visitors. Jonah looked at his watch. He did not think it was the driver of the horse-drawn wagon he arranged to transport him and his mother to the mineral springs. That was not due for at least 30 minutes. Hershel shrugged. He did not have any appointments this morning.

"Rivka, it must be your friends stopping for you on the way to school," Chaya-Raisa surmised. *Mama was probably right*, Rivka thought, so she jumped up, egg untouched, and kissed both her parents. Revealing the full length of her tongue to her brother, she grabbed her schoolbooks and left the kitchen. Hershel seemed to take that as his signal to leave, too. "Well, I'm off to the salt mines," he announced as he pushed himself up from the table and kissed his wife. "*For gezunterheyt* (have a good trip) my wife and son. I hope the baths prove beneficial today, dear." But before he took even one step, three figures appeared in the kitchen doorway, and one of them was Rivka.

Jonah smiled, then stood up, "Good morning, Edke. Good morning, Mirzsa."

"Good morning, girls," Hershel chimed in as he straightened his clothes and put his wallet in his pocket. Jonah and his parents were surprised to see Shayna's sisters in their kitchen at this hour of the morning, especially with such serious looks on their faces. "Is everything alright?" Jonah asked with concern in his voice. Edke looked over at her sister, then turned back to Jonah and his parents, "Oh, yes, well . . . we just wanted to talk to you."

There was a pause, then Chaya-Raisa asked diplomatically, "Is this something private?"

"No," both sisters said in unison as they shook their heads and looked at Jonah.

"Well, why don't we all sit down," Chaya-Raisa said as she began clearing the breakfast table. "Would you girls like something to drink— some tea or coffee?"

"No, thank you, Mrs. Kaufman, we just had breakfast and we can't stay very long," Mirzsa answered as both girls took a seat at the table. Rivka started to join them until her mother looked over at her and said, "You, young lady, go to school." The fourteen-year-old was about to protest, but her father intervened by saying, "Rivka, please listen to your mother." She looked dejected and said, "Everyone always treats me like a child."

"Come, I'll walk out with you," Hershel said, "Good-bye friends and family. I will see you later." He put his arm around his daughter and they left.

Jonah and Chaya-Raisa sat silently and politely as they waited for the girls to speak. The two sisters looked at each other, then at Jonah and

Chaya-Raisa. The younger one began to stutter, "When I got up this morning . . . well, I couldn't believe that she really did it." Mirzsa put her hand on her sister's arm, then jumped in to get to the point, "Jonah, we came over to tell you that Shayna left."

Jonah looked perplexed, "Left? *Vos meynstu* (What do you mean)? Left to go where?"

"She went to South America . . . to a city called Montevideo in Uruguay," Edke blurted out.

Jonah, who was now becoming as agitated as he was perplexed, said, "She didn't tell me she was going anywhere. When did she go? Why did she go?"

"The thing is," Mirsza continued, "she didn't want you to know because she was afraid you wouldn't let her go . . . I mean, that you would convince her to stay. She was planning it for a while, but, honestly, until I woke up this morning, I wasn't sure she would really do it." Jonah frowned. The secretive nature of Shayna's actions disturbed him almost more than her actually leaving.

"Why would I stop her? Don't you have cousins in Montevideo? Did she go to visit them? How long will she be away?" Jonah asked needing much more information.

"Yes, she is going to be staying with them," this time Edke answered, "but she did not say for how long."

Mirzsa put her head down and began to fuss with a napkin on the table in front of her as she confessed out loud, "it's my fault."

"Your fault?" Chaya-Raisa who had been watching her son's reaction entered the conversation. "Why would it be your fault, dear?"

"Because," Mirzsa cried out, "our father won't let her marry Jonah until I am married. And she is afraid he won't wait for her." As soon as she said those words, her face turned bright red and the pretty features of her face contorted as if she was about to burst out crying. Edke moved her chair closer to her younger sister and draped an arm over her shoulder to comfort her.

Jonah was silent as he stood up and began to pace. Suddenly, the room did not seem big enough to hold all his intense emotions. He and Shayna talked about marriage, of course, and he was aware of Moshe Ozdoba's edict. But had he been so busy taking care of his family that he did not see the signs that she was leaving? He was even more confused now because he was not sure if he was more upset with her or with himself.

"When did she leave?" Jonah asked, calculating in his mind how far away she must be by now. Did he dare try to go after her? Could he even find her or catch up to her? He looked over at his poor mother who had tears welling up in her eyes and realized the wagon would soon arrive to take them to the mineral springs. He froze. He could not abandon his mother.

"She left hours ago . . . while everyone in the house was sleeping," Mirzsa told him. "We're so sorry Jonah. We thought you should know."

For the first time in his life, Jonah felt his world turn upside down and inside out. His mind raced and he thought he was going to lose his breakfast. As he planted himself back down in a chair, the palms of his hands rose involuntarily and squeezed the sides of his temples. He knew Shayna was a strong woman. It was one of the many things he loved about her. Still, he had a hard time coping with the fact that she left this way. He took a deep breath and let it out with a sigh to gain his composure. His mother watched him. Edke watched him. Mirzsa's eyes were focused somewhere on the tabletop. After what seemed like a very long time, he looked at Shayna's sisters and said softly, "I appreciate that you both came to tell me."

Then he turned to Mirzsa and added, "This is no one's fault. Shayna makes her own decisions."

CHAPTER 4

1928–1930
Montevideo, Uraguay

The cure for anything is salt water—sweat, tears, or the sea.

~Isak Dinesen, *Seven Gothic Tales*

With her suitcase by her side, Shayna leaned over the railing of the huge ship as it docked in the port of Montevideo. She thrilled to the smell of the salty, sea breeze that caressed her face and the unfamiliar cries of the seagulls that flew overhead. It was almost three weeks from the day she left home. She was now on the other side of the equator and almost 8,000 miles from her *shtetl*. She marveled that she was really here. Two women on the ship passed by and waved to her, "Bye, Shayna, remember to keep in touch!" She smiled and waved back to them. Shayna always made friends wherever she went, so this time was no exception. She had spent some pleasant moments—eating, sitting in the sun and playing cards—with several nice people on the ship from Hamburg. Some of them were moving to Montevideo from towns in Eastern Europe. Others were on their way to visit family or returning from a visit with family. Still others were just on a sightseeing vacation to the subtropical destination.

Mindy Lipkovich, who married a year ago and was now Berkowitz, arrived at the port with her husband, Aaron, just before the ship carrying her cousin was ready to allow passengers to come ashore. Mindy searched for Shayna in the swarm of faces on the long line of people waiting to disembark from the oceanliner. "There must be hundreds of people waiting to get off this ship," she said to her husband. But she refused to give up and and was finally rewarded when she recognized her cousin's porcelain skin and delicate features in the crowd. Mindy waved and jumped up and

29

down to get Shayna's attention as she pointed her out to her husband. "There she is—recognize her from the picture?" Mindy asked. Then the line began to move as people came off the ship. When Shayna finally reached them, the cousins embraced warmly. Even though they had been writing to one another for years, they had not seen each other since they were children. Mindy introduced her husband, then wanted to know all about her trip as Aaron bowed gallantly to their visitor.

Shayna told them that being at sea was unlike any experience she ever had. When the ship was at sea with no shore in sight, there was no familiar point of reference from which to find balance. Her senses became overwhelmed by the sheer force of the salt-laden wind on her face, the baking heat of the sun on her neck and shoulders, and the expanse of sparkling water around her. "No wonder people once believed the world was flat," she announced, "the horizon seemed like the edge of the world . . . even though it was as beautiful as it was terrifying." She told them that the motion of the ship caused a thousand dancing fairies with lacy wings to perform impressively high ballet leaps in her stomach, reaching even to her throat. She found herself taking deep gulps of air at times until the feeling subsided. After two days, the fairies ended their performance and paraded off stage. She had, as they say, gotten her sea legs.

Later that night, Shayna and Mindy talked and laughed into the night while Shayna unpacked her suitcase. Her cousin lived in a large apartment with three bedrooms, two of which they used as rentals, but were currently vacant. Her husband worked as a clerk in an accountancy in downtown Montevideo while she stayed at home and managed the room rental business. Mindy showed Shayna to the first room down the hall. It had soft yellow lace curtains and a double bed covered with a white Matelasse bedspread that was decorated with pillows embroidered in every color of the rainbow. Shayna smiled when she saw the vase of fresh flowers on the bedside table. She reminded Mindy that she fully intended to pay room and board as soon as she got a job. "We'll talk about that later," her cousin responded good naturedly. Mindy watched Shayna take her dresses out of the suitcase and hang them in the closet. She remarked how talented a seamstress Shayna was. But, she added with a wink, "You're going to need some fancier dresses and shoes for Montevideo. We're more colorful here than the girls are in Poland. I know you want to start looking for a job, but let's go shopping tomorrow." Shayna nodded her approval.

The girls hugged and said goodnight. Shayna closed the door behind her cousin and got ready for bed, but she was not ready for sleep. She was much too excited from her world travels and there was so much on her mind. There was definitely someone on her mind. She got out her stationery and a fountain pen, made herself comfortable at the writing table in front of the window and began to write Jonah a long letter.

◆　◆　◆

The next morning, Shayna and Aaron sat at the kitchen table, sipping coffee, with a map of Montevideo spread before them as Mindy stood over tomato, onion, and cheese omelets sizzling in a frying pan. Aaron pointed out the important sites of the city, including the business district, the shopping district which was in the Old City that also contained government buildings, museums, and the most interesting architecture. Shayna listened intently as he explained this exciting new place to her. Aaron spoke to her in her familiar tongue of Yiddish even though there were many languages present in this kitchen. Shayna spoke Yiddish, Polish and some Russian while Mindy and Aaron spoke Yiddish, Polish and Spanish fluently. But like most Eastern European Jews at that time they were most comfortable with Yiddish. So, that was how they chose to communicate. Shayna brought up the fact that, because she intended to stay and work in Montevideo for an extended period of time, she hoped to add Spanish to her repertoire of tongues.

"Tonight, when I get home from work," Aaron offered, "I will start teaching you Spanish, if you'd like."

"Thank you," Shayna responded gratefully, "I would appreciate that."

"Okay," Mindy announced, "omelets are ready." Aaron picked up the map, folded it carefully, and put it away. Mindy brought the warm omelets over to the table along with a basket of rye bread and muffins and a bowl of fruit for dessert. The three of them sat quietly for a while, enjoying the delicious breakfast. Then they began to talk about family members they had in common back in Eastern Europe and the ones who moved here, like Mindy's parents, who Shayna would be seeing soon. Mindy's father and Shayna's mother were siblings who grew up together in Zbojna. Shayna told them about her parents and how she learned to bake and serve in their café. She spoke about her siblings and her life in Zbojna. She did not talk about Jonah and Mindy did not ask. She only told Mindy that she wanted to mail a letter home.

"Also, as I mentioned in my letters," Shayna added, "I am hoping to find work as a seamstress."

Aaron jumped in and said, "Tonight you can look for seamstress jobs in the Yiddish paper and I will show you where they are on the map. Then, if you want, I can even take some time off work tomorrow or the next day and show you where those places are."

"That is very kind of you, Aaron," Shayna responded politely, "I would really appreciate that." At that moment, Shayna noticed that Mindy was staring at her husband, and she was not smiling. *What do we have here?* Shayna wondered. Aaron seemed like a nice guy who was just being kind to her. She certainly had no designs on him. Maybe her cousin possessed a jealous streak or there was something in her relationship with her husband that made her feel that way. Whatever it was, Shayna wanted to keep an eye on this situation and be sensitive to her cousin.

Later that morning, the girls ventured out. Clutching their handbags, they made their way to the center of the city. Shayna was delighted by the new wonderland of sites and sounds that surrounded her. In every direction, she saw stylishly-dressed people, magnificent architecture, posh clothing stores and fine eateries whose windows displayed a panorama of the treats and delicacies they served. As she and her cousin strolled through the bustling city streets of Montevideo, Shayna spun around, looking up and down, then this way and that to take it all in. She closed her eyes and opened them again. Unbelievably, the scene was still there. Lovely scents filled her nose as perfumed men and women walked by.

Shayna was enchanted. She had been in this lively city for a short time, but already she was feeling like she could be happy living here.

"Let's go in here," Mindy said as she pointed to a store with rows and rows of brightly colored dresses, skirts and blouses. A counter in the center of the store held more sparkling, dangling bracelets, necklaces and earrings than Shayna had seen in her lifetime. She was almost overwhelmed as she walked up and down the aisles, taking in all the dazzling colors and stopping to feel the different textures of exquisite fabrics that were new to her. *What would it be like to work with these fabrics?* she wondered to herself. Mindy held up a bright yellow blouse trimmed with red and orange embroidered flowers on the pockets and the collar. "What do you think of this one?" she wanted to know. Shayna's eyes widened, but she wrinkled her nose, and answered, "Oh no, not for me. Those colors are too bright." She held up a light pink blouse, instead, that sported a more subtle black trim to show Mindy. "But this is just for fun, today," Shayna reminded her cousin, "I won't be buying anything new until I start earning money." Mindy smiled and continued looking through the racks, determined to find something attractive and affordable for her cousin.

◆　◆　◆

The next few days passed quickly as Shayna settled into her new home. She had not been there long when the first of many letters arrived from Jonah in which he told her how much he loved her and missed her. He did not seem angry with her for leaving without even a 'good-bye', but she knew from corresponding with her sisters, that Jonah was terribly upset when they told him she left. She missed him, too, and felt awful leaving him the way she did, but she did not miss Poland. Life was so vastly different here than life was there. She was not one for wishful thinking, but her mind could not help wondering . . . what if Jonah were here to share this with her. The nightlife, the art museums, the theater—those things did not exist in her Polish *shtetl*. As Aaron promised, he helped her get interviews and make her way around the city. She was Mindy's cousin, but Aaron was acting as though he was hers, too. She found a job she loved through the Yiddish newspaper, working for a dress designer. The woman's shop was less than two miles from Mindy and Aaron's apartment. She was excited to tell Jonah in her next letter to him. As much as she missed her family and wished Jonah were here, this adventure was much too thrilling for her to feel anything even resembling homesickness.

One evening when Shayna came home after work, exhausted but happy, she found Mindy sitting on her living room sofa and softly crying. Shayna raced over, sat down beside her and asked, "What is it, sweetie, what happened?"

"Nothing happened, I'm fine," Mindy stammered, wiping her downcast eyes, and clearly avoiding Shayna's.

"But something must be wrong to make you sit and cry like this," Shayna said.

"It's just hard sometimes," Mindy said as she choked back tears.

"What's hard?" Shayna asked and genuinely wanted to know.

"It's just that Aaron has been working long hours and you usually work late too and . . . ," Mindy stopped abruptly. "Never mind, it's really nothing—it's just that time of the month."

That night Shayna thought about Mindy and realized that it was too difficult for a recently married couple to be living with a young, single woman, especially when the wife was a bit jealous. Nothing was going on between her and Aaron, but it was too much of a strain for Mindy. Shayna did not want to hurt her cousin nor did she want to damage their relationship. She made a decision right then that she must move somewhere else. *But where?* she wondered. That quick-thinking mind of hers did not take long to come up with a solution. Tomorrow she planned to put an ad in the Yiddish paper stating that she was a young woman who just arrived from Europe and was looking for a fine family to live with. *Yes, that's perfect*, she thought, pleased with herself. It was the right thing to do. She wondered, too, about what she would tell Mindy and Aaron. She certainly did not want to hurt their feelings or tell Mindy that she knew there was a green monster in her eyes. No, she would just tell them she was very grateful for their help, but she did not want to take advantage of them. It was time for her to find another place to live.

Several days later the responses to her ad arrived and one in particular stood out. It was from a couple who was looking for a companion for their nineteen-year-old daughter, Pauline. Shayna was invited for lunch to meet their family and see their home. The family lived not too far away in a wealthy neighborhood. Their spacious home was larger than any home Shayna had ever entered. Lunch was served on a veranda overlooking a beautiful rose garden that made the home seem like a cottage in fairy tales Shayna read. The two young women took an immediate liking to one another and Shayna moved in a week later.

◆ ◆ ◆

The next several months passed by pleasantly for Shayna. She was pleased with her decision to leave Mindy and Aaron's house. Living with Pauline and her family was very comfortable, and Shayna and Mindy were able to stay on good terms. Love letters from Jonah were arriving on a regular basis—she would get one before she even had time to respond to the last one. They were even getting a bit more serious in that Jonah was saying he wanted to marry her. He asked her to please wait for him to save enough money to enable him to join her. Those words made her very happy, but in the meantime Shayna's life became a whirlwind of fun and social activity. There were not many Jewish people in Montevideo, but the ones who were there lived well and in a tightly-knit community. When she was not working at her job making beautiful and fashionable clothing for her customers, she enjoyed being a regular at parties and social events sponsored by the local Jewish Community Center. The charming Shayna was no stranger to flirting and she made many girlfriends and got the attention of more than a few boys. Two of the young men even convinced the modest Shayna to enter a beauty contest for a charity event for which she won second prize.

One young man, in particular, paid very close attention to Shayna. Mendel was actually a second cousin on her mother's side. He came from a wealthy family who owned and operated a furniture manufacturing business and he was one of their rising young salesman. Unbeknownst to Shayna, from the moment he met her, Mendel decided she was the woman he was going to marry. He spent hours dreaming of activities that might allow him to spend more time with her. Strict rules at the time kept young people from going out on dates unless they were chaperoned. Now that Shayna was living with a family, he hoped that would change. He wasted no time making arrangements to bring along a friend for Pauline so the four of them were able to go on dates, chaperoned by Pauline's father or mother. The four went everywhere together—dinner, dancing, theater, and parties—with Mendel's friend sticking close to Pauline and Mendel always by Shayna's side.

After a time, Shayna began to realize that she was being courted by not one, but two men. Jonah's letters were becoming more frequent and more serious. He indicated that he would definitely be coming. It was just a matter of time, and he wanted them to get married right away. The last letter also contained the sad news that his mother passed away. His father was utterly devastated and was left with Jonah's seventeen-year-old sister to care for. Jonah could not abandon his father—not now. He wanted to make sure his father was alright. But he promised to come soon—very soon. He concluded his letter with a heartfelt plea that she not marry anyone else. It was now very real to her that Jonah wanted to come to Montevideo and marry her. Yet these were just words. Jonah was far away and Shayna felt terribly sad about his mother. Her realistic nature kept her from getting too excited.

Then there was Mendel. He had a lot to recommend him. He was attractive and bright, even charming at times. And he had a good job, and came from a wealthy family. In fact he possessed only one flaw, but it was a big one. He was not Jonah. Because of that, Shayna never entertained any romantic feelings toward Mendel, and she made sure they were never alone. There were always other friends around when she was with him. Certainly nothing serious was ever said. From Shayna's perspective, they were just part of a group of friends having fun. Yet he was very attentive to her. In fact, he almost never left her side. *In his mind*, Shayna wondered, *was he courting her?* She knew immediately that next time she saw Mendel she must tell him about her boyfriend in Poland.

◆ ◆ ◆

Shayna, who had now been living in South America for almost a year, made another close friend—one who would prove pivotal in her life. Anchelita Schneider was a pretty eighteen-year-old girl who came from a wealthy family. She and Shayna met when Anchelita and her mother came into the dress shop to have a formal party dress designed for Anchelita. The two women spent many long hours there and while Anchelita was being fitted for her dress, Anchelita and Shayna became fast friends. Shayna, in fact, had become close to the whole family. One day Anchelita came into the store deeply out-of-breath, but very happy.

"Shayna," she called, rushing over to her friend, "I have wonderful news!"

Shayna looked up from her sewing project and smiled at her friend, "Sit down and relax . . . Catch your breath first."

"Remember we talked about how great it would be if you came to live with us while you were waiting for Jonah to come?" Anchelita continued. "Well, my parents think it is a fabulous idea! And mama wants to help you find an apartment for both of you to live in and . . . here's the best part," she paused now and smiled. Then she added, speaking quickly, "My parents want to make you a wedding," as she began bouncing up and down so hard she barely got the words out.

Shayna was truly overwhelmed. She put her sewing down, looked at her friend with a stern face, shook her head from side to side and said, "I cannot let them do that. It is too much to ask . . . much too much."

"No, it is not—we're practically family now," Anchelita responded. "And, it's going to be at our house." Shayna just sat looking at her friend in utter amazement. "Come on," Anchelita continued, "put your work away, let's go have some lunch and discuss the particulars."

◆　◆　◆

The port of Montevideo was crowded the morning that Shayna waited for Jonah's ship to arrive. Shayna stood in the bright morning sun breathing in the salty, sea air just as she did when she arrived a year and a half ago. This time, though, she was waiting for someone else's ship to arrive. She was surrounded by a gaggle of girlfriends almost as jumpy as she was as they all awaited the arrival of the mystery man from Poland. Anchelita and Pauline were here, along with cousin Mindy and three other girlfriends who came to be part of this occasion. One of the friends pointed out someone else they knew in the crowd. Shayna looked over to see Mendel several yards away and his friend who apparently came to check out Shayna's boyfriend.

Anchelita announced to everyone, "He came to see if Jonah truly exists! Mendel probably thought she made up a story of a boyfriend in Poland just to get rid of him." The friends all burst into hysterical peals of laughter and giggles.

The girls turned their attention to the massive vessel as it docked and its horn blasted out a loud bellow to announce its arrival. "He was so angry when I told him about Jonah," Shayna said to her friends. "He carried on about it, saying that I danced with him and that gave him the wrong idea. Can you imagine? He said I danced with him . . . who doesn't dance? I never even hinted that I wanted to be serious with him." The friends all murmured and nodded in agreement.

"People see what they want to see," Shayna philosophized.

The girls continued to chat and giggle as they waited anxiously for the moment that was drawing near. "It won't be long now," Mindy said, as she put her arm around her cousin and gave her a gentle squeeze. The passengers began to disembark from the ship as Shayna searched their faces, her eyes hungry for the sight of her man. Finally, there he was. The thick, dark wavy hair. The handsome face and square build. It was all packaged in a smart grey suit. He even wore a tie for the occasion. Her spirits soared. With a smile as wide as the horizon, Shayna began to wave as her friends followed her line of vision and joined in.

Shayna and Jonah were not given to public displays of affection, but their hug seemed to go on forever. "I'm not ever letting you go—not ever again," Jonah said quietly, but emphatically, into her left ear. They finally parted and looked at each other. When their lips met for their first kiss in almost two years Shayna's friends began jumping up and down, clapping and cheering wildly. Jonah looked a bit startled by all the attention. "Darling, I want you to meet some special people," Shayna told him.

◆ ◆ ◆

The next day, Shayna and Jonah were married. Shayna wore a beautiful, but simple white dress—nothing like the elaborate wedding gowns her customers so valued her for. And Jonah wore his best suit from Poland that Mrs. Schneider made sure was steam pressed to perfection. All of Shayna's South American friends and family were in attendance, except for Mendel who chose not to be there. Every surface of the Schneider's home was covered with flowers. They even fashioned a flowered *chupah* (wedding canopy) in the garden for the couple to stand beneath and say their vows.

The rabbi created a beautiful service in Yiddish and in Hebrew. After they each said "I do," tears welled up in Shayna's eyes when she looked at her husband. She had waited so long and everything was happening so fast, it was hard to grasp that it was real—that Jonah was standing right in front of her. Jonah lifted her veil and they experienced their first kiss as husband and wife. A breathless silence settled among the guests and more than a few women dotted their eyes with a tissue. Then Jonah's right foot shattered the champagne glass wrapped in a velvet cloth. Two souls became one. Loud clapping and cheers of "*l'chaim* (to life)!" burst into the air as everyone surrounded the beaming couple with love. A boisterous celebration followed with music and dancing and fine food that went long into the night. Shayna and Jonah did not let go of one another.

The entire experience was like something in a fairytale, not resembling anything the practical Shayna ever allowed herself to dream about. In the wee hours of the morning, the happy, but exhausted couple finally said their 'thank-yous' and 'good-nights' and waved as they stepped out into the hallway. The two walked hand in hand up a grand staircase and stood before the closed door to the room that Mrs. Schneider prepared especially for them. They embraced briefly, then Jonah opened the door and with his hand gently touching his bride's back, ushered her into a magnificent suite filled with fresh flowers.

◆　◆　◆

The last year and a half since Jonah stepped off the ship was a happy time for the couple. Jonah made friends and adjusted beautifully to life in Montevideo. Through Shayna's connections in the Jewish community, he found a job as a junior salesman in a men's clothing store. In the dress shop where she worked, she was promoted from seamstress to dress designer. She loved their cozy one-bedroom apartment. Anchelita and her mother helped her find one that was just perfect for them. It overlooked a pretty tree-lined street not far from her cousin Mindy's apartment. They also helped her decorate and furnish it beautifully. The best thing about it was that it was theirs—hers and Jonah's. At night, she cooked delicious meals and baked challah for *Shabbes*. They often entertained friends and family with Shayna preparing sumptuous meals for dinner or lunch on the weekends. She enjoyed showing Jonah around Montevideo, a place she had come to love. In a word, life was good. But very soon two letters would change everything.

The first one was from Shayna's sister, Edke. Shayna wrote to her parents, brothers and sisters religiously since she arrived in Montevideo almost three years ago, and she always looked forward to letters from home. Sometimes she opened them with a bit of anxiety since her parents were getting older. Now, it was here . . . the letter she feared. Edke told her that their dear mother passed away unexpectedly. When Sarah-Miriam did not get out of bed one morning their father thought, at first, that she just overslept. That was unusual, but she was tired lately. He tried to awaken her, but could not. He called the doctor who came quickly. He said it appeared that she died peacefully in her sleep. The family was shattered and they were all sorry Shayna was not there with them. Shayna felt her sister's tears through her words. They felt sad, too, that by the time she read this letter, the funeral will have passed. Waves of guilt washed over her. In her most recent letter to her parents, she told them that she and Jonah were discussing a visit home. They just needed to save enough money for the trip and take a leave from their jobs. Now, the realization that Sarah-Miriam was gone struck her like a knife in her heart. It was too painful to think that the last time she kissed her mama, which seemed so long ago now, was truly the last time. She put down the letter and sobbed in Jonah's arms.

Hershel's letter came a few weeks later. Jonah exchanged letters with his father and sisters on a regular basis since he moved to Montevideo. Hershel Kaufman had a big personality and his letters were always optimistic, full of grandiose ideas and happy stories of the births of grandchildren and successful business projects. He always said how he missed Jonah and Shayna and wanted to know when they would be coming home. This last letter sounded different. There were no glad tidings. There was not even a hopeful tone. This letter was filled with the opposite and was flavored with a sense of doom and desperation. Hershel had not been feeling well, and he recently fell and hurt his back. He had been unable to work for weeks. The only one home with him was Rivka who was good with household chores, but she was of no help with the business. He was worried about what might happen to his business if he continued to be unable to work. How would he support himself and the daughter who was still at home with him? The letter ended with these words: "Please come home. I need you."

Shayna and Jonah were shocked. They talked about different options. Was it possible for Hershel and Rifka to live with Rachel and her family in Lomza? No, Rachel's house was too small. In any case, that did not solve the problem of Hershel's business. And Rachel's husband was a hard-working tailor. He did not have the knowledge let alone the time to help with the lumber business. The business would fail and it was unfair to ask Rachel and her husband to support Hershel and Rivka. Jonah's older brothers were settled with their families in New York City and his sister, Esther, moved there with her husband just before Jonah came to Montevideo. Besides, Hershel was not asking for Jonah's other siblings. He wanted Shayna and Jonah. "Please come home, I need you," he wrote. Those words, from a man who rarely asked for help, touched them both deeply.

Jonah put his father's letter down. A silence hung in the room as heavy as a thick blanket of fog. Jonah knew how much Shayna loved it here, how much she wanted to stay and make this their home. For the first time in his life, he was torn. He was forced to either disappoint the woman he loved or the father he loved, and it broke his heart. They looked at each other. They reached the same conclusion at the same moment. No words were necessary. They both knew what they needed to do. Family was everything. Jonah looked into Shayna's sad eyes. They seemed to say, *What else can we do?*

The next few weeks were hectic for Shayna and Jonah. They gave notice at their places of business. They cancelled newspapers. They returned library books unread. They notified their landlord and arrangements were made for ending the lease on their apartment. They sent regrets in response to invitations to upcoming parties. Shayna struggled to finish a lavish wedding dress she designed for a friend whose wedding she would not attend. It was adorned with a galaxy of pearls woven into the bodice. She managed to finish it just in time. They said sad farewells to co-workers, family and friends followed by the requisite almost believable proclamations of, "We'll definitely see each other again" and, "Of course, we'll be back to visit." Shayna's girlfriends were especially sad, and the Schneiders threw Shayna and Jonah a sumptuous going-away luncheon at their villa.

"How can we ever repay you?" Shayna said as she hugged the Schneiders.

"Just be well," they answered graciously.

Everyone who had been at the wedding was there. Even cousin Mendel attended with his new girlfriend. Shayna was happy for him. With tears rolling down her cheeks, Anchelita Schneider embraced her friend for a long, long time and made her promise to write. Shayna nodded and choked back her own tears as she made her way around the room and hugged all these people who meant so much to her. She and Jonah wore matching lipstick stains in every shade of pink and red on their cheeks. Armed with tissues, many tried, but were unable to remove the telltale signs of the feminine embrace. Shayna and Jonah thanked everyone profusely and sincerely. All the help and the love had been indispensable to them. All these people were magnificent.

And then Shayna and Jonah were gone.

❧ CHAPTER 5 ❧

1930–1932
Zbojna, Poland

Sometimes when you open the door to the
past, what you confront is your destiny.

~Diane Setterfield, *The Thirteenth Tale*

The two sienna-brown horses pulling the wagon that carried Shayna and Jonah down the main street of Zbojna lifted their heads and snorted as they clip-clopped to a stop in front of Moshe Ozdoba's cottage. Jonah jumped down to the ground, turned, and helped his wife out of the wagon. Shayna brushed off her blue and white checked dress, belted at the waist and stood up straight. Arms akimbo, she furrowed her brows and looked around the main street of her former home. She felt strange being back here even though everything looked the same. The street was still a dirt road, but it looked dirtier and dustier than she remembered. Maybe she was the one that changed. She sighed. There was beauty in the village, too. The sky was a rich and cloudless blue. The green leaves on the sea of trees and shrubs around her were animated by a spirited breeze and seemed to be dancing a Tarantella. She had forgotten about the fragrant lilac bushes that were everywhere. They did not grow in Montevideo.

The happy shouts of children playing in the flowering fields wafted across the street to her ears. She was one of those children not so very long ago—playing, running, laughing—being called home to help prepare dinner. This thought slid easily to mama's kitchen with its heavenly aromas and the family sitting at the table, everyone talking at once, then obediently becoming quiet when their father cleared his throat to speak. A bird tending to a nest in a tree just above her caught her attention and snapped her mind back to the present. The nest was too high to see inside, so she wondered if the mama bird had eggs or baby birds in there. The mama bird. Her heart dropped like a boulder in her chest as she remembered her mama was no longer here. Even her mother-in-law was gone. At twenty, she was already the matriarch of her immediate family. She watched Jonah lift their heavy luggage from the wagon with ease and pay the driver who laughed and exchanged some pleasant words with him. Shayna took a deep breath and steeled herself. She called on the spirits of her iron will and sheer determination to take charge of mind and body. *She could begin again,* she thought, *and she would—right here, right now.*

For the next few weeks, Shayna struggled to adjust to being back in Zbojna. In some ways, it was not difficult because Montevideo already seemed like a dream. *Had she really been there?* she wondered. Planning for the future helped to keep the sadness from weighing too heavily on her. She and Jonah spent hours talking about the design of the new home they wanted to build and selecting the empty lot for the new home. There was one near her father's house that was perfect for them. It had enough land for sharing a potato garden with the relatives who lived behind them. There was a barn to keep milking cows for such time that, God-willing, they were blessed with a child. People were a big help, too. Her father's house, where the couple was staying in a spare room, was always full of people and activity. Her older sister, Edke, lived nearby with her husband, Meerche and their two children. Other relatives and childhood friends all came over to welcome Shayna and Jonah home. They brought warm hugs along with prepared meals, cakes and other delicious *noshes* (snacks) for the newly-returned couple. All were eager to hear stories about the exotic place they lived and offer them any help they might need to get settled.

Jonah immediately started where he left off helping his father with the lumber export business, but this time taking on a greater share of the responsibilities. His aging and convalescing father would be more of an adviser now than an active participant in the business. Shayna began thinking of ways that she, too, might bring additional income to the couple. She thought about opening a sewing shop, but then changed her mind. There was already a seamstress down the street, and this *shtetl* was too small for two seamstresses. Since her father closed his bakery and café after her mother passed, two new bakeries already opened in Zbojna. These bakeries did not provide spirits, but selling liquor and wine did not appeal to her. Besides, since there were now fewer restrictions on who can sell liquor, she reasoned to herself, it did not represent the good business opportunity that existed for her parents and grandparents. No, she thought, she needed to come up with an altogether different solution.

◆ ◆ ◆

One evening Shayna and Edke were in the kitchen preparing flanken and cabbage soup for dinner when a loud bang made them jump. It seemed to come from the front of the house. Moshe looked up from his newspaper spread on the kitchen table and exclaimed, "*Vos iz dos* (what is this)?"

Suddenly, there was Jonah standing in the kitchen doorway, looking much more excited, they all thought, than he usually looked after a hard day at work. With outspread arms, he greeted everyone, "Hello, my beautiful family!" Next, he slid over to a surprised Shayna. "Hello, my darling," he said, pulling her close, kissing her cheek, and beginning to hum and dance a waltz with her.

They all stared at him, eyes wide and expectant. When he saw their surprised faces, he said, "I'm sorry for the noise . . . I opened the door a little harder than usual . . . it's just that I'm so excited to show you something. Come. Come." He took his wife gently by the elbow, beckoning her to follow him.

"It's just outside. Come, I'll show you . . . *Tati* Moshe, you, too, and Edke . . . Come."

Edke put down the spoon that she was using to stir the cabbage soup and both women wiped their hands on their aprons. Hershel got up from the table and the three hurried after Jonah. Their interest was thoroughly piqued. What could have engendered so much excited happiness in him? They knew that he was certainly a happy man, but more often than not he was exhausted at the end of the day. They stepped outside into the cool glow of twilight. A crescent moon hung low in the darkening, eastern sky. There was just enough light from the sliver of sun balancing itself on the horizon to see each other dimly, but clearly. Jonah stood before his family, his palms facing outward and his fingers pointing downward, his handsome face sporting a broad smile. There was something at his feet, laying on the ground.

"*Gib a kuk* (give a look)," he said.

They all looked down, and Shayna spoke first, "What . . . what is this?" She bent down and with her right index finger poked at what seemed to be a canvas sack full of something.

"It looks like a sack of grain—maybe 10 or 20 pounds of it," she announced as she looked at Jonah quizzically. "You are excited about a sack of grain?" she asked as she crossed her arms, and lifted her right palm to her cheek.

Before Jonah was able to answer, Shayna turned to her father and sister and announced, "*Nu, mayn man iz a bisl meshuge* (my husband is a little crazy)."

They all shrugged and looked at Jonah who responded by posing another question to his wife, "Answer me this . . . Where can a farmer in Zbojna get a 20-pound sack of grain?"

Shayna thought about the location of the nearest dry goods store and answered, "Well, there's a store across the river in Ostroleka. Or, they can wait until Market Day and get it in Lomza."

"Exactly!" Jonah said with glee.

"Exactly, what?" Shayna wanted to know.

"Exactly the point I want to make," Jonah said. "They have to leave their farms and spend almost a day of travel to get the basic supplies they need."

There is a Yiddish proverb that states: A wise man hears one word and understands two. In this case, it was a wise woman and she heard more than two words. "Are you saying that we should open a dry goods store here in Zbojna?" she asked with raised eyebrows.

"That is what I am saying," Jonah said smiling broadly.

Moshe and Edke looked from Jonah to Shayna who was standing quietly and digesting this information. Her arms still crossed, she frowned and bent her head slightly downward and tapped her left foot, her mind almost visibly calculating the pros and cons and all the possible ramifications of this undertaking. Everyone was quiet. Only the distant voices of neighbors and the chirping of birds in nearby trees could be heard. When she finally came to a satisfying conclusion, she lifted her head. Everyone was looking at her.

"My husband," Shayna said, uncrossing her arms and walking toward Jonah, "is a genius."

◆ ◆ ◆

A few months later, they completed a new design for their home that accommodated a dry goods store. As with all businesses in Zbojna, Shayna and Jonah's store was to be a part of their home. They spent days and nights sketching different layouts with paper and pencil, then testing them out in their imaginations. Finally, they decided on a design in which the store occupied the front part of the house with the front door opening directly into the store. At the back of the store another door opened to the family's main living area which would consist of a bedroom and a kitchen along with a dining area. Behind those two rooms they planned to have a long room to serve multiple purposes. They would use it for extra inventory for the store and as a guestroom, when needed. Like many of their neighbors, they will also have a root cellar, a water pump and an outhouse.

As soon as the design was finished, work began on the house. When he was having a good day, Hershel the *Royte*, whose grey beard no longer contained any remnants of its former flaming glory, took it upon himself to oversee the construction of the new house. Jonah was more than happy for the help and was pleased that his father felt useful. Using his and Jonah's connections in the lumber industry, Hershel made sure to get only the best workers and was not pleased unless they brought the finest wood. Leaning on his cane, he barked orders at the toiling construction workers.

They smiled, nodded and waved back at him, then secretly winked at each other. Let the old man have some fun, their eyes seemed to say.

While their home was under construction, Shayna kept busy sewing curtains and quilting a bedspread for the new house. She also helped friends and family with some of their sewing projects. Jonah spent a few days a week taking care of the family lumber export business which had become his responsibility. On other days he and Shayna traveled to nearby towns on exploratory shopping trips and to establish relationships with the businesses that would be a good source of wholesale merchandise for the store. They visited friends and family who lived in and around the places they went, sometimes staying overnight. Jonah's sister, Rachel, was across the Narew river in Lomza and his cousins on his mother's side, the Finkelsteins, were in Ostroleka. Shayna's sister, Mirzsa, was in Nowogrod and her brother, Shmulke, was in Lomzatseh, which was a neighborhood on the outskirts of Lomza. They were all blessed with homes full of spirited children. Shayna and Jonah adored their nieces and nephews and loved to shower them with gifts and candy.

This world was far from Montevideo with its bustling streets and progressive attitudes. The Jewish people who lived there were not treated like an unwanted minority by the government or by society as they often were here in Poland. Shayna missed that and her friends and family who lived there, but thoughts of that time in her life did not enter Shayna's mind very much these days. She was too practical to long for something she could not have. Besides, her life here was too filled with family and friends and planning for a future to waste time looking back at what was or what might have been. Instead, she found plenty of joyful blessings in her life here. As it goes with blessings, there were never too many and one more would soon let itself be known to the intrepid couple. It was on one of those shopping trips that Shayna experienced her first ever bout of morning sickness.

◆　◆　◆

Several months later, Shayna and Jonah sat in the kitchen of her father's house after Moshe went to bed. The light of a kerosene lamp above the kitchen table cast a soft glow that faded as it reached the far corners of the kitchen. Outside an orchestra of nocturnal insects played a cacophonous symphony that the wind carried in through a partly opened window. Jonah got up and closed it when a chilly evening breeze entered and wrapped itself around a shivering Shayna. She pulled her sweater more tightly around her shoulders as he rejoined her at the kitchen table where they were sipping hot tea. A plate at the center of the table was piled high with sweet rugelach that Shayna baked that afternoon. Shayna watched Jonah enjoy one. She held up her hand and shook her head from side to side when he offered her one. She smiled as he took a second one, then reached over and brushed away a crumb that settled on his chin. Jonah swallowed, took a sip of tea, and looked as though he was gathering his thoughts.

"The house is almost ready," he said. "Tomorrow I'll begin stocking the store. I think we should schedule the furniture to be delivered—it will take a few weeks. I saw that you and Edke put the curtains up. They look very nice."

Shayna smiled and nodded as she stood up to clear some dishes from the table, revealing the swollen belly of a woman who was on the brink of motherhood.

"Can you please sit?" Jonah said as he jumped up and took the dishes away from her. "You need to take it easy. The baby is due in six weeks."

Shayna listened to her husband and sat down, but said, "You know I always need to be doing something."

"You'll have plenty to do after the baby comes and we move into the new house and open the store," Jonah said as he cleared more dinner dishes. "We need to talk about my father moving in with us. I'm a little worried about that."

She frowned and shrugged her shoulders, "You know he needs our help. Rivka will be getting married and moving out soon. He can't be alone."

Jonah thought about this and said, "I love my father very much, but he will have two married daughters who live nearby . . . and I'm concerned about you. This pregnancy has been so hard on you. How will you be able to take care of a new baby and an old man? And look at you, *maidele* (little girl). You're skin and bones. Women are supposed to gain weight when they are pregnant—not lose."

She knew he was right. Standing five feet, four inches tall, during her pregnancy Shayna had dwindled down to a mere ninety-eight pounds on the doctor's scale. Instead of acknowledging that, though, she said, "Your father doesn't want to live with his daughters. He wants to live with us."

"He wants to live with you," Jonah said, emphasizing the word 'you' and smiling at her. "I can't blame him." It was true. Hershel was crazy about his daughter-in-law. "Seriously, darling, don't you think it will be too much for you?"

"I'll be fine . . . it won't be too much for me," Shayna responded reflexively, waving her hand in the air. Then, thinking a bit more about Jonah's question, she said, "Maybe you're right. I have a cousin who needs a place to live. She is only fifteen and she could be a big help with the baby. Why don't we invite her to move in with us?"

"She's the one who was recently orphaned?" Jonah asked.

"Yes, *nebekh* (unfortunately), poor thing," Shayna answered.

Jonah thought about this as he stood up. He nodded, kissed his wife on the head, and cleared the rest of the dishes. Just like that, the matter was resolved.

◆　◆　◆

Two months later on Monday, February 1, 1932, a light dusting of powdery snow covered Zbojna in a soft, white blanket. Inside Moshe Ozdoba's house it was warm and dry, but a drama was unfolding. Chaya-Sarah Kaufman, so named for her grandmothers Chaya-Raisa and Sarah-Miriam, of blessed memory, was about to make a dramatic appearance. A midwife attended to her mother who had been in labor since the night before. Her father was in the room with them. Her grandfathers, aunts, uncles, cousins and friends were gathered in the living room. Some of them were there last night when the first agonizing pain gripped her mother's body just as the family was sitting down for dinner. All of them were aware that Shayna's pregnancy was a difficult one, and they were worried. Some were pacing. Some were wringing their hands. Some sat silently as they all prayed to God almighty for a healthy mother and baby.

Hershel Kaufman looked at his watch. It was ten o'clock in the morning. His daughter-in-law had been in labor for fifteen hours. He looked up and his eyes fell on Moshe Ozdoba's face. It was impassive. Maybe it showed a bit of fear, Hershel thought. Both men were of different temperaments, but were strongly bonded over the love of their children united in marriage and their shared grief of missing their wives. Now, their eyes, softened by age and weariness, met across the room. They both blinked slowly and nodded to one another over yet another shared moment in their lives.

Above the quiet in the room, someone suddenly cried out, "Shhh—listen."

Everyone was visibly startled as the door to the bedroom flew open and allowed the shrill, but welcome sound of a crying baby to escape into the rest of the house. All eyes were on Jonah Kaufman as he stood in the doorway, sweat beading on his brow, showing more exhaustion than one was accustomed to seeing in a man of twenty-five years. He paused for just the smallest of seconds, gulped in a breath of air while everyone else held theirs. On the exhalation, he joyfully cried out, "My daughter, Chaya-Sarah, has arrived. She weighs five pounds."

◆ ◆ ◆

For the new parents, the next few weeks were unfortunately fraught with more pain and anxiety than joy. Shayna developed an infection in her left breast and found it almost impossible to nurse her child. One morning Edke looked at the burning red area on her sister's body and said, "You need to go to the doctor . . . now." Within an hour, Shayna, holding her baby, was bundled into a wagon cushioned between her husband and her sister for the hour ride to Lomza where Shayna's doctor had an office in the local hospital. Two hours later, Chaya-Sarah was tucked in next to her mother on a hospital bed in a white-washed, antiseptic-smelling room that Shayna shared with two other women. White linen screens on wooden frames afforded each some semblance of privacy.

A nurse came over to her to take the baby. "Let me put the baby in the nursery, dear. You'll be more comfortable," she told Shayna as she reached down to pick up the squirming pink bundle with coffee colored hair laying in the bed next to her.

Shayna glared at her with the fierceness of a lioness whose cub was being threatened by a pack of hungry hyenas, "No, thank you," she said sternly, "my baby is fine right here."

At first, Shayna's infection seemed to be healing, and everyone was relieved. After a few days, it became red and inflamed again. This time Shayna developed a high fever. Everyone—even the nurses—became frightened for her. The next few weeks would prove difficult for everyone involved. Edke stayed with her sister. She slept in a fourth bed in Shayna's hospital room that was not being used. Jonah came by horse drawn wagon each day from Zbojna, sometimes twice, juggling his time between his businesses and his family.

"I'm going to have to operate to remove this infection," the doctor said gently to Shayna and her sister.

"Whatever you have to do, doctor," Shayna said anxious to get back on her feet and go home.

"Unfortunately, there will probably be a scar," the doctor said later to Edke when he thought Shayna could not hear him.

The surgery was successful although painful and unpleasant for Shayna. She would later tell her family and friends that because the doctor was unable to tolerate the smell of ether, she needed to be wide awake for the procedure. "What could I do?" she told them. "I had no choice, but *danken Gutte* (thank God), I'm alright." She also reported that the baby stayed by her side the whole time. "The nurses wanted to take her from me . . . I wouldn't let them . . . I didn't let them even touch her."

When the doctor was confident that the infection cleared and the incision was healing adequately, Shayna was able to go home. She was ecstatic.

Jonah and Edke helped her out of the hospital and into a wagon. Still in a weakened state, she rode home wedged gently between them, cradling her baby in her arms. She winced in pain when the bumpy ride jostled its passengers even though her companions tried to lean toward her and keep her body stable. Nevertheless, she and her companions were grateful that she was coming home. Looking at his wife, Jonah was overcome with emotion and had to remove a handkerchief from his breast pocket to dry his tears.

After the hour ride, the wagon pulled to a stop in front of their home on the main street of Zbojna. A group of people were gathered in front staring at the front door. One of them was reading aloud the note that Jonah left on the door indicating that the store would be opening soon. When they heard the wagon approach, they turned around and someone cried, "Here is Jonah and look . . . Shayna is back!" They all ran over and surrounded the wagon, greeting the family and welcoming Shayna home after the two-week absence. News travels fast, especially in a small *shtetl*, but apparently the news of Shayna's recovery had not. One woman was less than subtle at demonstrating this when she called out, "It's wonderful to see you. We thought you died!"

◆　◆　◆

A warm and colorful July arrived in the tiny village west of the Narew river. Wildflowers were in bloom everywhere and the many varieties of birds, having returned from their winter migrations, filled the air with melodic, territorial songs. A steady stream of horse-drawn wagons, some covered, some not and troikas carrying people and goods made their way up and down the busy main street. Shayna fully recovered from her recent ordeal and even gained back some weight and strength. The family moved in to their new home along with Jonah's father, Hershel, and Shayna's cousin. She proved to be a big help with Chaya-Sarah who, at six months, was beginning to crawl.

The store had been open for four months. Shayna and Jonah made sure it was fully stocked with sacks of grain, wheat, flour, honey, and sugar. Farming and gardening tools and equipment were on display in one corner along with lanterns and lamps, gloves and ropes, buckets and brooms. Kitchen utensils as well as pots, pans, strainers, and dishware lined one long shelf. Glass jars for preserving jam and pie plates for baking were on another. Several shelves were devoted to sewing items such as bolts of cloth, pins and needles, thread, ribbons, and silk. A penny candy barrel stood in front of the counter behind which there was a locked drawer where cash was kept. Two windows lining the front wall on either side of the door and one on each side wall were dressed in sunny yellow curtains that kept the room bright during the day. The store was busy whenever it was open which was seven days a week. Shayna and Jonah made the decision to keep their store open for a few hours on Saturdays, in spite of it being *Shabbes*, as a courtesy to their Polish customers whose religious beliefs prohibited them from shopping on Sunday. They also decided to keep the store open for a few hours on Sundays in spite of legislation in Poland that forced the closing of stores on that day. This law was passed strictly to hurt Jewish commerce which would typically be closed on Saturdays, but Shayna and Jonah's intention was not to engage in political or religious activism. They did this as a courtesy to their Jewish customers whose religious beliefs prohibited them from shopping on Saturday.

Sunday morning, Jonah and Shayna opened the store for business as usual. No customers had arrived yet so they were busying themselves dusting, restocking shelves, and counting the cash reserves in the drawer. As was typical, Shayna's cousin was in the house watching Chaya-Sarah. Whenever she watched Chaya-Sarah, Papa Hershel watched her. He adored his granddaughter and was extremely protective of her. That was the reason that Shayna and Jonah were surprised when the door between the family living area and the store opened suddenly and Hershel appeared. He quietly closed the door behind him, and walked over to them. He looked very distressed and seemed slightly out of breath.

"*Tati*, is everything alright?" Jonah asked his father.

Hershel took a deep breath and, looking at Shayna, said in a loud whisper, "I saw your cousin pinch Chaya-Sari."

"What?" Shayna and Jonah asked in unison as they looked at each other, then back at Hershel.

"Yes, the baby was crying and she went over to her and pinched her arm hard," he said still breathing heavily and now crossing his arms. "It left a mark."

"She did it on purpose?" Shayna asked him. "Are you sure it wasn't an accident?"

"Yes, I'm sure," Hershel said shaking his head from side to side. "It was no accident."

Shayna and Jonah exchanged looks of horror. Shayna jumped into action, leaving the store immediately to go and find her baby girl. When she came upon Chaya-Sarah being held by her cousin, she gently, but firmly took the baby from her. She told her cousin that she was planning to watch the baby and needed her to help in the store today. Shayna wasted no time finding somewhere else for her cousin to live—someplace where there were no young children in the house.

The next day was a typical Monday afternoon in the store, except that Shayna held Chaya-Sarah on her left hip as she stood behind the counter. She was exchanging pleasantries and news of the day with two female customers as a third searched through the barrel of candy. She was in a good mood. Her daughter was with her and no longer in harm's way. She enjoyed the social rewards that accompany being a shopkeeper. People stopped in to shop, but they often stayed to chat with the amiable proprietress. Jonah was there, too, to join in the socializing since he usually reserved Wednesdays or Thursdays for merchandise buying trips.

Suddenly the front door opened and two men, Polish farmers, burst into the store. They were arguing loudly. All heads turned toward the sound of the commotion. The women gasped as they saw the men begin to shove one another. Jonah who was kneeling to adjust some merchandise near the floor, quickly stood up, walked over to the men, and ushered them outside. They initially resisted, but Jonah was insistent and they finally relented. Once there, they continued to shout, gesticulating wildly and pointing fingers at one another.

The first farmer looked at Jonah, and roared, "His dog jumped my fence and killed two of my chickens . . . He owes me money."

"You can't prove it was my dog that did it. You can't even prove two of your chickens are gone," the other yelled.

"How about the chicken feathers I saw in the mouth of that mangy mutt of yours? What do you say about that?" the first farmer yelled back with hate in his eyes.

"I never saw any feathers in my dog's mouth," the other hollered back.

The first farmer rolled up his sleeves, spat into his palms and raised two fists high in the air, his mouth in a tight knot and his chin thrust out in defiance. The other man quickly responded by doing the same. Jonah did not waste a minute. He immediately positioned himself between the two men, then stretched out his arms wide to distance them from one another. While working to physically keep the men separated, Jonah said sternly, in his best Polish, "Listen to me, both of you, this can be settled by discussion—not fists."

Everyone in the store gathered at the windows and watched Jonah as he tried to break up this altercation. Shayna involuntarily brought her right hand up to her mouth, her eyes fixed on her husband. Another woman gasped. No one was able to hear what the men were saying, but the tension in their body language told them everything. The women were sure something violent was about to occur. After a few more strained moments, however, the men began to back away from one another and assumed a more relaxed position. Unbelievably, the three of them walked away from the main street in the direction of the farms and were soon out of sight. Everyone inside continued to stare at the spot where the men last stood. They were still in shock over what they saw and what they realized might have happened. Then they all slowly turned to each other and began talking at once.

"Your husband is a brave man," one woman said to Shayna as she brought items up to the counter for purchase. Another woman getting in line behind her agreed.

Shayna heard the women, but was silent for a moment. She clearly looked worried. While making sure Chaya-Sarah was secure in her left arm, she took a hard candy from the penny candy barrel with her right one, unwrapped it nervously, then absent-mindedly placed it in her mouth. It was peppermint, but she did not notice. Then she answered the woman, "Hmmm . . . I hope my brave husband comes home in one piece."

◆　◆　◆

That night at the dinner table, an excited and unharmed Jonah regaled his father with what happened in and outside the store that day. After following the men back to their farms, he checked out their properties, assessed the situation, and gave them each another chance to repeat their side of the story—calmly this time. After listening to their arguments, and thinking for a moment, Jonah hit on what he thought was a workable solution.

"I told them that the fenced area around the chickens needs to be higher. It was obviously too easy for a dog—or a fox or wolf, for that matter—to jump over it. So, I told the farmer who owned the chickens that I would provide him with fencing materials from the store at a fair, wholesale price. Then I asked the farmer with the dogs if he would agree to pay for part of the materials—say twenty percent."

Hershel slapped the table and cried, "Son, I'm so proud of you! You have muscle and brains! So what happened?"

"The farmers both stood for a long time staring at each other and thinking. I thought it was a good idea, but I don't know these men very well and I had no idea what they would say or do, so I was a little nervous," Jonah said. He took a few bites of the potato *kugel* (pudding) on his plate.

"*Nu*, what did they say?" Hershel asked.

"First, one agreed to my terms, then the other," Jonah answered smiling.

"Ha!" Hershel cried.

"But," Jonah continued, "I told them they had to shake hands on it . . . and I wouldn't leave until they did." He cut a piece of the tender brisket in his plate and brought a forkful to his mouth.

"*Nu*, did they?" Hershel asked.

"They did," Jonah said laughing. "They shook hands."

Hershel was laughing now, too, and slapping his knees. "What a great story," he bellowed.

Just then, Shayna entered the kitchen after nursing Chaya-Sarah and putting her to bed. "Shhh, please, the baby is sleeping," she scolded her father-in-law. "I guess Jonah told you the story."

"Yes, he did," Hershel said enthusiastically, but in a softer voice. "And, as usual, I am very proud of my son. As I am of you, *tayer maidele* (dear girl). You have both become successful shopkeepers and you've given me a beautiful granddaughter. You've made an old man as happy as he could possibly be."

"I'm very glad, *tati*," Shayna smiled at her father-in-law, then looked at her husband. "And, thank God, those men didn't hurt you. *Fintster iz mir* (darkness was over me) when I saw you standing between those two *khayes* (animals)."

Jonah was not the only one telling the story that night. The story was, in fact, repeated at dinner tables all around the *shtetl* Zbojna. It would be repeated the next day, too, and the day after that. The story's trajectory would lead it even beyond the perimeter of their village and contribute to changing two things in Jonah's life in Poland. One was that, from now on, whenever any of the local Polish farmers or anyone, for that matter, was involved in a dispute, they sought out Jonah to settle the crisis. He literally became the King Solomon of Zbojna. Heated arguments ended summarily as soon as the parties involved decided to bring the matter to Jonah, agreeing beforehand to go along with whatever he determined was a fair solution. The other effect was that, from this day forward, whenever people talked about Jonah, they referred to him as Jonah the *Shtarker* (the Strong One). Some people said he earned that name because of his physical strength and courage. Others believed it was because of his strength of character. Most assumed it was a little of both.

✌ CHAPTER 6 ✆

1936
Zbojna, Poland

Eastern European Jews created a culture that venerated the
Sefer, book of religious learning, but whose people laughed at
themselves. It was a culture that put its people, familiar with
poverty and hardship, on speaking terms with God. It was a culture
unique in all Jewish history, and Eastern European Ashkenazic
Jewry, which fashioned that culture, was the wellspring of Jewish
creativity for Jewish communities throughout the world.

~Lucy Dawidowicz, *The War Against The Jews 1933–1945*

Like her parents and grandparents, Chaya-Sarah's childhood world consisted of forests and flowers and a four-block length of dirt road—the Jewish section and main street of her tiny *shtetl* Zbojna. It held wonders aplenty for the charming, curious girl with the long coffee-brown *tsepelach* (braids) and enormous doe eyes. She was surrounded by a loving community of aunts and uncles, cousins and friends. Her uncle Yudke's children lived just a few doors down the street, and her best friend, Edke, who for some inexplicable reason had the nickname of Edkelkee, which was even longer than her name, lived only two houses away. The two played for hours pretending one was Queen Esther and the other her faithful servant or they dressed a doll as the baby Moses and carried him around in a basket.

Chaya-Sarah loved to visit the cows in the barn behind her house and hear their rich lowing sounds. She pulled up clumps of grass to feed them and laughed as their hairy lips tickled her fingers. She always helped at milking time and enjoyed a warm glass of milk fresh from the cow. Beyond the barn was the large potato patch that they shared with Jonah's uncle. Mama taught her how to identify the ripe potatoes that grew on their side and pick them at just the right time for eating. Sometimes at dinner she heard her parents talking about the fact that Jonah's aunt and uncle often took more than their share of potatoes from the garden. Shayna and Jonah did not mind as long as their daughter had enough to eat. So they both just laughed, good-naturedly and Chaya-Sarah joined in the fun.

At four, Chaya-Sarah was tall enough to reach into the penny candy barrel in the store, which she did whenever she pleased. She always took extra pieces of candy for her playmates while Shayna and Jonah watched her, lifted their eyebrows, and smiled. She knew she had permission to do so, and they were pleased their child was generous. To the left of her home and across the street lived a family with a large, stone well in their backyard. Chaya-Sarah's backyard had only a metal pump for her family's water supply so this charming structure was endlessly fascinating to her. Whenever she saw someone getting water from the well, she ran over to stand and watch the lever being spun over and over and around and around. When, finally, a full, dripping bucket of mineral-rich water appeared someone always offered her a glass of cool water.

One warm spring day, Jonah and Shayna closed the store for lunch and the family headed to the woods for a picnic and to gather mushrooms. If Chaya-Sarah had to choose a favorite time, and she had many, it would be when she and her parents crossed the dirt road, walked through the fields of wildflowers and lilac bushes and ventured into the woods. Sometimes other family and friends joined them, but today it was just the three of them. As they walked, Jonah pointed out all the nests in the trees. He stopped to lift Chaya-Sarah onto his shoulders to enable her to glimpse any baby birds that might be inside. Once, from her bedroom window, she stood transfixed as she watched two baby robins struggle to the edge of their nest and take their first flight. She peered into the nest her father held her up to, but this time the baby birds were gone.

"There are no baby birds in here, *tati*," she announced sadly as he lowered his daughter gently back down to the ground.

As they approached the woods, she smelled the pine and the fir trees and felt the squishy moss and lichens that grew beneath them. She loved the forest—its smells, its sounds, its textures. The darkness of the arboreal world made it seem like a magical kingdom to her, one where fairies and sprites might jump out at any moment. Sometimes, depending on which way the wind was blowing, she would get a whiff of the pungent odor of the turpentine factories that were not too far away, but that was not the case today.

When they reached the forest, Shayna pointed out a good spot, and Jonah lifted his arms wide and floated a large blanket down to the ground. Shayna sat down, straightened her skirt and made herself comfortable alongside the basket of carefully wrapped sandwiches, pastries and fruit. Jonah joined her and they both settled in to enjoy this relaxing moment together. Chaya-Sarah, on the otherhand, was too excited by all the wonders of the forest to waste her time relaxing, so she skipped off to pick wildflowers, always keeping her parents in sight.

After they finished lunch, which for Chaya-Sarah consisted of two bites of a sandwich and some fruit, Shayna leaned back on a tree. She kept an eye on her wandering daughter as Jonah put his head gently in his wife's lap and closed his eyes. "My poor father used to love to come on picnics with us, but now he can barely walk," Jonah said with sadness.

Shayna sighed and stroked her husband's thick hair, "He hasn't been eating much lately, either. Maybe I can coax him to eat some mushroom soup tonight—that's one of his favorites. My *tati* is not doing so well, either. He used to love to read and study Talmud, but now he seems to be tired all the time and just sleeps."

"Oy, if only our mamas could be here with them," Jonah mused out loud. Shayna nodded and continued stroking her husband's hair.

Not wanting to make them both too sad, he changed the subject, "What's going on with Hersheleh? Is your brother serious about the woman from America?"

"Oh, yes," Shayna answered, "I think so. She seems very nice, and she has her eyes on that handsome brother of mine. He'll probably go to America with her and get married. Her family is wealthy. They'll have a nice life." Their conversation was interrupted by two bunches of daisies being held under their noses.

"Wow! So beautiful," Shayna and Jonah both said to their daughter. "Thank you." Chaya-Sarah kept some for herself. She liked to pretend they were tall lion people with manes of petals and green leafy paws. She made a den of pine cones for them and put them on the blanket next to her father.

"It's time to find some mushrooms," Shayna announced. Jonah stood up, taking care not to disturb Chaya-Sarah's lions, and gallantly gave his wife a hand to help her to a standing position. Shayna brushed off her dress and rifled through the basket for the bag she brought along for the hunt. Chaya-Sarah told her lions she needed to leave for a while, but she would be back. Then she jumped up and raced ahead of her mother, stopping briefly to jump into a mound of crunchy, brown leaves. It was easy for her to turn the search for the succulent fungi into a lively game. Suddenly, she knelt down and pointed excitedly to a group of large mushrooms growing near her feet. "Look, mama, are these good ones?" Her mother taught her that certain mushrooms were poisonous which meant that they made people sick, if they were eaten.

Shayna bent over to look at the mushrooms her daughter was pointing out. "No, no, *maidele*, those are *nisht tsum esn* (not for eating)," Shayna answered gently, but firmly. Shayna knew of a very unfortunate incident involving children and poisonous mushrooms. She shuddered at the thought and silently vowed to make sure her daughter learned to accurately distinguish between the edible mushrooms and the poisonous varieties.

Shayna stood up, looking at another area that seemed promising, "Come, maybe we'll find some over here." She ambled toward a dark, shady area near a tall fir tree and lifted a large clump of moist, green moss.

"Here we go. Look at this," Shayna said. Underneath the moss grew four large, dark capped mushrooms with even darker stems. Shayna pointed out the differences in appearance between these and the other ones Chaya-Sarah found. She then showed her daughter how to remove them from the ground without damaging the fragile stems. Chaya-Sarah helped her mother gather the mushrooms into a bag, then raced back to her father to show him what they found.

Later that night, back in her kitchen, Shayna transformed them into a delicious and savory soup the entire family enjoyed.

◆ ◆ ◆

Some months later, Shayna and Jonah received a succession of very important and consequential news. The first item they discovered was that Shayna was carrying their second child. She was due to deliver the baby in the spring of 1937. They were both thrilled. Chaya-Sarah would be five by then and old enough to be of some help to her mother around the house. At least that was what they hoped. The second item was in a letter that arrived from New York. It was a heartbreaking story.

Jonah always looked forward to letters from his family in New York and always read them aloud. Unaware of the contents, Jonah smiled as he opened the letter from his brother Srolke in America. "Let's see what the news is from America," he said with excitement. Shayna sat near him at the kitchen table eager to hear how the family was doing. Strangely, he stopped reading almost as soon as he started. Jonah's eyes had involuntarily read ahead when he felt the floor shift suddenly as if it were made out of sand instead of solid wood. He sat down at the kitchen table as Shayna placed a hand on his shoulder. She did not have to see the color drain from his face to know that he just read devastating news.

"What is it?" she asked as her heart began to bang uncomfortably inside her chest.

Jonah looked at her, but did not answer immediately so she took the letter gently from him and began to read the words out loud. "Dear Jonah and Shayna, I am so sorry to have to tell you the terrible news that Shlemke died suddenly . . ." She put her hand over her mouth. The letter went on to say that it was probably a heart attack. They both looked at each other. Shlemke was not an old man—far from it. He had just celebrated his forty-sixth birthday. Nor was he sick. In fact, in his last letter, he was feeling good. Taped to the letter was a rectangular piece of newspaper, carefully cut from one of the Yiddish newspapers in New York City. It was his obituary. It stated the standard items found in such an article.

He leaves his wife, Sarah-Gitta, and four children, Abe, Raye, Edith and Miriam. His two brothers, also in New York, are named along with their families as are his brothers and sisters in Poland and his father, Hershel.

"This is so terrible," Shayna cried. "I'm so sorry for Sarah-Gitta and the children."

Jonah shook his head still trying to comprehend this news as another distressing thought came into his mind. "How are we going to tell my father?" Jonah asked. "He is already so sick—this will kill him."

They both silently worried over this for a while, then Shayna answered with another question, "Why do we have to tell him?"

"How can we not tell him that his eldest son died?" Jonah asked almost choking on the words, his eyes growing moist. They both became lost in their thoughts, again, then Jonah shook his head and said, "You know, you're absolutely right, he doesn't have to know. He shouldn't know. We'll tell Rachel and Rivka that we decided not to tell him."

Just then, a surprise with braids jumped out from under the table. Chaya-Sarah had quietly entered the kitchen while Shayna was reading the letter and scurried under the table holding two cloth dolls. That spot was her favorite cozy nest when adults were sitting at the kitchen table. It allowed her to play by herself, but at the same time enjoy the comfort of her parents being nearby. So engrossed were Shayna and Jonah in their conversation, they were not even aware that she was there. Shayna and Jonah both looked at their child with concern. Shayna quietly asked, "Chaya-Sari, how long have you been there?" The child just shrugged. Shayna realized that she needed to get to the point, "*Maidele*, did you hear what *tati* and I were talking about?"

"Yes," Chaya-Sarah answered. Shayna and Jonah each looked at the other and wondered what she actually heard. They needed to find out without repeating the actual words.

"What were we talking about, *maidele*? Jonah asked. "Do you remember what we said?"

"Um," Chaya-Sarah pointed to one of the dolls she was holding, "Mama, this doll has a torn dress."

"Yes, I see, I'll go right away and fix it, but your father asked you a question," Shayna said, then she repeated the question for her four-year-old.

"You said that Shlemke died," Chaya-Sarah announced brightly. Death was not something she understood, but she was all too capable of saying the words and repeating them to her grandfather.

"Listen, darling, you must not tell your grandfather," Shayna said sternly. "He is an old man and it will upset him too much." When her child did not respond, but only seemed to be distracted by her dolls, Shayna continued, "Chaya-Sari, are you listening to me? Let's not tell Papa Hershel. It will be our secret, okay?"

"Yes, mama," she answered dutifully. Then the child with the long, brown braids and the cloth dolls charged out of the kitchen to find her grandfather and tell him exactly what her parents did not want him to know.

◆ ◆ ◆

The news of his son's passing was a terrible shock for Hershel Kaufman who had not seen him since he went to America more than ten years ago. Hearing the words from his sweet Chaya-Sarah helped to soften the blow even if only a little. Five months later and probably unrelated to this incident since his health had already been failing, Hershel the *Royte* died peacefully in his sleep. His family and the people of Zbojna all mourned his passing. During the *Shiva* (initial period of mourning) neighbors sat with Shayna and Jonah and shared amusing stories about the legendary lumber man. He was well-liked in Zbojna and beyond. Shayna and Jonah told everyone they were grateful that his was a full life and that their daughter and his other grandchildren had given him so much *nakhes* (joy and pride) in his last years. Shayna helped Jonah write the difficult letter to Jonah's brothers and sister in New York which they tempered with these positive thoughts.

Not long after Hershel passed, Jonah and Shayna knew that it was time for the family to visit the U.S. Embassy in Warsaw and apply for visas. They had spoken often about moving to America, but it was not a consideration while Jonah's father was alive. They would never have left him. Current events spurred on their desire to leave as quickly as possible. Economic sanctions on Jewish people in Poland were getting tougher and vicious pogroms were becoming a common occurrence. On top of these unsavory local conditions, the news out of Germany grew more alarming every day. Now that Jonah's father passed, getting an American visa was foremost on their minds. It was an overwhelming fact of their lives that so much was riding on this single piece of paper. Like a magician's wand, that paper was the sorcery they needed to begin the process of transporting themselves to America. Shayna and Jonah were more than eager to follow Jonah's siblings to New York and start a new life there.

They would soon learn that it was going to be much more difficult now to get an American visa than it was for Jonah's brothers and their wives in the 1920s. America was still experiencing the trauma of the Great Depression which resulted in many people fearing that immigrants would drain government resources or worse, take jobs that American citizens needed. At the center of the American immigration debate was United States president Franklin Delano Roosevelt. How he handled the situation would be a matter of debate for decades to come, but one fact was incontrovertible. The country's immigration laws were tougher than ever before just at the moment in history when the Jewish people needed America's help the most.

The main force working in favor of the desperate immigrants were the Jewish Americans who were vocal about their concerns for family and friends caught in the hostilities heating up in Europe. The first thing Jonah knew he needed to do was get two letters from sponsors in America. Sponsors needed to provide proof that they not only had a job waiting for him in America, but if that job did not work out, they would be able to support the person being sponsored. In their letters, the two sponsors were also required to provide evidence of their own employment and financial situations. Even with two sponsors such as these, many visa applications were rejected. Without the sponsors, it was not even in the realm of the possible. Another issue that Shayna and Jonah were concerned about was that because of the difficulty of getting a visa for even one person and the expense of traveling to America, they were not certain they were going to be able to leave together. This was a stressful thought, but they only knew they had to try.

As soon as Jonah received the sponsorship letters from his brothers in America, the family from Zbojna boarded a wagon for Warsaw to visit the American embassy. There, they completed application forms for the entire family and submitted them along with copies of their birth certificates and the letters of sponsorship from Jonah's brothers. With Chaya-Sarah walking between them and holding both her parents' hands, Shayna and Jonah felt cautiously optimistic when they left the American Embassy in Warsaw.

❧ CHAPTER 7 ❧

1937
Zbojna, Poland

I cannot understand / The wild, mad lines / Written on
the misted window-panes, / By a withered twig.

~Rachel Korn

"Please pass the *kreplach*," Nachman asked his wife, Rivka, who was at the other end of the table. Rivka picked up a large bowl of the savory dumplings stuffed with chopped flanken and onions and passed it to her brother, Jonah, who passed it to Nachman.

"These are delicious, honey," Nachman said as he helped himself to a few more.

"Yes, they are excellent—just like my wife's," Jonah said with a wink and a nod to his younger sister.

"That's a great compliment. My sister-in-law is an excellent cook," Rivka answered, smiling sweetly.

Across from Jonah sat his nephew who was five-years-old and his niece who was three. The two youngsters began to giggle loudly as they tossed food into each other's laps. They both got scolded gently by their parents, but continued nevertheless. "That is enough," their mother announced. "If you both don't stop immediately, you are going to bed—no dessert." The siblings stopped abruptly, put their hands by their sides, lowered their heads and cast embarrassed looks at their uncle Jonah.

"Guess what?" Jonah asked, addressing his niece and nephew. "After dinner, I'm going to show you both some magic tricks using coins . . . What do you think of that?"

"Yay!" the duo cried in unison. Jonah smiled as the children's faces lit up, and they went back to their respective meals.

"What keeps you out overnight . . . more lumber orders tomorrow?" Nachman asked his brother-in-law. It was the spring of 1937, and it was not unusual for business to keep Jonah away from home overnight. He spent the day in a nearby forest, overseeing the delivery of an order of wood for one of his regular customers. He needed to be in Lomza tomorrow so rather than go home and come back the next day, he decided to stay in Lomza for the night at his sister's house.

"No, tomorrow I need to make some purchases for special orders," Jonah answered. Lomza's market on Thursdays was the closest market of its size and offered a wide variety of goods. Market day in Lomza brought vendors and merchants and their wares from nearby villages and towns and was a major weekly event in the area. Jonah and Shayna went there often—sometimes two or three times a month—to purchase items for their dry goods store as well as for the family's personal needs. With Shayna so far along in her pregnancy, Jonah wanted her to stay home, near the midwife.

"Oh," Nachman said. "I didn't realize you and Shayna offer that service for your customers."

"Yes, we started doing it a few months ago," Jonah answered, sitting back in his chair and loosening his belt. "The customized orders give us a lot of extra work, but it is a convenience the customers appreciate, especially the farmers, and the extra income helps us pay for tax increases and other expenses."

Nachman shook his head in agreement as he finished another mouthful of his dinner. He and his father were Kosher butchers so he was well aware of the rising tax burden on Jewish businesses and other expenses.

"Rivka," Jonah turned to his sister. "Thank you, dear. The meal was delicious."

"My pleasure. Anytime," Rivka said as she smiled at her brother and stood up to clear the dishes. The men got up and went out the front door to have a smoke as the children scampered away from the table to look for coins for their uncle to perform magic tricks.

Later that night, after dessert was eaten and the magic tricks were performed, Jonah closed the door to the guest room where he slept and opened his suitcase. He took out a picture of Shayna and Chaya-Sarah and placed it on the table beside his bed, removed his watch and got ready to go to sleep. He did not realize how exhausted he was until his head was on the soft, feather pillow and his weary eyes closed. His last thoughts before falling asleep were of his wife and daughter. He did not like leaving them, especially overnight. He decided that this was the last trip he would make for a while. Shayna was due to deliver in just a few weeks, and he wanted to be sure he was home when the baby arrived.

◆　◆　◆

Shayna closed the store a bit early the day her husband was away to spend more time with Chaya-Sarah. She decided she wanted to give her five-year-old an important lesson in the art of making cherry preserves. The sweet, red fruit was in abundance this time of year and it was the family's favorite for pies and to slather on thick slices of challah. Now, Chaya-Sarah stood proudly on a chair, stirring the large pot of crimson sauce while her mother held her securely around the waist.

"It smells so good, mama," her daughter proclaimed as she took a deep breath over the aromatic, boiling froth.

Mama's kitchen was a sacred place where all kinds of delicious alchemy transpired. Chaya-Sarah felt it a very special privilege to be asked to help her mother in the kitchen, but now her arm grew tired of stirring the thick liquid. She jumped off the chair, and let Shayna take over. When the sweet mixture was ready, Shayna carefully poured it in even amounts into seven glass jars she had lined up on the table. Shayna covered these, not too tightly, then put six of them on the bedroom window sill for cooling. She would normally put the jars on the kitchen window sill, but that was already covered with young sweet potato plants that Shayna was sprouting.

After the six jars were placed neatly on the bedroom window sill, Shayna noticed there were cherry stains everywhere, including Chaya-Sarah's button nose. She wet a *shmatte* (cloth rag) and removed all traces of cherry sauce from Chaya-Sarah's face, hands and neck. Then she saw some on her knee. "How did this get here? Was your knee hungry?" Shayna teased her daughter and they both laughed. "Now put your shoes on, please. We're going over to aunt Edke's for dinner." Shayna took a kitchen towel and wrapped it around the lone jar of jam left on the table. She thought it made a nice gift for her sister's family.

They had a quiet and pleasant evening at Edke's house. Shayna talked and laughed with her sister and brother-in-law, Meerche. She was grateful to have an appetite as she thought of her last pregnancy when she could barely eat at all. As usual, though, Chaya-Sarah barely ate anything before she ran off to play hide-and-seek with her cousins.

"What am I going to do with a *shtikl oysgetrunkn maidel* (piece of dried-up little girl)? She is so thin. She doesn't like food," Shayna told her sister and brother-in-law, shaking her head in defeat.

"Maybe you just have to find the right food. Maybe she is just a finicky eater," Edke suggested.

"I've tried everything. I make her a *pekele* (small package) with a sandwich and a piece of kugel . . . you know, when she goes out to play or goes to temple with Jonah. Or, I try to feed her *guggle-muggles* (milk, honey, and a raw egg) to fatten her up."

"Those are good ideas," Edke responds.

"You think? She doesn't touch any of it and Jonah gets so annoyed with me . . . he thinks I'm bothering her too much. 'Leave her alone,' he says, 'she's fine the way she is.'" Shayna laughed thinking of the scenario that has played out so many times and will probably replay many more.

After dinner, Shayna helped her sister clear the dishes, but Edke insisted that she stop and that she and Chaya-Sarah leave immediately because it was getting dark. Everyone blew kisses to one another, and Shayna thanked her sister for a wonderful meal. Edke waved her hand dismissively, "Thank you for the jam. I can't wait to try it."

Mother and daughter walked home slowly, enjoying the quiet of twilight and the stillness of the air. It seemed like even the birds were asleep. They both watched the colors of the sky turn into radiant purples and pinks as the evening sun melted into the horizon. "It's so beautiful, mama . . . I wish *tati* could see it," Chaya-Sarah said wistfully.

"Maybe he can," Shayna answered. Chaya-Sarah wrinkled her nose and thought deeply about how this could be true when she was distracted by the sight of a horse coming their way. She watched it come closer, framed by the brilliant sunset. Shayna waved as she recognized the farmer and his wife riding in the wagon behind the horse. It was unusual to see wagons out this close to sunset. Like all rural villages in Poland at the time, Zbojna streets were not lined with any lamps. Unless a bright moon hung in the sky, when the sun went down, the village was cloaked in a blanket of darkness brightened only by the tiny flickering of fireflies and the occasional soft glow of a kerosene lamp in a window. *Well,* Shayna thought to herself, *they are only a few minutes from their farm. They will be home before the night is completely dark.*

Shayna was glad when they reached their front door. She bent to pick up the evening paper and glanced at it as they walked in the door. She locked the door behind them. The headline was distressing. Apparently, there had been a recent increase in pogroms all over Poland, and some occurred north of Warsaw, close to where they lived. Too close. Several people in Jewish neighborhoods were killed. She shivered even though the air was warm and absentmindedly caressed her pregnant belly. She will be happy when Jonah gets home tomorrow, she thought.

"Mama, I'm thirsty," Chaya-Sarah cried. Shayna tossed the paper on a chair, and poured her a glass of water from the pitcher in the kitchen.

"After you finish, let's get ready for bed," Shayna told her. "It's been a long day and mama is tired." Chaya-Sarah finished her drink, then skipped merrily off to the bedroom.

Soon mother and daughter were comfortable in the matching pink floral nightgowns that Jonah brought home for his girls after a recent buying trip. In the soft glow of a kerosene lamp, Chaya-Sarah played with the flowers on her gown as she sat down in a chair by the bedroom dresser and readied herself for the bedtime routine that she and her mother both enjoyed so much. Mama would take her braids apart slowly, then very carefully so as not to cause any pain brush out her daughter's long, dark hair and remove any knots or tangles. As she did this, Shayna would sing to her, which she began to do now. As always, mother and daughter became lulled, like two babies being gently rocked in a cradle, by the rhythm of the brush gliding through Chaya-Sarah's hair and the sweet sound of Shayna's voice.

> *Tumbala, tumbala, tum-balalaika*
> *Tumbala, tumbala, tum-balalaika*
> *Tumbalalaika—shpiel balalaika* (play balalaika)
> *Tumbalalaika—freylach zol zayn* (merry we'll be)

When the song ended and Chaya-Sarah's long, soft curls were unencumbered by braids and free of knots, Shayna kissed the top of her daughter's head. She walked over to her side of the bed which was near the window and checked the jars of cherry preserves on the window sill. Satisfied that they were cooling nicely, she turned out the lamp as they both climbed into the double bed that usually held three of them. Jonah typically read bible stories to Chaya-Sarah as she drifted off to sleep, but tonight Shayna was too tired to fill that role. Chaya-Sarah kissed her mother goodnight and said, "Mama, can you sing more?" As Shayna began to sing softly, the little girl nestled into her mother's body and kissed her pregnant belly.

"Goodnight, baby," she said tenderly. "Mama?"

"Yes, *maidele*?" Shayna's eyes were already closing.

"When the baby comes will you and *tati* tell me the name?" Chaya-Sarah asked.

"Of course we will tell you. We just don't like to say the baby's name before it comes. It's bad luck." This satisfied Chaya-Sarah who closed her eyes and soon fell into a deep slumber.

◆ ◆ ◆

At three o'clock in the morning, a rectangular sliver of moonlight made its way into the otherwise dark room and landed on the end of the bed near Shayna's right foot. Mother and daughter had already been asleep for hours so they did not see it. An owl hooted outside their window, but they also did not hear that. Shayna was too far away in a dream to sense anything happening in the room around her. It seemed like she was in Montevideo, but she could not be sure. Dreams can be so strange. She was wearing a soft, flowing white dress and she was with Jonah who looked dapper in a black jacket. His thick hair was slicked back with hair gel the way the men in Uraguay liked to wear it. She smiled at him. She felt so happy. He held her lightly in his arms, then twirled her around to the soft beat of a Latin rhythm. They must be near the ocean because she heard the soothing sound of waves behind the music although she did not see the water. She sensed that Chaya-Sarah was there, too, playing on the sandy beach, but she did not see her.

Quite suddenly a thunderous noise came crashing into her dream. The happy feeling began to dissipate, but Shayna did not understand the disturbance. She felt a sense of confusion, even in the dream. The sound of shouting men filled her dream and finally drowned out the music and the sound of the waves. She could not tell what was being said, but she knew the men were angry. She felt frightened. Before she could figure out what was being said, the dream was shattered by an earsplitting explosion. Her eyes flew open, but she still felt groggy from the dream. The noise seemed so close. Oddly, she could feel something, too. Something sharp stung her face and her arms, and there was wetness, too. Was she still dreaming? She was not sure. Then a scream pierced the air around her and Shayna knew she was awake. This was real. Her body bolted to an upright position and she struggled to make sense of what was happening. It did not take her long to realize that Chaya-Sarah was screaming.

"Mama," she cried, "something cut me!" Shayna tried to steady her trembling muscles and collect her thoughts. Chaya-Sarah's screams abated and became whimpers when she felt her mother sit up next to her.

"I'm here," Shayna managed to say in a breathless voice. "Mama is here." As her eyes adjusted to the darkness, she looked down at her daughter. What she saw shocked her. Both she and her daughter were covered with grey rocks of every size surrounded by what seemed to be shards of broken glass. And there was something else. It was wet and shiny and red like blood. Shayna's breath caught in her throat like a trapped bird. The blood was everywhere. She and her daughter were covered with it. She looked up and around the room. Where the window had been was now a gaping hole directly to her right. The chill of the night blew in and struck her face and arms. She looked down at the bed and her mind began to piece together the puzzle of what had just happened. The voices she heard must have come from people outside her window who threw rocks into her bedroom. The rocks broke the window, covering her and Chaya-Sarah with an avalanche of glass and stones.

She blinked a few times and felt the panic rising in her chest. *I have to get up*, she thought. *I have to turn on the light*. Her mind began to run through a checklist of things she must do. *I have to stop the bleeding*. Over and over she repeated the list as she lifted herself out of bed, taking care not to cut herself on the glass that was all over her and on the floor. As she stood up, a torrent of rocks and broken glass fell from her nightgown to the floor. She heard her daughter whimper, so she yelled to her, "Don't move, *maidel*, don't move. Mama's coming."

She reached for the kerosene lamp to turn it on, but the lamp was not there. *It must have been knocked over*, she thought. Her nostrils were suddenly filled with a pungent, oily odor. Kerosene. *It must be all over the floor. Vey iz mir* (Woe is me). She knew she had to get over to her daughter's side of the bed and she had to walk through the darkness. Lighting a match was too dangerous. She placed her feet carefully on a floor which was an obstacle course of broken glass, rocks and slippery kerosene. She tried to step lightly and quickly, but it was impossible to avoid the mess. In the dim light, she was not able to see what was on the floor. A sudden stabbing pain sliced into her left foot like a knife. She sucked in a loud breath, then cried out.

"Mama?!" Chaya-Sarah called out in response.

"I'm okay, I'm okay. Just stay still. I'm coming," Shayna said as she lifted her left foot and removed a chunk of glass that lodged in her throbbing heel. She sucked in a breath and winced as she put her bleeding foot back down on the floor and began to move again. It felt as though her body weight had doubled in the last few minutes. Her hand instinctively went to the underside of her swollen belly as if her baby needed support. She worried that the baby might be hurt, but she first had to reach Chaya-Sarah, she told herself. *I have to stop the bleeding.* She continued to move to her daughter in the dim light in what felt like slow motion, repeating over and over to herself: *Stop the bleeding. Just stop the bleeding.*

When she finally got to the other side of bed, Chaya-Sarah who was not moving, but only whimpering, lifted her arms up to her mother and made a moaning sound. "I can't pick you up right now. Wait, *maidel.* Wait, just one more minute," Shayna said breathlessly as she turned on the kerosene lamp on that side of the room. The light flooded a room that looked foreign to them both. Almost every surface of the room was covered in shards of glass that shone like an army of crystal knives. At least a dozen rocks were strewn about like pirates sitting atop their booty. It looked like the entire scene was spotted with pools of deep, red blood. Shayna gasped, then jumped into action.

"Stand up and lift your arms," she said as she began to carefully remove Chaya-Sarah's nightgown.

"Don't move. I need to see where you're cut," Shayna explained. Her heart beat wildly and she was as out-of-breath as if she had been running for an hour. She carefully checked her daughter's body in the lamplight to see where the blood was coming from. Not here. Not there. She looked over the smooth surface of the young skin and found nothing but a small cut in her right index finger where she must have touched a piece of glass. She checked her again, her eyes, her head, her ears. Where was all the blood coming from? Chaya-Sarah was fine. *Is it me?* she thought. *Is it the baby?* With a cold feeling of dread, she lifted the skirt of her nightgown and looked down at her legs. There was nothing. The crimson streaks she expected to see were not there. She tried to take a breath, but could not get a full one. Then she noticed that her left hand had smears of blood on it. She held her hand up to her face. She could not see where the blood was coming from. She also thought it was strange that it was not acting the way blood usually behaves. This blood seemed thicker and it felt tacky to the touch. She brought her hand up close to her face to get a better look. As her hand got closer, she paused and became confused. Her nostrils did not fill with the cold, iron smell of blood as she expected. Instead, she found herself smelling the subtle, but sweet perfume of cherry preserves.

It's not blood, Shayna thought, and took a deep breath. All at once, everything made sense to her. The rocks hurled through the window destroyed the jars of cherry preserves and spread glass and cherry jam onto them and onto the bed. She felt some sense of relief, but her mind was still racing. Maybe it was from the shock or the sudden exertion or both, but her body began to shake violently. She tried to steady herself and think of what to do next. There was still glass everywhere. *I need to get both of us into fresh clothes*, she thought to herself. She looked over at Chaya-Sarah who was watching her mother wide-eyed and silent. Shayna stumbled to the dresser, opened the top drawer and willed her trembling limbs to obey her as she tried to take out clean nightgowns for the two of them.

Shayna changed both of them quickly, then lifted her daughter into her arms and out of the bed. Just as she did that, loud banging on the front door made them both jump. Chaya-Sarah nestled her face into her mother's neck and squeezed her eyes shut. Shayna took a deep breath, got her balance and began walking toward the front door. There was the loud knocking again. Shayna felt as though her heart was banging in time with the knocking. Chaya-Sarah began to cry. As she approached the door, she heard the frantic words of her sister and breathed a sigh of relief.

"Shayna, open the door! Shayna, are you there?" Edke cried. "Please open the door!"

Shayna's hand shook as she fumbled with the lock. She pushed open the door and saw Edke standing in a robe, tears streaming down her face, her hair a dark, disheveled mass on her head. Behind her was her husband, Meerche, holding a lantern. "Oh my God, are you alright?" Edke asked. "Is Chaya-Sarah alright?" She looked at Shayna's pale face and tried to take Chaya-Sarah from her, but the child would not let go of her mother.

"Yes, we're alright, I think. They threw rocks into the house. There was glass and jam . . . I thought it was blood . . ." Shayna trailed off. "I . . . I need to sit down."

"Blood?" Edke asked. Meerche put an arm around Shayna and guided her, with her daughter clinging to her, into a kitchen chair while Edke lit the kerosene lamp over the table.

"Vey iz mir," Shayna exclaimed as she sat down with a thud, placing her right elbow on the table and her head in her right hand.

Edke kneeled down by her sister and saw the streaks of red, "You got hurt?"

"No, no, Chaya-Sarah got a small cut, but this is cherry jam," she held up her hand to show her sister. "What about you . . . the kids . . . *tati* . . . is everyone alright?"

"Thank God, we're fine," Edke said. "They broke two windows in the kitchen. I was so worried about you and Chaya-Sarah with Jonah being away, but Meerche would not let me leave the house until he was sure those *chalerias* (horrible people) were gone."

When he saw that his niece and sister-in-law were not harmed, Meerche walked out of the room for a few minutes. When he came back, he reported the damage to the rest of the house. "Wow, the bedroom is in bad shape," he said, "it's a mess and it looks like there is blood everywhere."

"The cherry jam we made today," Shayna sighed. "I put the jars in the bedroom window to cool. *Vey iz mir,* I thought it was blood, too."

"You and Chaya-Sarah will come over and spend the rest of the night with us. Tomorrow we'll clean up the bedroom," Edke announced and everyone silently agreed.

Edke put her arms around her sister and kissed her head. "Are you able to stand up?" she asked. Shayna nodded as she struggled to get up still holding Chaya-Sarah. Her brother-in-law rushed to her side to help her.

"What do they want from us?" Shayna wondered out loud. "What did we ever do to them?"

"Vey iz mir," Edke said as she followed her sister and husband out of the kitchen.

◆ ◆ ◆

Early the next morning, Jonah ate his breakfast quickly, hugged his sister and her family and left. He was eager to get the day's work done and go home to his wife and daughter. He waved to an eastbound wagon that was already almost full of people. The driver pulled over and stopped for him. "Can you drop me in the market square?" Jonah asked. The driver nodded and as Jonah began to climb aboard, he heard people talking about something that happened in Zbojna last night.

"Excuse me," he asked as he sat down and the driver prompted his horses to start moving. "What happened in Zbojna last night?"

One man looked at him and shook his head, "It was a vicious pogrom. At least six men were seen runnng through the main street and throwing rocks into windows of Jewish homes. They even set fire to . . ." The man did not get to the end of his sentence before Jonah jumped up and yelled to the driver to please stop because he must get off immediately. The driver raised his eyebrows and mumbled something under his breath as he pulled to the side of the road and slowed his horses to a stop.

"I'm sorry for your trouble," Jonah said as he handed the driver a few *zloty*. He apologized to the other passengers, grabbed his suitcase and jumped off the wagon. There would be no business in Lomza today. He must get home. He flagged down the next wagon going in the other direction and jumped aboard. The hour ride from Lomza to Zbojna was the longest hour of his life. His heart thrummed so hard it felt as though it was trying to escape from his chest. He was sure the other passengers could hear it. Every time the wagon stopped to pick up or drop off passengers, he was barely able to control the urge to jump off and run home. His girls. The baby. *Please God*, he prayed, *let my family be alright.*

When the wagon finally stopped in front of his house, he jumped off so fast he forgot to pay the driver. "Sorry, sorry," he said as he raced back with the money. Then he turned, took five running leaps and burst through the door of his house.

"Shayna! Chaya-Sarah! Where are you?"

He entered the kitchen just as mother and daughter were eating their breakfast. They both stopped immediately and Chaya-Sarah ran to him.

"*Tati*!" she cried as he wrapped his arms around her, then opened his arms to let his wife in. After a long hug and establishing that everyone was alright, at least physically, he sat down and listened to his wife and daughter tell him everything that happened.

Tears filled his eyes as he listened. It pained him that he was not there to protect his family.

◆ ◆ ◆

The next day, the family's bedroom was back to normal except for the wooden boards covering the broken window. There was a clean blanket on the bed and the floor had been swept several times. Things can be repaired, but people, especially hearts, are harder to heal. Shayna was overcome with an extreme fatigue and a sense of forboding since last night. She could not seem to calm herself. There were other casualties, too. In addition to the terror felt by everyone, Edkelkee's father suffered a concussion when a large rock hit his head as he slept and an elderly man was cut so badly that he was in a hospital in Lomza, fighting a serious infection. Another neighbor's home was burned to the ground. The family just managed to get out in time. The Jewish people of Zbojna reacted as best they could to the attack, using whatever resources they had. Windows were reinforced with shutters. Beds and chairs were moved away from windows. The Kaufman's store began to stock better locks for doors. Fathers resolved not to do business that took them too far from home. One family decided to move to a bigger city believing there would be safety in numbers.

In her spotless bedroom, Shayna lay in her bed, but she was not resting. Ease and comfort were distant dreams for her. Even though the baby was not due for almost two months, she started feeling labor pains in the early hours of the morning. Worried about the health of his wife and baby, Jonah called for the midwife. He would not have to worry for long. She got there quickly, examined Shayna and informed him that this was no false labor. The baby was coming and it was coming fast.

"The baby's head is showing!" the midwife cried out. "Push! Push!" Family and friends who gathered in the house heard this and were holding their collective breaths. Chaya-Sarah was playing on the kitchen floor with some of her cousins and she heard it, too, but more than that she felt the excitement and the tension in the room. She looked up at Edke and asked, "Is the baby here?"

"Soon, *mameleh* (little mother)," Edke said not even trying to hide the tension in her voice. "I think your brother or sister will be here very soon."

The family and friends heard a few more minutes of shouting, then there were no more sounds coming from inside the bedroom. Just silence. Everyone looked at one another. Edke got up slowly and began to walk to the bedroom door, but stopped suddenly when the door began to open. Everyone turned to stare as Jonah stepped out and looked around the room. His eyes were red. "Mirzsa, Edke," he called out, "please come." The sisters looked at each other and got up quickly. They both walked through the door and Jonah followed, closing it behind them. Once in the room, the sisters looked anxiously at the midwife who was holding a tiny, still bundle, then they looked at their sister and they knew immediately. Shayna was sitting up with her face cradled in her hands as her body was wracked by waves of silent sobs. They ran and embraced her.

"It's because of the pogrom," Shayna moaned softly. "Those *chalerias* (horrible people) killed my baby." She leaned into her sisters for a few moments, appreciative of their support, then sat up straight. "Please," Shayna said, "I need to hold him." Jonah was sobbing now as he took the body of his son, who never breathed a single breath, and passed it gently to his wife. She held her stillborn child and rocked him gently in her arms as Jonah sat beside her on the bed and placed his arm around her trembling shoulders. Shayna's sisters sat down on the other side of their sister and burst into tears.

"A *kleyne yingel* (little boy)," Edke moaned, putting her face in her hands.

The midwife walked over to the grieving couple, placed her hands on their shoulders and said, "I'm so sorry, dear friends. Is there anything else I can do?"

Jonah looked at the midwife with pained eyes and said, "Can you please tell Yudke to bring the rabbi?"

"Of course," she answered as she gathered her things to go.

Jonah looked back down at his wife and son. As the midwife opened the door to leave, everyone in the room became aware of a skirmish taking place just outside the door. Jonah and Shayna's sisters looked up to see Chaya-Sarah emerging from the center of it and charging through the door. Mirzsa jumped up and tried to keep her from entering the room, but the child struggled against her crying, "I want my mama and *tati*!"

Shayna lifted her head and said, "It's alright. Let her come in." Then she motioned for Edke to take the baby.

Chaya-Sarah ran to her parents and her father lifted her onto his lap. She looked at him, saw the tears on his face then her mother's. Disturbed, but not knowing why, she asked to see the baby. There was a pause as Jonah collected his thoughts. With great difficulty, he gently explained to Chaya-Sarah that the baby went to heaven to be with God. When she asked why, he told her it was because that was what God wanted.

"But why does God want that? Why doesn't he want us to have the baby?" Chaya-Sarah asked, needing to know more.

"We don't always understand why God does something," Jonah told her in a breaking voice. Chaya-Sarah frowned, thinking hard about her father's words.

"God always knows the right thing to do, *maidele*," Jonah added softly. Chaya-Sarah sat quietly absorbing this new information about how the world worked as Jonah looked lovingly down at his daughter's face. When tears started rolling down her cheeks, Jonah lifted her and moved her to the bed between him and his wife. Shayna, who was unable to speak any words, hugged her daughter as Jonah wrapped his arms around them both. The family of three began to rock together slowly as they cried . . . and cried . . . and cried.

1938
Zbojna and Ostroleka, Poland

No matter what ones economic or social status, and regardless of
whether one resided in the humblest of hovels on the outskirts
of the shtetl or the grandest of brick buildings lining the market
square, each house became a palace and every man a king, every
woman a princess ready to welcome the Sabbath Queen.

~Yaffa Eliach, *There Once Was A World*

For the family that lived on the main street of Zbojna, not too much
changed in their daily routine since that sad spring day nine months
earlier. The family businesses were doing well and keeping Jonah and
Shayna busy every moment of every day. Chaya-Sarah started first grade
and was a smidge taller, but still thin, much to Shayna's dismay, and she
was just as mischievous as ever. A few weeks ago she climbed a tree in front
of their house after being warned many times not to climb trees, fell off
one of the lower branches and skinned her knee badly. Her father tried
to soothe her with soft words as he picked her up and carried her into the
house so her mother could clean and bandage the wound, "Shhhh, Shhhh,
don't cry, *maidele*. Don't cry."

She answered him with a new phrase she started using when she cried,
but only since she lost her baby brother, "I'm not crying, *tati, mayn harts
veynt* (my heart is crying)." The words touched her parents deeply, but
they did not know where she got them.

One Wednesday afternoon, Chaya-Sarah dashed into the store after
school, her braids flying in every direction. Shayna was checking the
amounts in the cash drawer behind the counter, and Jonah was clearing
the December holiday decorations from the store. They decorated all year

long for the many Jewish holidays like Rosh Hashana, Chanukah, Sukkot, Purim, Tu Bishvat, and Simchat Torah, but they also began to put up a colorful tree in December out of respect for their non-Jewish customers.

Shayna and Jonah both immediately stopped what they were doing and looked at their daughter. Two customers in the store were curious, too. On the counter before them Chaya-Sarah placed one *groshen* (fraction of a penny) and looked at her parents, smiling broadly.

"What's this?" her mama asked.

"I got this in school today! I knew the answer to a bible question!"

The proud parents looked at each other, their faces beaming. "That's wonderful!" Shayna cried out.

"The rabbi held his hand up really high over his head, then he dropped the coin on the table," Chaya-Sarah continued. She demonstrated by standing on the tips of her toes and lifting her right hand as high as it could possibly go. "He tried to make it look like it came from God, but I know the rabbi did it."

"We are so proud of you," Jonah announced as he picked up his daughter and proudly waltzed her around the store. The two women in the store cheered and clapped at Chaya-Sarah's accomplishment.

"How much candy can I buy with this?" the happy girl wanted to know. Her mother explained that it would buy two pieces of candy from the barrel.

"You save your money," her father told her, laughing. "Everything in the store is already yours."

They were even more impressed a few weeks later when she wrote her name using Hebrew letters, the typical way that Yiddish was written. Her father taught her to read when she was four, but the writing he left to her teachers. He bought her books from the Yiddish booksellers he met in his business travels or borrowed books from the library down the street. When he read to her he pointed out the words and encouraged her to read along with him. Like many Jewish families in Poland at the time, literacy was highly valued so it was not unusual for children to be reading long before they started school. One of Chaya-Sarah's favorite nighttime routines, after her mother brushed her hair, was to choose two books, climb into bed and read with her father.

Right now, though, she wanted to play with friends. "Can Edkelkee come over and play?"

"Yes, of course," Shayna said. "First, go and change into your *shpiel* (play) clothes, and wear your coat if you go outside, please," Shayna said.

◆ ◆ ◆

The next day was Thursday which was typically a big day in Jewish neighborhoods in Poland and around the world. The Jewish street in Zbojna was no exception. Not only was it market day in nearby Lomza, but it was also the day before *Erev Shabbes* (Sabbath Eve), and preparations for welcoming the Sabbath Queen would begin. White table linens and cloth napkins were washed thoroughly and hung out to dry on backyard clotheslines strung between trees. Fine *Shabbes* dresses and suits were scrutinized and cleaned or mended as needed. Some people shopped for what they needed for the *Shabbes* meal—fish, chicken, meat, fruits, and vegetables—at the local greengrocer. Others jumped into horse-drawn wagons for the hour-long ride to Lomza, preferring a large market for their shopping. Jonah was among those traveling to Lomza while Shayna stayed home and took care of the store. He left very early in the morning so he also had time to purchase supplies and special orders for the store. Since the vicious pogrom last year and its sad aftermath, he no longer stayed away from home overnight, so he planned to be back before dark tonight.

A steady stream of customers paraded in and out of the dry goods store that day. Shayna barely had a minute to herself, but somehow managed, while she was tending the store, to run through a mental inventory of her preparations for *Shabbes*. Edke and her family were planning to join them for the *Shabbes* meal along with Shayna's father, Moshe. Her holiday table linens were already cleaned, starched, folded and ready for tomorrow night. Her dress and Chaya-Sarah's, too, were cleaned, pressed and hanging in the closet as was Jonah's suit.

She thought about the meal preparation that needed to start tonight after she closed the store. The *Shabbes* meal always began with the challah and was followed by the gefilte fish with its zesty grated horseradish sauce all of which she liked to prepare the night before. After they cooled, Jonah will put the fish and the horseradish in the cold cellar. The challah can stay out overnight. *Let's see*, Shayna's planning continued to the next day. She would be devoted to meal preparation tomorrow while Jonah took care of the store. *I will make the chicken soup tomorrow morning along with the knaidlach (matzoh balls) which must be nice and firm, the way Jonah and Chaya-Sarah like them.* For the main dish, she would make a roast turkey with a side dish of *kasha mit varnishkas* (buckwheat groats with bow-tie egg noodles) seasoned with fried onions. Edke was bringing a sweet carrot-plum *tzimmes* (stew) as another side dish. For dessert, Shayna planned to bake an apple pie in the late afternoon to be served warm right from the oven.

She stopped her thought process to chat with two customers, complete their purchase transactions and thank them. She congratulated one lady on becoming a grandmother for the first time. Her mind then continued to plan. *Tomorrow morning, while the soup is cooking, I'll clean the house from top to bottom, change the linens, and polish the candlesticks and all of the serving dishes. In the afternoon, I will prepare the pie and the turkey and while they are in the oven, I will wax the floors. After that, the kasha must be prepared. When Chaya-Sarah comes home from school, I need to wash her hair and braid it after it dries.* Suddenly, she remembered she was out of floor wax. She made a mental note to get an extra can when she closed the shop tonight. It was a good thing Jonah bought so much of that from the market in Lomza. Everyone who has been in the store today was buying one or two cans of it.

Her mind went back to the planning. There should be just enough time near the end of the day tomorrow for her to help Chaya-Sarah put on her dress and join her father for Friday night *Shabbes* services before dinner. She sighed, feeling comfortable that everything was under control as she looked up and greeted the next customer entering the store.

◆ ◆ ◆

The next night, Shayna smiled to herself and chatted with her sister as everyone sat down at the *Shabbes* table that was covered with a beautiful white table cloth and dishes that Shayna and Jonah received as wedding gifts in Montevideo. The *Shabbes* candles that Shayna lit earlier in the evening cast a magical glow over the faces of her family. She beamed with pride at her handsome husband and beautiful daughter. The children were laughing and giggling at some private joke, but grew obediently silent as the adults lifted their wine glasses to begin the *Shabbes* dinner. Jonah gave his father-in-law the honor of reciting the *kiddush* (blessings) over the wine. Chaya-Sarah's eyes sparkled with fascination as she watched the candlelight dance on the long silvery strands of Papa Moshe's beard as he spoke. *"Baruch atah Adonai Elohaynu Melech Ha'Olam, borei peri ha'gafen* (Blessed art Thou, Lord, our God, King of the Universe, who creates the fruit of the vine)."

Everyone said, "Amen," and the adults each took a sip of wine.

Jonah stood up and sliced into the soft challah as he recited the *motzi* (blessing over the bread), and Shayna passed the bread around. *"Baruch atah Adonai Elohaynu Melech Ha'Olam, ha-motzi lechem min ha-aretz* (Blessed art Thou, Lord, our God, King of the Universe who brings forth bread from the earth)."

Everyone said "Amen" and enjoyed a few bites of Shayna's delicious challah. There was a moment of silence in the room as if all were privately savoring the transition from their busy work week to the sacred *Shabbes* and its otherworldly sense of contemplation and serenity. Then, all at once, serving plates of food were passed around the table and at least four conversations started. Many topics were covered on a wide variety of subjects including what the children learned in school or preschool, the health and wellbeing of family members in America, weekend plans, taxes, a bit of innocent local gossip, fears about what was going on in Germany, and the state of affairs of the Jewish people in Poland. All discussions were peppered with loud and happy howling about how delicious everything was as Shayna bustled around the table, making sure glasses and plates were kept full. By the time the apple pie made an appearance, everyone announced they were too stuffed to eat another bite. Even so, no one was able to resist at least one slice of the warm, sweet confection from Shayna's kitchen. In fact, the pie was gone before the evening was over.

◆　◆　◆

The next day was a typical Saturday. In the morning Chaya-Sarah wore a pretty, new dress and her dark hair was freshly combed and braided into two perfectly even strands as she held her father's hand and accompanied him to *Shabbes* services at the synagogue down the street. She carried the *pekele* (small package) of food her mother gave her that she more than likely would not even open. While the adults in the congregation sat with their prayerbooks and listened to the rabbi, Chaya-Sarah played with the *tsitsiss* (strings) on her father's *talis* (prayer shawl), carefully braiding and unbraiding them. When that got boring, she went outside to play with the other children. By noon, father and daughter were home, sitting at the kitchen table with Shayna for a *Shabbes* lunch of chicken soup, chopped liver, and smoked fish. After lunch Shayna and Jonah opened the store for a few hours so their non-Jewish customers could shop. Chaya-Sarah played outside with her cousins and friends, returning only for a drink of water or some candy, until her parents closed the store and called her in for dinner.

Sunday, too, was a typical one. The family enjoyed a relaxed and leisurely morning together. It was the one morning Jonah gave himself time to sit back and read the Yiddish paper. After breakfast, they put on their coats and went out for a stroll and some fresh air. They waved to neighbors and stopped to chat with friends and family who were also out enjoying the day. Chaya-Sarah proudly named all the winter birds she was able to identify, like the buntings and the waxwings. When they returned, Shayna made her family lunch, then she and Jonah opened the store for a few hours in case their Jewish customers needed anything. Chaya-Sarah played outside with her cousins and friends, returning only for a drink of water or some candy, until her parents closed the store and called her in for dinner.

The next morning, the family awoke and started their weekday routine. Shayna got Chaya-Sarah dressed for school and the family sat down for a quick breakfast. Holding her books and a bag her mother packed with lunch, Chaya-Sarah kissed her parents who were finishing their coffee and joined her friends who were on their way to school. After Chaya-Sarah left, it was business as usual for the Kaufmans. Shayna finished cleaning the breakfast dishes, prepared a pie and put it in the oven to bake. She then joined Jonah who was already in the store chatting with customers. Shayna took her place at the cash box so Jonah could be free to do the heavy lifting. Periodically, she darted back into her kitchen to check on the pie that was in the oven. She did not stay in the kitchen long because there was a steady stream of customers. The first business day after the weekend was usually a busy one in the store and this Monday was no different. In short, it was a typical Monday morning until the moment it was not. That moment was when everyone smelled smoke. Shayna noticed it first. She lifted her head and sniffed the air deeply. She looked over at her husband and was about to ask him if he smelled smoke when a neighbor burst into the store.

"There is smoke coming out of your kitchen window!" he shouted.

Everyone in the store stopped what they were doing and looked at Shayna and Jonah with alarm. Since Shayna was nearest the back of the store, she reached the door that led into the kitchen before Jonah did. A cry stuck in Shayna's throat as she opened the door. The curtains on the east wall were ablaze with bright yellow flames that were pushing dark columns of thick smoke into the air. Before she could even shriek, Jonah ran past her into the burning kitchen.

"Stay back," he shouted. "Everyone out." Jonah stopped for a split second and looked at his wife. "You, too," he said as he turned and raced out to the water pump in the back yard.

Shayna turned and ushered the customers who were still in the store outside. Once she knew everyone was safe, she ran back into the store and opened the door to the kitchen. Shayna could not stand idle while there was a fire raging in her home. With fear hammering in her chest, she watched the hungry flames devour everything they touched and noticed the large patches of blue sky where the wall and ceiling used to be. She started to run to help Jonah, but he stopped her.

"Don't you dare," he said sternly. "Go outside . . . now." Her husband was rarely stern with her so she reluctantly obeyed.

Jonah and the men continued to run back and forth between the fire and the closest water pumps, bringing buckets of water to throw at the burning house. Others gathered to watch in horror as the thick, black smoke rose high into the sky. Fires were not unusual in these homes made of wood, but it was always terrifying to see.

What seemed like hours, but was probably more like twenty or thirty minutes later, the men were able to extinguish the fire except for a few red embers scattered throughout the wreckage. An exhausted Jonah stood next to his wife in their front yard with family, neighbors and friends, surveying what was left of their home. Gone was the entire east wall of the house, half the interior walls, and much of the roof. Almost half of the merchandise in the store was burned or smoldering, and the kitchen was a blackened shell of its former self.

"Did it start in the kitchen?" someone asked.

"Maybe it was a spark from the oven that started burning the curtains," one lady suggested. "That's what happened to my sister's house in Nowogrod."

People continued to murmur their ideas and suggestions as they placed hands on the shoulders of Shayna and Jonah, spoke their regrets and offered to help in whatever way they were able. Edke put her arm around her sister's waist and the two women stared into the blackened mess that was once a home. "Let's see what we can save," she said. "Then you'll pack some clothes and stay with us tonight."

Jonah put up a sign in front of their house that read 'Fire Sale'. That afternoon and the next day, people came and emptied the store of its salvageable merchandise that Shayna and Jonah sold at half price. The next night at Edke's house, Shayna's brother, Yudke came over to offer his support and discuss next steps with the family. As they all sat around the table after dinner, drinking tea and eating *mandel-broyt* (almond cookie), Moshe expressed gratitude that it was just damage to property, and no one was hurt. They all agreed and listened attentively as Shayna and Jonah told them of the plans the two of them made. They wanted to rebuild a new home in Zbojna, but they needed to live across the river in Ostroleka while the home was being built. Ostroleka was a much bigger town than Zbojna so it offered many apartments for rent, and as they all knew, Jonah had family there. Jonah planned to go there tomorrow to find a furnished apartment to rent and make arrangements for the family to move in the next day or so.

◆   ◆   ◆

Two days later, the family of three rode on a horse-drawn wagon with most of their belongings in four suitcases of various sizes. Some of the family's belongings and furniture were moved into the homes of Shayna's sister and brother until the family moved back. They were heading south for what would be a twenty-mile journey to Ostroleka. They made this trek before to visit family and friends who lived there or for shopping trips to obtain merchandise for their store. With her hands curved over the side of the wagon and her chin resting on her hands, Chaya-Sarah watched the cows and sheep, fields of crops, wildflowers and trees of the forest go by. She laughed and called out to her parents to look when they passed a dog chasing some chickens and some children chasing the dog. When the scenery began to blend into a steady haze of trees and grass, she leaned on her father and put her head on his shoulder. Jonah put his arm around her and kissed her head as she closed her eyes.

After an hour and a half, the wagon finally reached the Narew river. There was no bridge here. The only way to get across the river was by boat or raft. Chaya-Sarah stared wide-eyed as the horse pulling their wagon was led onto a large, flat raft made of gigantic logs lashed together by many layers of twine rope. A man aboard the raft held out a sugar cube and gently coaxed the horse to come on board. The horse stepped gingerly onto the raft as water sloshed up through the openings between the logs and the raft tilted under the weight of the horse and wagon. *How can the raft hold something as big and heavy as this wagon full of people and a horse?* Chaya-Sarah wondered as she watched closely. She turned to her parents, but they were deep in a serious conversation as the man steadied the horse. Obviously, the men as well as the horse had done this before. They seemed to know what they were doing. Certainly, Chaya-Sarah had seen it before, but she never got tired of watching it. Soon, a man on the raft put his thumb and index finger between his lips and blew two loud whistles. He then pushed a huge oar up against the dock and the raft began to float gently away from the shore. She watched with fascination as the man used the oar to guide the raft through the water. When she had seen enough, she made herself comfortable between her parents for the remainder of the journey down and across the river.

◆　◆　◆

Ostroleka, a town 75 miles north of Warsaw where Jonah was born, was home to a community of over 4,500 Jewish people. Living here while the new house was being built in Zbojna would be comfortable for the homeless family, Jonah thought. His uncle, his mother's younger brother, Fivel Finkelstein, his daughter, Rivka, and two sons lived there. A large and ancient forest that was nearby meant that Jonah would be able to conduct his lumber export business while the family was there. The town also offered a wide variety of merchandise and services in a cornucopia of markets, salons and emporiums. With a few cars passing by on its many paved roads and a lot of people riding bicycles, Ostroleka also had two- and three-story buildings that gave it a modern, progressive feel to the family from the tiny village. Jonah rented a second-floor apartment with a kitchen and one large room for everything else—living, sleeping and eating. A large, picture window in the apartment looked out over the Narew river and a scenic park where the family could take walks and Chaya-Sarah could spend many happy hours chasing ducks and squirrels.

The year they lived in Ostroleka was a productive one for the family and peppered with memorable events. While they lived there, Shayna and Jonah redesigned their new home in Zbojna, and built it on the same property as the old house. Chaya-Sarah was enrolled in school where she contracted measles that forced her to stay home for weeks. Sadly, while they were there, the family received news that, Shayna's father, Moshe, passed away. They returned to Zbojna on one of their many trips back to attend his funeral.

One afternoon, after the family was in Ostroleka for a few months, the three of them arrived at uncle Fivel's apartment where they were invited for lunch. Fivel and Jonah's families were very close. Fivel's daughter Rivka, recently married, and one of her brothers were there, too. Rivka, who was also good friends with Shayna, often visited and stayed with the family in Zbojna, especially before she got married.

After a very pleasant meal, everyone was invited to make themselves comfortable in the living room for coffee and cake. Once there, Chaya-Sarah sat on the floor in front of her parents and played with her doll as the adults became engrossed in conversation. The afternoon was passing pleasantly for the adults, but the bored little girl grew tired of playing alone with her doll. She stood up and faced her parents.

"Can we go to the park now?" Chaya-Sarah asked, leaning on the pretty, floral-print skirt that covered her mother's knees.

"Not this minute," Shayna answered, "but we'll go soon."

"You promised we could go to the park after lunch," the child insisted.

"Yes, we will, but in a little while. Your father and I are in the middle of a conversation. Please play with your doll," Shayna said.

"I want to go to the park now," Chaya-Sarah demanded.

Shayna looked at her husband as she stood up, took her child's hand and walked her to the other side of the room. "Please don't embarrass us," Shayna begged her daughter. "The adults are going to talk for a bit longer. Now, sit down and be a polite young lady."

Chaya-Sarah sat down obediently, but she crossed her arms in front of her. She watched her mother go back to the couch, sit down and continue talking and laughing with the others. Her lips pursed, the scolded girl looked around the room for something to do. Her eyes fell on a pair of scissors lying on the table. She was not allowed to play with Shayna's sewing scissors and here were these scissors so close, she could almost touch them without standing up. The temptation was too great. She eyed her mother to make sure she was busy. Shayna was safely engrossed in conversation. Then she grabbed the scissors and held them in her hands. They were heavier than she thought they would be. She put her fingers in the holes like she had watched her mother do and began snipping the air around her, enjoying the whooshing sound the blades made when they slid against one another. She was starting to lose interest in this game so she looked around the room for something she could really cut. She turned to her left and caught sight of her father's brown leather jacket hanging neatly on a chair. It was a new jacket that her mother gave him as a birthday present. She wondered what it would feel like to cut, if she would even be able to cut it. The urge to move the scissors near her father's jacket and find out proved to be irresistible. She looked again at the adults, especially her mother. They were completely focused on one another and oblivious to her activities. She positioned the scissors below the back of the beautiful jacket and began cutting. The soft leather yielded to the sharp scissors and came apart. It was easier than she thought. Too easy. She kept going. She was fascinated. She did not stop until the scissors reached the collar and the jacket was almost split completely up the back.

"Chaya-Sari, what are you doing?" Shayna yelled. The shocked Chaya-Sarah jumped away from the jacket and dropped the scissors. Shayna ran over and picked up the damaged jacket. "*Guttenu*, she cried. "What have you done to your father's new jacket?!"

Chaya-Sarah shrugged sheepishly and looked down at the floor. Shayna fumed as she glanced over at her husband who raised his eyebrows, but was quiet. She announced angrily that it was time to go home, and apologized to everyone for this disruption. The family gathered up what was left of their coats and said their thank-yous and good-byes. After they walked out the front door, Shayna leaned down and told her daughter that there would be no park visit this afternoon and that her father would certainly be punishing her for this terrible act when they got back to their apartment.

◆ ◆ ◆

Later that night, Shayna sat at their dining room table, struggling to repair her husband's jacket with a needle and thread. After dinner, she had cooled down from the day's upsetting event, but was still wondering how to teach her recalcitrant daughter better manners. Jonah, on the other hand, had found it extremely difficult to punish his daughter or even conjure any feelings that slightly resembled anger. He did try to be stern with her for the sake of discipline and to respect his wife's wishes, but it did not work. Whenever he tried, he and his daughter would invariably burst into raucous peels of laughter at his feeble attempt—each privately knowing that it was a sham. This time was no different.

On the other side of the room, Jonah was stretched out in bed, reading to Chaya-Sarah from one of her many Yiddish children's books. Chaya-Sarah, her head resting comfortably on her father's shoulder, was trying to read along with him, but beginning to skip words as drowsiness overtook her. Finally, the sleepy child was no longer able to fight the weight of her eyelids and they shut completely. Jonah paused to make sure she was asleep, then slowly closed the book and slid it onto the nightstand. Very carefully he began to wave his free arm in the air in an attempt to get his wife's attention. It was not working so he tried snapping his fingers lightly.

Finally, Shayna looked up and saw him pointing to their sleeping daughter. She put down her sewing, and quietly walked over to the bed.

"Honey, please turn out the light. I can't move," Jonah whispered.

Shayna walked over and pulled the blanket up under her daughter's chin, then turned out the light on Jonah's side of the bed.

"Come to bed, it's late," Jonah said.

"In a minute," Shayna answered as she returned to her sewing basket. She held up the jacket to scrutinize her repair work. She shook her head in dismay as she realized that it looked terrible and was probably not reparable. With a sigh, she put away her sewing basket and quietly got ready for bed. After she turned out the light, got settled in bed and closed her eyes, Jonah whispered, "Honey, I've been thinking."

"Oy, you scared me," Shayna answered. "I thought you were sleeping."

"I was thinking about the store—maybe we shouldn't open it, again," Jonah continued.

"No, why not?" Shayna asked. "It's been good for us, no?"

"Yes, it has, but expenses have become so high because of increasing taxes and the large amount of inventory we have to keep."

"That's true," Shayna said quietly as she considered his words. "On top of expenses, we have some farmers who still owe us money."

"And it's very time-consuming," Jonah continued, "God-willing, we will get our visas soon so we can leave."

"But who knows when . . . and would we make enough money from just the lumber business?" Shayna answered.

Jonah considered this and said, "My parents certainly did. And I can always take on more customers, if necessary."

"Darling, that was a long time ago and there is more competition from big companies. And you said yourself that expenses are higher now," Shayna reasoned.

"All of that is certainly true," Jonah said. "Maybe we can sell something else for extra cash when the lumber business is slow."

"What could we sell?" Shayna asked.

"Well, I was thinking," Jonah lifted his head slightly so he was able to glance down and to his left to make sure their conversation was not disturbing Chaya-Sarah. She was sleeping peacefully on her father's shoulder. He adjusted the blanket to make sure she was still covered, then he laid his head back down on the pillow. He looked up at the ceiling and whispered, "I was thinking maybe we should sell bicycles."

CHAPTER 9

1939
Zbojna, Poland

The Jews have three velten: die velt, yeneh velt and Roosevelt. (The Jews have three worlds: this world, the next world and Roosevelt).

~Jonah J. Goldstein

Chaya-Sarah was laughing with unbridled joy, but no one could hear her because the wind was pushing the sound of her voice behind her along with her airborne braids. She sat on the handle bars of her father's new bicycle as they flew down the main street of Zbojna with a volley of screaming children running after them and people lined up on both sides of the street clapping and waving. It was not that the people never saw a bicycle before. The paper delivery man rode one and so did the postman. But no one who lived in Zbojna owned one yet, and their village had never before had a bicycle shop and certainly not one that, this very day, was having its grand opening. To add to the excitement, this was the first time they saw one of the village children riding shotgun on the handlebars of a bicycle.

Shayna was standing on the sidelines feeling nervous about her daughter's seeming precarious perch on Jonah's bicycle. When the excitement got too much for her, she went back into the new house to tend to her batches of sugar cookies that she was baking for today's grand opening. Their new house opened directly into a kitchen and living room area instead of into the dry goods store as the old house had. A bedroom for the family of three was at the back of the house. The bicycle shop was situated on the left side of the house with a doorway into the living room and an outside entrance with a cobblestone walkway leading to the street. Shayna removed a new batch of cookies from the oven and set them aside to cool. One plate with the sweet treats was already in the bicycle shop sitting on the counter for the customers who were examining the bicycles on display there. Another tray of cookies that she made earlier was now cool enough so she piled the sweet treats high on a plate and brought them outside.

◆　◆　◆

The family had moved back to Zbojna in January, a full year after the fire in their previous home. It took Jonah approximately two months after that to purchase bicycles from neighboring towns and cities, transport them to Zbojna and set up the bicycle shop. By late April, as the first purple lilac bushes were beginning to bloom, it was time for the grand opening of the shop. A month later, Jonah sold ten bicycles to fellow villagers and four more to customers passing by on the main street of Zbojna. Shayna had a bicycle, too, and she used it not only for the leisurely afternoon and Sunday rides with her husband and daughter, but also sometimes as a means of transportation when visiting a neighbor down the street or someone in another part of the village.

It had been three years since the family trekked to the American Embassy in Warsaw to submit their visa applications. Not a moment has passed in all those years that Shayna and Jonah did not privately stress over the question of when and if the visas would arrive. Nor were either of them ever free of concerns about the tightening of American immigration quota laws, rising antisemitism in Poland, and the ever present threat of war. Inspite of all these worries, they were practiced in the art of putting on brave and happy faces for each other most days and even relaxed and casual ones when the mail was delivered. Regarding the latter, they each realized, what would be the point of getting anxious every time the mail came just to find—day after day, month after month, year after year—there was nothing in the mail to be excited about?

Jonah was in the bicycle shop helping a neighbor and his young son when the the post was delivered that day in late June of 1939. Shayna heard the familiar ring of the postman's bell, but she was busy in the kitchen, so she did not rush to get the mail. She had a challah in the oven and was now preparing dough to make rugelach. The door opened between the shop and the living room and there was Jonah standing there, looking bright and happy. "Mmmm, it smells good in here," he said as he walked up behind his wife, put his arms around her waist and kissed her on the neck. "And we just sold another bicycle."

"Yeah? That's good," Shayna said somewhat preoccupied with the dough she was pounding. "Oh, I heard the mailman just now."

Jonah kissed her, again, then walked to the front door, stepped outside and brought in the mail.

"Honey!" he called out with a slight tremor in his voice as he ran into the kitchen and sat down at the table. "Shayna, we have something from the American Embassy."

"Wait, I'm coming." Shayna could not hide the excitement in her voice as she put down the dough, wiped off her flour-dusted hands on her apron and came running over to Jonah's side.

They both stared at it as if a magic genie was about to jump out and grant them three wishes. Jonah's strong hands almost shook as he carefully tore open the envelope. He took out the one piece of official-looking paper that was inside and unfolded it. It was a letter.

"What does it say?" Shayna could not wait a moment longer.

Jonah's words came out in slow motion as if time were stretching out before them. "It says that they regret to inform me that my visa has been delayed. Its status is Pending, but I should receive a notice in a few months regarding any change in status."

Jonah looked up, but at nothing in particular. Shayna continued to stare at the letter as her hands distractedly squeezed the fabric of her apron. Disappointment and fear hung in the air like a dark cloud bringing a storm as Chaya-Sarah, who had been at school all day, burst through the front door. "I got another *groshen* today!"

That afternoon, like most afternoons throughout that spring and summer, Jonah lifted his daughter, positioned her carefully on the handlebars of his bicycle and made sure she was holding on securely. He then got on the bicycle carefully and whisked them through the tree-lined streets of Zbojna, pointing out interesting animals and foliage and waving to neighbors and friends. Chaya-Sarah loved these afternoons with her father and it was the only way for her to experience the thrill of riding. Bicycles were not yet available in smaller sizes and when she sat on the adult-sized bicycle, her feet did not reach the pedals. Sometimes Shayna joined them, but only when the leisure activity did not interfere with her cooking or sewing responsibilities or Jonah was able to coax her away from them.

One week after Jonah opened the disappointing letter from the American Embassy, another one arrived. They thought that this was strange, but it contained a long-awaited message. This one indicated that the status of his visa was Approved. Jonah and Shayna looked at one another. Which letter was the right one? And was only Jonah's visa approved? The only way to find out was to go back to the American Embassy.

◆ ◆ ◆

Two days later, the family was on a wagon coming back from Warsaw where Jonah picked up his passport at the U.S. Embassy. Apparently his visa was approved, but just as they feared, only his was approved. The light of their happiness was darkened by the realization that Jonah must go to America without his wife and daughter. Shayna and Jonah sat quietly, each with their private fears and concerns while Chaya-Sarah did not fully understand this yet.

"*Tati*, can I see your passport?" Chaya-Sarah asked, fascinated by what looked to her like a miniature book. Shayna's immediate reaction was to say 'no,' but her father cannot say anything but 'yes' to his precious girl.

"Just be careful with it," he said as he winked at his frowning wife and handed it to Chaya-Sarah. She took the blue-covered booklet and gently turned the pages. She stopped when she got to the page that contained the picture of her father in the corner.

"You look so serious, *tati*," she said, looking up at her father and laughing.

"You mean I look like this?" Jonah asked as he frowned and displayed an extremely serious face.

"Yeah," Chaya-Sarah laughed as she jumped into his lap and tried to mold his cheeks back into a smile. "Be normal again."

"You mean like this?" he said as he made another silly face and began to tickle her.

◆　◆　◆

Less than a week after receiving his visa, Jonah began packing. He fought back tears as he prepared for the long journey that would take him away from his wife and daughter. Leaving his family was the hardest thing he had ever done. As he chose what items to bring with him, it was impossible to comprehend that he was actually going to do this, but both he and Shayna knew it was the only way. He needed to secure employment in New York City and send money to her as she and Chaya-Sarah awaited the arrival of their visas, which, he prayed, would come very soon.

He packed carefully, folding his clothes neatly into a sturdy, but worn, leather suitcase. A gentle breeze brought in the smell of lilacs through an open window, billowing the lace curtains, and imparting to his every breath a sweet aftertaste. Mired as he was in feelings of despair and worry, this brilliant, sun-drenched July day just taunted him with promises it could not keep. He looked over at the blue cover of his passport laying on the dresser. This humble booklet whose pages the slightest spark would easily reduce to a pile of ashes in mere seconds was a mighty thing. It meant that he was able to leave his home, the country where he was born thirty-two years earlier and start a new life in a better place. His heart sank when he thought, again, that it also meant he must leave his family, but this opportunity might be his family's only hope of emigrating. It was also important that he leave immediately. No one knew the future, only that the storms of war were brewing and had been for years. It was only a matter of time before Germany invaded Poland. He had no choice. He must go to America, then help his family join him. Nevertheless, the thought of leaving them brought him excruciating pain. *Joy and sorrow—must they always go together?* Jonah wondered.

◆　◆　◆

Chaya-Sarah sat silently between her parents on the wagon ride to Ostroleka. She was barely able to muster any enthusiasm for the raft ride across the river so heavily did the thought of her father leaving weigh on her mind. Jonah put his arm around her and gave her an affectionate squeeze. From Ostroleka, the family boarded a train to Warsaw, the city where he must part with them. He did not want this trip to Warsaw to be laden only with sadness so he and Shayna decided that the family should stay a few nights in the busy city, taking in a show, trying some new restaurants and just generally enjoying their time together. In keeping with that theme, Jonah picked a hotel to stay in that would be considered luxurious to his family of modest means.

While Jonah was checking in at the hotel desk, Shayna and Chaya-Sarah stood at the center of the cavernous lobby with its dark chestnut walls and swirling marble columns. Shayna lifted her eyes to marvel at the huge, neoclassical paintings on the walls around her as Chaya-Sarah danced around, running her hands over the columns and enjoying the smooth, cold feel of the stone on her skin. The elevator ride that took them to their room on the sixth floor was a first for Chaya-Sarah. She was anxious about getting into the confined space, but her parents were finally able to coax her into getting in with them. Once she got over the initial fear, she decided she loved riding the elevator so much that she would beg her parents on many occasions to ride up and down the elevator with her just for fun. Another first-time experience awaited Chaya-Sarah in the hotel room. She never saw indoor plumbing before. She was unable to stop herself from turning on the faucets and playing with the water in the bathroom sink and the bathtub. And her parents did not try to stop her.

While in Warsaw, the family spent a few hours in a Thomas Cook Travel Agency office where Jonah booked his passage to America on the S.S. *Washington.* The ship would depart from the port city of Danzig for the United States with one stop in London. Once that was done and he had his ticket, they tried to distract themselves enough to forget why they were there.

The population of Warsaw in the 1930s was over one million and even though the Jewish people were only ten percent of the population of Poland, they accounted for thirty percent of the population of War-saw. This large Jewish population as well as liberal attitudes of the 1930s helped support a flourishing Yiddish theatre in Warsaw and was part of the reason the city was an important European center of Jewish culture. The family took full advantage of this in the days before Jonah left. There were so many Kosher eateries and delicatessens, it was difficult to pick one. Entertainment was plentiful, too. With over a hundred Yiddish acting troupes performing in seven Yiddish theatres, they easily found a show to attend. They strolled through markets that seemed to go on and on with no end, passing vendors who displayed strange-looking fruits and other merchandise from exotic places.

◆　◆　◆

On the morning of July 19, 1939, after spending two enjoyable days together in Warsaw, Jonah and Shayna repacked their bags and, with their daughter, walked out of their hotel room for the last time. After a light breakfast at the café in the lobby, Jonah checked out of the hotel and paid the bill. It was time to go to the train station where Jonah would board a train for the four-hour ride to Danzig.

At the station, the family of three walked together alongside the monstrous, huffing locomotive. Finally, Jonah stopped and turned to his family. "This is where I get on," Jonah said as he coaxed his face into a smile for them and lifted the feather-light Chaya-Sarah into his arms.

"*Tati*, I don't want you to go!" Chaya-Sarah cried into his shoulder.

Jonah's eyes met his wife's. They both read all the emotions there that they dared not express—doubt, fear, desperation, uncertainty, love. Was this the right thing to do? War had been looming on the horizon for years, but no one knew when it would happen. This seemed the only thing to do. "Sha, *maidele*, sha, don't cry," he said as he held her tightly. I'll see you very soon, God-willing. Before you know it, you and mama will be in America with me!"

He pulled Shayna into the embrace. Shayna held on to her husband, her head on his other shoulder. "We won't say good-bye," Jonah said. "We'll just say so long."

How do you say 'so long' when you don't know how long? Shayna thought, but she whispered, "*Zol zayn in a guter sho* (good luck for a safe arrival), darling."

"Remember everything we discussed," he said quietly. "I will write as soon as I get to London and then again from New York." The platform was getting crowded with travelers boarding the train and others standing and waving to them. A sudden burst of white steam seemed to signal the train's impatience to get moving. Shayna and Jonah released one another. He lowered his daughter gently to the ground, held her head softly in his hands and kissed the top of it where the two braids mama plaited this morning met. He kissed his wife, picked up his suitcase and began to walk away, but then almost immediately turned and came back. He hugged them and kissed them again and then again, "I love you both so much. Don't wait for the train to leave. Go home now, please."

Shayna nodded in agreement. The lump in her throat stopped any sound from escaping. With a final wave and a smile for his wife and daughter, Jonah picked up his suitcase, turned and disappeared into the train that would take him to a ship bound for America.

◆ ◆ ◆

Shayna and Chaya-Sarah sat in silence for most of the melancholy ride back to Zbojna. Chaya-Sarah put her head on her mother's shoulder. "Can you sing something, mama?" she asked.

Shayna was not in the mood for singing, but she wanted to please her daughter. "What should I sing?" Shayna asked as she tried to think of a happy song that might cheer them up.

Chaya-Sarah wrinkled her nose and thought about this. "Can you sing the song about the little orphan boy who has to sell cigarettes in the rain?" she asked.

"*Papirosn* (Cigarettes)?" Shayna asked somewhat surprised. "But that song is so sad, *maidel*."

"I want that one, please," Chaya-Sarah begged.

It seemed to match the mood of the day perfectly so, in her softest soprano, Shayna began to sing. She sang it as it was traditionally sung— with the first part in Yiddish and the second in Russian. Since Chaya-Sarah only understood the Yiddish words, maybe she would be spared some of the harsh reality of the story. "*A kalte nakht a nebldike finster umetum shteyt a yingele fartroyert un kukt zikh arum* (A cold night, foggy, and darkness everywhere a boy stands sadly and looks around) . . . *Koyft un hot oyf mir rakhmones, ratevet fun hunger mikh atsind* (Buy and have pity on me, save me from hunger now)." When Shayna got to the end of the long ballad, she breathed a sigh of relief. It told of such a bitter tale.

"Mama," Chaya-Sarah said as she looked up at her mother.

"Yes, *maidel*?" Shayna answered.

"Can you sing it, again?" Then she snuggled in closer, put her head on her mother's shoulder and closed her eyes.

◆　◆　◆

Two days later, back home in Zbojna, Shayna was clearing the breakfast dishes when both she and Chaya-Sarah heard the ringing of the postman's bell as he rode by on his bicycle. The mail was delivered daily, when there was mail. Usually something arrived at least two or three times a week. Sometimes there were letters from family in America. Those were always written in Yiddish and Chaya-Sarah was proud that she was able to read those. She sometimes insisted on opening and reading them to her parents, stopping frequently to ask about words she did not know. Other letters, though, were in Polish. These were usually tax bills or other messages from the county or the federal government which Chaya-Sarah was not yet able to read. Before his visa arrived, Jonah was planning on starting to teach her Polish.

"Maybe there is something from *tati*!" Chaya-Sarah cried out as she flew out the door. Shayna, of course, knew that was impossible since he just left and was, in fact, still in Danzig, waiting for his ship to depart. She was not even sure if he boarded the ship yet.

Shayna followed her daughter out the door, wiping her still damp hands on the white, cotton apron tied around her waist. The summer air was fresh and sweet and the morning sunlight carpeted their front yard with leaf-shaped shadows dancing in the breeze. One of their neighbors passed by in a troika being pulled by a shaggy horse. Shayna waved and nodded to the man as he tipped his cap to her.

Chaya-Sarah opened the mailbox and brought her mother one envelope and a folded newspaper, the Yiddish daily that Jonah liked to read first thing every morning with his coffee. "I think this one has *tati*'s name on it," Chaya-Sarah announced as she pointed to the envelope.

Shayna looked at the official looking envelope that bore her husband's name in Polish. 'Jona Kaufman' was written in bold letters. She glanced next at the return address in the upper left corner of the envelope which read *Military Headquarters-Polska, Warsaw, Poland*. She took in a quick, startled breath, and beckoned her daughter back into the house.

"Is it for *tati*?" Chaya-Sarah asked as she followed her mother and closed the door behind her.

Shayna sat down and, with slightly trembling hands, opened the crisp, white envelope, set it on the table and unfolded the several layers of official looking sheets of paper within. Her heartbeat quickened when she read the words on the first page. She read them, again, and realized she was looking at Jonah's conscription papers for the Polish army. The shiny, embossed Polish military stamp and the date he was to report for duty—August 5, 1939—stared up at her. That was just two weeks away. Her mind was racing as she furrowed her brow and turned to her daughter. "Yes, *maidele*, it is for *tati*, but he is not here," she said the last words slowly as if she was just realizing their great significance.

"He is not here." she said, again. "But most importantly," and these words she enunciated distinctly, "He is not in Poland!" She looked at her daughter and said, again, "Your father is not in Poland." With that, she jumped up, took her daughter's hands in her own and began twirling her around the kitchen.

"He is not here! *Tati* is not here!" she sang.

Chaya-Sarah smiled with delight at her mother's happiness, but she was confused, "Mama, why are you happy that *tati* is not here?"

Shayna stopped dancing and sat down again to be eye-level with her child. "*Maidele*," she began as she held the papers in front of her. "These are your father's conscription papers, drafting him into the Polish army, but your father is in Danzig. Danzig is a free city that Poland and Germany are fighting over—but it belongs to neither country. He is safe. They cannot get him there!"

"Oh, so that's good," Chaya-Sarah nodded happily.

"Yes, that's very good," Shayna replied. It was so good, in fact, Shayna could barely believe their good fortune. If those papers arrived even a day or two before . . . she almost stopped herself from continuing that line of thinking, but the reality was that the timing was remarkable. If Jonah had not been in the free port of Danzig, if he was anywhere in Poland when the conscription was issued, the authorities would not have let him leave. He would have been required to report to Polish army headquarters by the date indicated on the letter. Two of her older brothers, Shmulke and Sholem, were already drafted into the Polish army. She felt sad for them because they were forced to spend long periods of time away from their families for military training and, worst of all, were unable to go to America.

Shayna hugged her child, "Let's get you dressed and ready for school."

Ten minutes later, Shayna stood in the doorway and watched Chaya-Sarah, with her brown-black braids gleaming in the sun and her books under her left arm, skipping down the street alongside her friends. She watched them disappear into the Yiddish schoolhouse at the end of the street. Then Shayna turned, went back into the house, and tore up the papers.

✦ ✦ ✦

By early August, the first of Jonah's letters started to arrive. Shayna already wrote him a few letters since he left and addressed them carefully to his sister's apartment. Shayna loved writing to Jonah, but nothing felt better than getting a letter from him. The air was always tinged with an energy and excitement Shayna found difficult to put into words. As usual, she sat down at the kitchen table while Chaya-Sarah climbed into her lap. She allowed her daughter to open the envelope, but scolded her to be careful not to tear the letter. Shayna took the letter with trembling hands and read the beginning which was always about how much he loved them and missed them. Chaya-Sarah listened intently as her mother read the words that told of his adventures and misadventures both on and off the ship. He wrote about the interesting people he met along the way and how, in an effort to avoid eating non-Kosher meat, he limited himself to tuna fish for lunch and dinner. The problem was that he was so sick of it, he never wanted to touch it again!

Most of Jonah's stories delighted and amused them, but one was shocking and frightening to the mother and daughter. The story began in London. The ship was docked there for a day, so Jonah decided to leave for a few hours and see some sights. He also realized that he would like to get a shave. He looked around the foreign city wondering how to find a barber. He saw a policeman and decided to approach him and try to ask for help. Unfortunately for Jonah, he and the policeman had no language in common. While Jonah spoke Yiddish, Polish, Hebrew and some Russian, the officer spoke only English. Jonah tried his best to act out a pantomime of a man getting a shave while the policeman watched him carefully and tried very hard to figure out what Jonah was trying to say with his performance. The officer kept shaking his head and putting up his hands and saying, "No, No, No," but then, finally, motioned for Jonah to follow him.

Jonah smiled thinking that the officer must have figured out what he was trying to say. He followed the policeman around the corner and for the next two blocks. *How polite*, Jonah thought, *the officer is even holding the door open for me.* Jonah walked in with the officer following directly behind him. This is the strangest barbershop I have ever seen, Jonah thought. It must be for police officers only. There are so many of them here. At that moment Jonah saw the prison cells with the bars in front of them and realized he was in a police station. He also became aware that the officer was guiding him and not gently into one of the cells. Jonah resisted as the officer tried even harder to push him into the cell. Several other policemen came over to see what the scuffle was about and give their fellow officer a hand.

"What seems to be the trouble here?" one senior officer said.

"Well, I'm not sure, sir," the officer who brought Jonah in answered, "but this man does not speak English and I believe he was threatening to slit his throat or someone else's. I thought it would be best if I bring him in to the station."

The senior officer checked and did not find Jonah in possession of any kind of a knife. He looked at Jonah and asked loudly, enunciating the words very carefully, "How can we help you?"

Jonah looked at the man and, again, began to pantomime getting a shave. The first officer looked horrified. "See what I mean? He wants to slit his throat." The other officers all looked at Jonah, but said nothing. So he tried it again, but this time more slowly.

The senior officer repeated Jonah's motions, then looked at him questioningly. *Yes*, Jonah thought as he nodded vigorously. *You have it!*

"Bloody Hell!" the senior officer said. "This man's not going to kill himself or anyone else. This man is looking for a place to get a shave!" The men all started laughing heartily which made Jonah laugh, too.

"Rogers," the senior officer barked, looking over at one of the officers who had been watching the proceedings. "Show this gentleman to McCabe's Barber Shop."

Jonah, of course, could only imagine what the officers were saying to one another based on their body language and the outcome. He ended the story by saying that it took him a while to realize that the first officer thought Jonah was threatening him or that he wanted to commit suicide. Mother and daughter both laughed until they cried.

"Mama, read it again!" Chaya-Sarah cried, and Shayna read this story and the others over and over again. They both stared at the pages as if the words written by Jonah's hand were about to magically jump off the page and transform themselves into the man himself.

∾ CHAPTER 10 ∾

1939
New York City

Not like the brazen giant of Greek fame, / With conquering
limbs astride from land to land; / Here at our sea-washed, sunset
gates shall stand / A mighty woman with a torch, whose flame /
Is the imprisoned lightning, and her name / Mother of Exiles.

~Emma Lazarus, *The New Colossus*

It was the afternoon of Thursday, August 3, 1939 when Jonah first stepped off the S.S. *Washington* and onto American soil. The tremendous feeling of exhilaration that filled him was tempered by the harsh reality that he was here without his wife and daughter. Even the salty, summer breeze that blew off the ocean into the port did little to assuage that pain. As he had been doing, Jonah would soothe the ache by writing letters to his wife and daughter. He sent one from London and wrote another letter during the ship's Atlantic crossing that he planned to mail as soon as he arrived in New York City.

In his correspondence with Esther, Jonah insisted that no one meet him at the port. His brothers and brother-in-law were working and he certainly did not want the women to have to *shlep* to the port. When he got into the taxicab, the driver turned around and smiled, "Hey, where ya goin', buddy?" Jonah smiled back at the driver, shook his head and said, "No English." He showed the driver the piece of paper with his sister's address. The driver nodded, turned on the meter in the cab and said something into a microphone that was connected by a cord to his dashboard. As the cab began to move, the rush of movement around him along with the sounds of yelling people, blaring car horns and screeching tires coming in through his partially opened window was overwhelming.

Never had he seen so many vehicles, buildings, and people or heard so much noise in one place at one time. He wrote his family that it was like a thousand Warsaws.

Esther and her husband Izzy lived in a second floor apartment on Nelson Avenue in the Bronx. The eight-story building which was owned by Jonah's father's older brother, Sender, was near Yankee Stadium. Sender Kaufman, who was now known as Samuel to his business partners, came to America in 1910 and did well financially through investments in real estate. Samuel owned part of a garment business and several office buildings in Manhattan as well as two residential apartment buildings in the Bronx where many family members from Poland now lived.

When Jonah arrived at Esther's apartment, he was greeted by her, his brothers' wives Rose and Nettie and his brother Shlemke's widow, Sarah-Gitta. The four women gathered around him, hugging him and painting red and fuscia lipstick streaks on his cheeks and jaw. His sister directed him to the dining room table which was spread with a feast fit for an Ashkenazi king. There were bagels and lox, herring and smoked white fish, sliced tomatoes and onions, sweet kugel and egg salad. Before long, everyone was slicing and shmearing and throwing out questions in Yiddish. The women all wanted to know everything about Shayna and Chaya-Sarah and details about his trip aboard the ship. Esther was so happy to see her brother that she seemed unable to stop fussing over him. She kept squeezing his hands, then jumping up to bring him a fresh cup of coffee when the old one was still half full. She told him that Izzy would be home tonight around seven as would his brothers and the rest of their families.

The best part of arriving in New York after being reunited with his New York family were the letters from home. When he got to Esther's apartment, there were three waiting for him from his wife and daughter. He read every word over and over with tears in his eyes. The pain of missing them seemed impossible to bear. He distracted himself by spending time with his New York family, finding work, and planning for the future—a future that he prayed included his wife and daughter.

The first Monday after he arrived, Jonah put on his best suit and boarded a subway for the hour-long ride to Manhattan to meet his uncle in his seventh avenue office building. Jonah would later write his family in Poland that riding the subway was like being in an underground world in a Jules Verne novel. He also compared it to feeling like a grain of rice in a stuffed cabbage. Back outside he brushed off his suit and made his way to the right building. His uncle shook his hand, offered him a seat and exchanged a few brief pleasantries with his nephew.

"The only job I have for you right now," he said removing the cigar from his mouth, "is running one of the two elevators in this building." Jonah nodded as this information sank in. It did not occur to him that he would be operating an elevator, but in truth he had no idea what kind of a job his uncle would offer him.

"The hours are eight to six," Sender continued unprompted. "I prefer you take a half hour for lunch, but you can take an hour as long as you coordinate with the operator of the second elevator. The important thing is to make sure you both don't take lunch or any break at the same time. The guy who currently works one elevator is leaving at the end of this week. He can start training you today, if you're interested."

Without even a discussion of salary because Jonah was happy for any work, he responded, "Yes, I am interested and I can start right away."

Although he had little experience riding an elevator and certainly no experience operating one, Jonah got comfortable quickly with the controls and idiosyncrasies of an elevator built in 1925. It was a large elevator car that held up to eight average weight people if it was not also carrying large boxes or other over-sized merchandise. He learned how to discreetly make a quick judgment about how many people to allow on at one time. He also needed to perfect the use of the heavy lever that controlled not only starting and stopping the elevator, but also the speed at which it moved. His training went beyond the technical aspects of elevator travel. He also discovered that some ladies liked to wear accoutrements that floated around or behind them that easily got caught in the grating of the elevator's inner metal door. As a result, he learned his first complete sentence in English which he recited as he slid closed the door: "Please step away from the door." He also became very good at calming passengers when the car got stuck between floors as it did at least three or four times a week. He distracted them with jokes and lighthearted banter in Yiddish or broken English while he struggled to manipulate the lever and get the elevator moving again.

The work itself was tedious and it did not pay well, but he did not mind. He certainly hoped to find a better paying job someday soon, but in the meantime he was grateful to be working and earning some money. He also enjoyed meeting people, and people enjoyed meeting him. The hordes of people who came in and out of the building every day quickly noticed the charming elevator man. Women of all ages flirted with him unabashedly. Some did not even make an attempt to hide their sidelong glances at the ring finger of his left hand to see if he wore a wedding band. Even the men gave him a big smile when they greeted him, and he was pleasantly surprised to find that some of the people spoke Yiddish.

One of those Yiddish speakers was a distinguished looking older gentleman who got on Jonah's elevator several times a day. The man engaged him in conversation on the rides to and from his office on the twentieth floor. He seemed to take a special interest in Jonah. One morning after Jonah had been working for several weeks, he told Jonah he would like to take him to lunch whenever Jonah was able to take a break. The next day at noon the two men crossed the busy New York street in front of their building and walked into a delicatessen.

"This place has the best corned beef sandwich in the world," the man said as they walked through the door and found a table. The conversation flowed and lunch was very pleasant for both men. They talked easily and covered many topics. The man asked Jonah about his life in Poland. He already knew that Jonah's wife and daughter were still there and that Jonah fervently hoped that they would soon be able to come to New York. He was very curious about the work that Jonah did when he lived in Poland, and listened with great interest as Jonah told him about his many business ventures. After talking a bit, Jonah turned the questioning around and asked the man what he did for a living.

"I'm in the *shmatta* (clothing) business," the man said smiling. "I manufacture and sell a line of women's dresses and ready-to-wear items, men's suits and some children's clothing. My brothers and I have been doing this for years, and thank God, we have done very well." Jonah enjoyed the company of the soft-spoken man with the kind, intelligent eyes and was eager to hear everything the man was willing to share about his business. The conversation eventually began to slow as they each polished off the corned beef on rye they both ordered along with the accompanying half-sour pickles and potato salad. They sat back in their respective chairs with the blue vinyl seat covers and each man took a deep breath.

"That was excellent," Jonah said.

"Agreed. Would you like some coffee?" the man asked.

"Yes, I would, thank you," Jonah answered, and the man called over the waiter. As the waiter poured two steaming cups of the rich-smelling brew, the man started talking again. "Tell me something, Jonah," he paused as if he were trying to find the right words. "Why is a man with your tremendous business experience and dynamic personality working as an elevator attendant?"

Jonah smiled as he added a saccharin tablet to his coffee, "Well, you know, my English is not very good . . . but I am working on it. And my uncle Sender who, as you know, owns the building where we work, offered to find me a job. This seems to be the best he can do right now."

The man nodded. He took two cigars from the inside of his jacket pocket and offered one to Jonah, which the younger man gratefully accepted. They were both quiet as they lit their cigars and enjoyed the first aromatic, smoke-filled puffs. After a few minutes, the man leaned forward and put his elbows on the table. He smiled at Jonah and with a sly wink said, "I don't want to steal you away from uncle Sender, but I would like to make you an offer."

Jonah straightened in his chair and looked at the man with great interest, all the while trying hard to appear nonchalant, "Oh?"

"I'm looking for a good salesman and I think you would be excellent, young man. Here's what I'm thinking. Come and work for me as a junior salesman. I will teach you the garment industry and I will pay you twice what you are making now." The man leaned back in his chair and took another puff of his cigar. Jonah could only stare at him, forgetting even how to blink, as the man continued, "After you learn English, I will promote you to salesman and double your salary, again. And I'm talking about your base salary before commission."

◆ ◆ ◆

That night at the dinner table, an excited Jonah told his sister and brother-in-law about his job offer. He was thrilled and they were thrilled for him. Esther told him that he must give uncle Sender notice right away so he can take that job. Jonah agreed to take the new position as soon as his uncle found a replacement for him and Jonah trained the new person.

"I will now be able to reimburse both of you for rent and groceries," he told them, but they both waved their hands and balked at the idea. Later that night, Jonah sat up in bed and, with great excitement, described every detail of the day's lunch in a letter to his wife and daughter. He read it over to make sure he did not leave anything out, then folded it neatly and put it in an envelope along with some American dollars and a promise that more will soon be coming. He sealed it and addressed it to his home on the main street of Zbojna, halfway around the world.

Early the next morning, Jonah climbed up the grimy subway stairs and walked onto the sidewalk of the bustling Manhattan street. He squinted in the bright summer sun as his eyes adjusted to the light after having been in the dimly-lit subterranean world for an hour. He marvelled at the tall buildings that looked like they were trying to stretch themselves high into the cloudless blue sky. The street vendors were already out with their carts ensuring the atmosphere was suffused with the appetizing smells of steaming breakfast sausages, warm pastries and hot coffee. As he approached his office building, Jonah stopped at a mailbox. He looked at the envelope in his hand, checking the address one more time to make sure it was right. He smiled, thinking of Shayna reading it with Chaya-Sarah on her lap, and dropped it into the mail slot. The day was Thursday, August 31,

1939. International letters traveled the same way people did, on transatlantic ships, and took the same amount of time, approximately two weeks. He had every reason to believe that in two weeks his letter would be in her sweet hands. Unfortunately, that is not what happened. Shayna, in fact, would never receive this letter.

CHAPTER 11

Early September 1939
Zbojna, Poland

Noble Jewish people, you are in Europe /
Like a statue shattered in the East. /
Scattering your fragments everywhere / You
carry on each an eternal hieroglyphic.

~Cyprian Norwid

The afternoon of September 2, 1939 was typical of early autumn in Zbojna. The dark shadows cast by the trees that reached high into the sky were beginning to grow even longer as the days grew shorter. The leaves of green on the great oak and elm trees were slowly transforming into rusty oranges, burnt yellows and rich reds. It was also a typical Saturday on the main street with one possible exception—the traffic was particularly heavy. Usually there was less traffic on *Shabbes*, but other than that, everything seemed ordinary. An air of spiritual calm and contemplative repose settled like a soft mist on the Jewish section of Zbojna. Morning services at the synagogue were over and the midday meal was eaten. Kitchen tables were cleared and the leftover food wrapped and put away. People sat back and tried to enjoy the sacred respite from their worldly cares.

Chaya-Sarah and Edke's children were outside playing with other cousins and friends while Shayna and Edke sat at Edke's kitchen table after lunch, finishing their coffee and reading the most recent letter from Jonah. The letter arrived yesterday which meant that he wrote it mid-August, after having been in America almost two weeks. The information in the letter was technically old news, but Shayna was happy for any news from Jonah. Edke laughed as Shayna read Jonah's humorous descriptions of the people in New York City and the detailed stories about his new job as an elevator operator.

"I know I should be grateful that Jonah has a job and, believe me, I am," Shayna told her sister. "But I never thought Sender would give Jonah such a menial job."

Edke shook her head, "I'm surprised, too. How does Jonah feel about it?

"Well, you can hear in his letter that he is trying to sound cheerful, but I'm sure he's disappointed," Shayna said.

"Have you told anyone else about it?" Edke wondered out loud.

"Only some people in the family. It's nobody else's business," Shayna said as she rolled her eyes, then laughed. "Can you imagine what the people in this town would think if they found out Jonah the *Shtarker* went to America to become an elevator boy?"

They both laughed as Shayna rose, hugged her sister and thanked her for lunch. Shayna's brothers and sisters were close and always looked out for one another. Since Jonah left, her siblings were especially concerned that she and Chaya-Sarah not be alone for *Shabbes* and other holiday celebrations.

"Come back for dinner," Edke said. "You can help us eat the leftovers from last night."

The bright afternoon sun assaulted Shayna's eyes as she walked out the front door and looked across the yard. She tented her right hand to shade her eyes and get a better look. The main street was crowded with a steady stream of horses and wagons plodding eastward. *Where is everyone going?* Shayna wondered. When her eyes adjusted to the light, she stopped suddenly. For Shayna it was a moment when the hairs on the back of her neck stood up. *That is an alarming sight,* she thought as she glimpsed a horse-drawn wagon full of bearded religious men making its way down the main street. *Religious men and rabbis do not travel on Shabbes,* Shayna said to herself. She wondered what circumstance would possibly cause them to do that. She did not wait long to find out. She walked quickly across the street, then stood and waited for the wagon of religious men to reach her. As the wagon got closer, she waved her arms at the driver, beckoning him to stop. It slowed immediately and came to a full stop directly in front of her.

"*Gut Shabbes*, gentlemen," Shayna said.

"*Gut Shabbes*," they all greeted her politely.

"Sorry to stop you, but I was wondering why you are traveling on *Shabbes*?" Shayna asked.

The men, most of them rabbis, looked at each other in dismay. One of them murmured, "I guess here they don't know." They all shook their heads from side to side, their eyes now cast downward. One older rabbi, who was sitting in the wagon closest to Shayna, leaned over and offered her a simple response, one that would change her life forever, "Madam, I'm sorry to tell you that the Germans have invaded the western part of Poland." Shayna gasped, her hand involuntarily leaping to her mouth. The man continued to further clarify why religious men were travelling on *Shabbes*. "Our yeshiva sent us away yesterday when the German army crossed into Poland and began bombing our town. We are going to our sister yeshiva in Vilna." Shayna just stared at him, her mind struggling to comprehend the meaning of the words she just heard. Her heart, however, understood right away and began to gallop at an impossible speed.

Another man touched the arm of the man who spoke to Shayna and gently said, "We have a long way to go."

"Yes," the man responded, then turned back to Shayna. "I'm sorry, but we must go. *Zay gezunt* (be well)."

Still staring, Shayna barely whispered, "Yes, *zay gezunt*," and stepped back as the horses slowly began pulling the wagon forward. Her legs felt leaden, like they weighed a thousand pounds each as her mind tried hard to absorb this reality. Was it truly here, the moment that for years they feared, but hoped would never come? The road was so congested with wagons and horses because everyone was running east, away from the side of Poland that bordered Germany. It all made sense to her even though it did not feel real. She moved one foot, then the other, slowly at first, then faster and faster back toward her house. Her legs were moving, but they did not feel completely connected to her brain which was just waking up to a new and terrifying world and beginning to spin extremely fast and in many different directions. Yet, somehow her legs seemed to be directing her to one goal which was to get out of there and go east, like those religious men.

She burst through her front door barely noticing the pleasant potato-onion aroma that hung in the air from the kugel she made yesterday. She ran straight to the radio that sat on the coffee table in the living room. She turned it on and moved the dials around the way Jonah always did to try to get a station. There was nothing but static. She turned around, ran back out the front door and raced toward Edke's house almost tripping on the large tree root that grew in front of her house. Her sister was still in the kitchen when Shayna opened the front door and reappeared. Before Edke could react to seeing her sister back so quickly, Shayna announced breathlessly, "Germany has invaded Poland!"

"*Oy meyn Gut*! *Vey iz mir*!" Edke cried. "You heard it on the radio?"

"No," Shayna said still out of breath completely out of proportion to the distance she had run. "I stopped a wagon full of rabbis and religious students that passed by. They came from the west. They told me they are running from the Germans." The two sisters stared at each other.

"What should we do?" Edke asked as she grabbed her sister's arm. This question came more from shock than any lack of planning. For years, there was constant talk and worry about an invasion, but no one knew when it would occur. Even now, they could not be sure what exactly was happening or what they should do about it. All they had were someone else's words. They both instinctively went to the front door, stepped outside and looked around. The birds flew in a clear, blue sky above and children played among the wildflowers. They knew the words of the religious men were horrifyingly real, but at this moment life still seemed so normal.

"If they are invading from the west, then we need to go east, like the rabbis," Shayna thought out loud. "Maybe we should all go to Mirzsa's house right now."

"Is there room for all of us there?" Edke wondered.

"If it gets too crowded, Chaya-Sarah and I can go to one of Jonah's sisters," Shayna continued thinking out loud. "Rachel is in Nowogrod and Rivka is in Lomza and, of course, we can always go to Shmulke in Lomzatseh."

Edke nodded in agreement. "I can't leave now. Meerche went to visit his brother. The kids are with him. They won't be home until later. You and Chaya-Sarah should go. We'll meet you in Nowogrod," Edke said.

Shayna paused momentarily and looked at her sister. Then she hugged her and said, "Leave as soon as you can. I'm going to tell our brothers."

Shayna raced over to the homes of both Yudke and Sholem and told them as well as everyone she passed on the way of the news of the invasion. She knocked on the doors of a few friends and neighbors to tell them, too, and urged them to pass it on. Everyone was shocked. No one had heard anything about this. News of the invasion had not reached this part of Poland. On her way back home she intended to look for her daughter, but thought better of it. *Let her play a little longer with her friends*, Shayna thought. In the meantime, she would get ready to go.

Back in her bedroom, Shayna froze momentarily. Thoughts and questions were fighting each other for attention in her mind. *What should I bring and how much should I bring? When will we come back? Will we come back? What about the bicycles? There are a few still left to sell. That's money we will need. And what about the rest of our money? I must bring all our money, but I'll need to keep it in a safe place.* She tried to think of where that was. She had both *zlotys* and American dollars that Jonah folded in with his letters and some were received from his brothers in America. She thought of how easy it was to lose that money or for someone to steal it, and it was all they had. She could keep the money inside the embroidered coin purse where she now kept extra money in a drawer. Yes, that was what she decided she would do—place the coin purse inside her leather handbag—the one with the metal clasp that was not easy to open.

Shayna placed a leather suitcase on the bed and quickly filled it with some clothes for her and Chaya-Sarah. She grabbed one of Chaya-Sarah's cloth dolls—the one she sometimes slept with—and placed it tenderly on the folded clothes before snapping the suitcase shut. She tucked the satchel full of money into her handbag, then thought, again, of the bicycles. It was inventory and that meant money, but she must not worry about that right now. If the Germans were invading Poland from the west, how long would it take them to get here? She tried to calm herself as she walked into the kitchen and began to prepare some sandwiches and cut up pieces of leftover potato kugel to take with them. She did not want to just show up at her sister's house and expect there would be enough food for them.

While she was making the sandwiches, she had time to think of Jonah. *What was he doing right now?* She thought of the time difference and realized he must be just starting his day. That meant he was probably on his way to temple for *Shabbes* services. That was something he would never miss, wherever he was. She finished making the sandwiches and wondered if Jonah knew about the invasion. There was certainly no time to write a letter now. Maybe she could write him from Mirzsa's house. Then she realized that was a ridiculous thought. There was a war going on. A war. Was that what this was? A war between Germany and Poland? If it was anything like the invasion of Czechoslovakia or Austria, it was not a real war. Germany just invaded those places and took over. She remembered the last war she was in and found it hard to believe that it was happening again. She pictured herself as a child running from the *Hallerczykis* with her brother. Would those beasts return or would this war bring something else? Something even worse? She shuddered when she thought of her child and felt a stabbing pain in her gut as it dawned on her that, at seven-years-old, Chaya-Sarah was the same age now that Jonah was at the start of the last war. Her stomach lurched at the realization. She needed to find her daughter now and leave immediately. She missed Jonah so much at this moment, but she willed herself to think only of the next step she needed to take, and that step was protecting her child.

Shayna rushed out of her house with her purse and the suitcase that held everything she thought they might need that she was able to carry. She began a mad search for her daughter in back yards, front yards, potato patches and everywhere in between, all the while calling out her name.

She felt anxious as she saw the afternoon sun getting lower in the sky and noticed the steady stream of horses and wagons heading east on the main road in front of her house. *Where is Chaya-Sarah?* Then she thought of the well. Sure enough she spotted her child's sweet *keppie* (head) bobbing up and down in the neighbor's yard down the street. She and her friend were leaning over the well as her friend's mother was getting water. The two girls were giggling as they watched the sloshing bucket being lifted up above the wet rocks.

When Shayna reached them, her tension got the better of her. "Chaya-Sari, didn't you hear me calling you?"

"No, mama," Chaya-Sarah answered, "we're just getting a drink of water."

Shayna greeted her neighbor, then said, "Okay, have a drink, then we have to leave so please say good-bye to your friends and let's go." Before Chaya-Sarah staged a protest, Shayna turned to her neighbor, pulled her aside and quietly told her the message spoken by the religious men. The woman's eyes grew wide with shock, fear and disbelief.

"Yes, it's true," Shayna told her. "Look how many more wagons there are on the road than there usually are. People are running away." The woman looked at the road then back at Shayna with eyes that reflected pure terror.

"Oh my God, you're right," the woman said as she put her hand to her face.

"Mama, I want to play a little longer," Chaya-Sarah cried. "It's still light out."

"No, we have to leave right now," Shayna insisted. "We're going to *tante* (aunt) Mirzsa's house tonight."

"We are?" Chaya-Sarah loved to travel and loved her cousins so her question was a hopeful one as she stood up.

"Yes, you can play with your cousins Volf and Dvayrie," Shayna said as she brushed the grass and dirt off Chaya-Sarah's skirt. "Come." Shayna took her daughter's hand and looked at the woman. Their was fear in both their eyes as they each said "*Zay gezunt*" to one another. Then she and Chaya-Sarah turned to make their way to the main road.

◆　◆　◆

Mother and daughter stood by the road for a long time trying to wave down a passing wagon to carry them east to Nowogrod. Many wagons passed by, but they were all full. One driver took pity on the young woman standing by the side of the road with a suitcase and a child, and stopped even though his wagon was full. "I have some room, if you don't mind sitting on the floor," he said kindly. Shayna thought for a moment, then thanked him and waved him on. The sun was getting lower in the sky, but there had to be another wagon that would have a seat for them. They only needed one. Her wisp of a girl could sit on her lap. Shayna shifted her weight from one leg to another and looked at her daughter. Chaya-Sarah was bending to pick a dandelion from the side of the road. She stood up with it in her hand, took a deep breath and blew into the fluffy white sphere. The child laughed as she watched her breath and then the wind carry the white petals in every direction. Shayna looked at her daughter. She felt a physical pain as she thought of her child's innocence and realized the frightening new reality they now faced. How she wished she could protect Chaya-Sarah from all this. Before she dwelled too long on those thoughts, she saw a wagon approaching that looked like it might have room for them. Shayna waved as it got closer and hoped that it was not completely full. Thankfully it was not. The driver stopped and asked Shayna where they were going.

"Just across the river to Nowogrod," Shayna said. He gave them a nod and a smile that was missing two front teeth, and motioned for them to come aboard. Shayna lifted Chaya-Sarah in first. Then she put her suitcase into the wagon, placed her foot on the metal step and hoisted herself in. She looked around and found some room on a side bench toward the back, lifted the suitcase and guided Chaya-Sarah toward the empty spots. The driver must have been waiting for her to be seated because he did not prompt his horses to begin moving until she and Chaya-Sarah were secure in their seats. The wagon began moving and took its place in the parade of horses and wagons moving east.

Shayna took a deep breath and glanced at the faces around her. Maybe she would find a familiar one among the strangers. She recognized no one. These faces were all unknown to her, and she noticed that not one of them was looking back. All eyes were cast downward. They were not the vibrant faces of industrious people going to market or happy people going to visit family in distant towns or cities—faces it would be easy to strike up a conversation with. No, these were not those kinds of faces. These faces wore a kind of weariness and deep, impenetrable fear that was covered in the grime of long distances and unknown destinations. The faces filled her with an uneasy feeling.

◆　◆　◆

Almost an hour after leaving Zbojna, the wagon reached the town of Nowogrod. With almost 800 inhabitants, it was four times the size of Zbojna. It was known for its scenic beauty by people who were blessed with the luxury of time and the inclination to notice its gentle, rolling green hills that provided beautiful bird's-eye views of the winding Narew river. Shayna and her family picnicked there on several occasions, but for the most part Nowogrod was a place where relatives lived and a stop on the way to Lomza.

As Shayna saw them approaching their stop, she gently roused Chaya-Sarah who had fallen asleep with her head in her mother's lap. "Wake up, *maidele*," Shayna said softly stroking her daughter's head and shoulder, "We're almost there." The wagon slowed and the horses nickered and whinnied as they came to a stop on the side of the road. The driver turned around and announced, "First stop Nowogrod. The next stop on the eastside of Nowogrod will be the last stop tonight. Step carefully please." Without his top front teeth, the words came out with a funny lisping sound, like his tongue was in the wrong place.

"Mama, he talks funny," Chaya-Sarah whispered as she giggled. Two children nearby heard her and laughed, too. *Would that the world were really the happy place these children believed it was*, Shayna thought, as she helped her daughter from the wagon and picked up their suitcase.

They had a four-block walk to Mirzsa's house. Shayna paused to nod to a woman she spoke with on the wagon whose story struck fear in her heart. The woman and her husband and child saw trucks filled with German soldiers enter their Polish town which was near the border of Germany. They heard shots fired and saw planes dropping bombs on buildings and homes. There was chaos in the streets and fires burning everywhere. They escaped from their burning house and made it onto a wagon that was fleeing from the ravaged town. "*Zay gezunt,*" Shayna said as she and the woman hugged one another and went their separate ways.

When Shayna finally knocked on Mirzsa's door, the sun was disappearing beneath the horizon. Both she and Chaya-Sarah heard the sounds of many voices coming from inside the house as the door opened. "Shayna! Chaya-Sarah!" Chaim Ladowicz, Mirzsa's husband, was surprised to see his sister-in-law and his niece. "Come in, come in!" They walked into a room full of people. "Mirzsa, your sister's here and your niece," he called out to his wife who was in the kitchen. Mirzsa came out of the kitchen, wiping her hands on her apron. She hugged her sister and kissed Chaya-Sarah on the head.

She looked concerned to see her sister, but only said, "I'm so glad you're here. Dinner is almost ready. You know Chaim's family." Mirzsa pointed to the other people in the room. Shayna looked around, smiled and nodded. She was greeted by Chaim's older brother and sister and their spouses. The women all cooed over Chaya-Sarah. "She's adorable and getting so big," someone said and they all agreed.

"Why don't you go into the bedroom?" Mirzsa asked Chaya-Sarah. "Volf and Dvayrie are there entertaining their other cousins." Chaya-Sarah looked up at her mother who nodded to her, then flew off in the direction of her cousin's bedroom. Once she was out of the room, Mirzsa looked at the suitcase, then back at her sister's face. "What's happening? Are the Germans in Zbojna?" Mirzsa asked with alarm.

"No," Shayna said. "I don't think so." Shayna told the story of how she saw the traveling religious men and was suspicious because it was *Shabbes* so she spoke with them and found out about the invasion. She added that she told Edke and Yudke so they might be coming here, too, but she was not certain. Everyone in the room nodded with a knowing look of despair in their eyes.

"I hope they come," Mirzsa said. "But who knows if we'll be safer here? Chaim's family will tell you their story, but right now dinner is ready." Mirzsa went back into the kitchen, declining offers to help. Shayna reached into her suitcase, brought out the sandwiches she made for the trip and followed her sister into the kitchen. "Listen, I made these two sandwiches and I have potato kugel. Chaya-Sarah and I can eat these for dinner. You have enough people to feed." Shayna said as she presented her sister with the wrapped food she brought.

"*Red nisht keyn narishkaytn* (stop talking nonsense), there is plenty of food," Mirzsa responded. "Chaim went to the greengrocer this afternoon to buy more food when his family arrived. He'll put the sandwiches in the cold cellar. You can have them for lunch tomorrow." *Tomorrow*, Shayna thought to herself. *What would tomorrow be like?* The word seemed like a foreign concept, vague and shapeless. For the first time in her life, she had no plans for tomorrow.

Mirzsa looked at her, "I know it's hard with Jonah so far away. Are you okay?"

"Oh, sure, I'm terrific," Shayna said sarcastically, then she softened and smiled at her sister. "Listen, we're all in the same boat."

"I'm glad you're here," Mirzsa said and kissed her sister on the cheek. "We have to stick together. Can you tell everyone to come to the table? Dinner's ready."

Everyone seated themselves at the kitchen table that was not really big enough to hold as many people as were there. The children sat on the laps of their parents and still some people were not able to get close to the table so they needed to keep their plates on their laps. Everyone did their best to get comfortable and enjoy the meal, chatting quietly as they tried to keep their fears in check and their conversations neutral in front of the children. They asked about Jonah and talked about other family members who were in America. In no time, the children finished their two bites of food, asked to be excused from the table, and ran off to play. The adults were able to speak freely. Shayna listened intently to Chaim's family's story which was similar to the one told by the woman in the wagon. They were forced to flee when German soldiers invaded their town.

"Those *makheshayfes* (witches) burned our homes to the ground," Chaim's sister said as she began to cry. "What do they want from us? We're just poor people. What did we ever do to them?" She stopped suddenly, choking on her words. Everyone's eyes looked as desolate as their hearts felt. Her husband put his arm around her shoulders.

"We're not hurt and we're together," Chaim told her. "That's the important thing."

◆　◆　◆

That night was a sleepless one for Shayna. There were not enough beds for everyone so the men and women separated into two groups and organized themselves into beds like giant human puzzles. It was impossible for anyone to get into a position even remotely conducive to sleep. Chaya-Sarah was invited to join her cousins on the floor in the children's room, but she chose to press her slight frame next to the warmth of her mother instead. Even though there was hardly room for her, Shayna was happy. She always preferred Chaya-Sarah to be nearby and even more now. As she put her head on her part of the pillow, Shayna's mind felt as agitated as her body, but the sound of her child's rhythmic breathing calmed her at least a little. Still, staying here was not going to work. There were too many people in this house. While her body was twisting and turning throughout the night, her mind came to the realization they should go to Lomza and try their luck at Rivka's house. Jonah's sister's house was a bit bigger than Mirzsa's so maybe there would be more room for them there.

The next morning, although she barely slept, Shayna was happy to get out of bed. She stood up, stretched, and looked out the bedroom window. She smiled to herself when she saw Chaya-Sarah was already running around behind the house and playing with her cousins. Shayna watched her stop to help Mirzsa take a pail and begin to milk the family cow. *At least my daughter will be fortified with fresh milk today*, Shayna thought. As usual, she fretted that her child was not eating enough. She stretched her neck first to the left and then to the right in an attempt to smooth out the knots that developed overnight. After washing and getting dressed, Shayna went into the kitchen and found her sister breaking open eggs over a frying pan for breakfast.

"Good morning. How did you sleep? Or, maybe I should ask, did you sleep?" Mirzsa said to her sister.

"How could anyone sleep?" Shayna smiled as she answered with another question. Then she realized that her sister gave her the perfect opening, "I think maybe it would be a good idea if Chaya-Sarah and I go somewhere else," Shayna did not look directly at her sister, but instead started to set the kitchen table for breakfast.

"No, you should not go anywhere else," Mirzsa said adamantly as she turned to her sister. "You should both stay here with us!"

"Darling, it's too crowded here and it's not fair to you and your family," Shayna reasoned.

Mirzsa shook her head and frowned. "It's perfectly fair. We want you to stay. Anyway, where would you go?"

She looked at her sister now, "I think we will go to Lomza and stay with Jonah's sister, Rivka. She has a large house and, hopefully, she'll have room for us."

Mirzsa thought about this. She knew her sister was right. Her house did not accommodate this many people. Still, she was about to protest, again, when Shayna put her hands on her sister's shoulders. "I think this will be the best for everyone."

"Will you at least stay and have breakfast with us?" Mirzsa demurred. She knew that once her sister made up her mind, there was no point in arguing.

After breakfast, Shayna and Chaya-Sarah hugged everyone, wished them well and left the house in Nowogrod. They walked the four blocks to the main road in the hope of finding a wagon to take them eight miles east to the city of Lomza. As they got closer to the main road, Shayna was able to see it was congested, again, with horses and wagons filled with dusty and road-weary people. Shayna felt a stab of fear. *Are all these people fleeing from their war-torn cities and towns?* She wondered. *How many are there? Hundreds? Thousands?* She saw, too, that there were many people waiting alongside the road for transportation, which only added to her anxiety. Families of travelers stood in clumps like bunches of wilted daisies, watching and hoping for empty seats on a passing wagon.

Shayna found a shady place for them to stand and wait. Finding a wagon with room for them might easily take a while—a long while. The unwelcome idle time gave her fertile mind too much space in which to ruminate about the current situation and think about her husband. *My poor Jonah must be sick with worry*, she thought. He had no way of knowing whether or not his wife and daughter were safe. She, herself, did not know if they were safe. She wondered if the fighting would reach them or if it would be confined to the border towns. She was a well-read woman, but not at all versed in tactical military maneuvers. Suddenly, she was overwhelmed with a feeling of helplessness she had never known before. The only remedy was some kind of action. She needed to move.

Shayna took Chaya-Sarah's hand and said, "Let's walk. Mama has *shpilkes* (inability to sit still)."

"Okay," Chaya-Sarah said.

Mother and daughter turned east and began walking down the road toward Lomza. They were not alone here, either. Other people with suitcases and bags grew tired of waiting for a ride and decided to do the same. Along with the others, Shayna and Chaya-Sarah trudged steadily eastward with the dirt road on their left. Spreading out to their right were fields scattered with flowers, high-growing grasses, and leafy bushes all framed by the dense forest beyond. The air smelled sweet with the earthy scent of autumn, except when a fast-moving wagon went by and kicked up a cloud of dust from the road. Chaya-Sarah got excited and pointed to an arrowhead-shaped flock of black storks that jetted above them across a cobalt blue sky dotted with puffy white clouds. She called her mother's attention to other birds she recognized, then ran to pick wildflowers and bring them back to her mother. Even with all this flora and fauna to entertain her, it was not long before the child who ran in mad circles all day when she was at play grew tired of walking alongside the road.

"Mama, can you pick me up?" Chaya-Sarah asked as she squinted up at her mother in the noon-day sun.

"Can you walk just a bit longer?" Shayna asked.

"I'm so tired," Chaya-Sarah groaned.

Shayna stopped, put down the suitcase, lifted her child in her arms, picked up the suitcase and began walking, again. For once she appreciated that her daughter was feather-light, but being that she was also carrying a suitcase and already bone tired, she knew that this was not going to be easy. After almost a half hour, Shayna's pace slowed. An ache in her shoulders got stronger and her legs felt weaker. Just at the moment she began to wonder how much longer she would be able to go on, she heard a loud snorting noise directly behind her. She stopped, turned and saw two huge marble black eyes framed with long, dark lashes blinking back at her. The mottled grey horse was standing so close she felt the animal's warm breath on her skin. She looked above and beyond the gentle face to see a young, male driver sitting in front of a somewhat dilapidated cart.

"Good day, ma'am," a sandy-haired driver with orange freckles called out to her in Polish as he tipped his cap. "You look like you could use a ride."

"Yes, we most definitely could." Shayna did not even try to hide her relief.

"Where are you going?" he asked.

"We're going to Lomza," Shayna responded.

"Well, that's easy. Not to be impolite, ma'am, but you look like a woman of some means. Am I right about that?"

Shayna looked up at the driver, "Yes, I have money. I can pay you." She was not looking for charity and appreciated that the man needed to make a living.

"Then hop on board. I have just enough room for you and your child," he said brightly as he jumped down to give her a hand.

❧ CHAPTER 12 ❧

Mid-September 1939
Lomza, Poland

Thus, a dark night in which were concealed night
moves such as mankind had never before experienced
descended on much of Europe . . . Poland and
Czechoslovakia had disappeared from the map.

~Robert Kee, *1939: In The Shadow Of War*

When they arrived in Lomza, Shayna stepped off the cart and lifted her daughter out. She paid the driver who tipped his cap and prompted his horse to continue trotting. Shayna stood beside her daughter and looked around the bustling city square. The city of Lomza seemed strange to Shayna. With its many commercial buildings and population in the thousands, she was familiar with its big town feel. She had been here many times to visit family and friends, to shop on market day, or to see doctors when necessary—like the time she needed surgery right after Chaya-Sarah was born. Something was different now. The streets were teeming with people rushing madly in every direction, filling the air with an uncomfortable sense of urgency. Even standing still, strangers collided with her as they hurried by. "*Antshuldik mir* (excuse me)," they said as they stared straight ahead and continued moving.

"Mama, there are so many people here," Chaya-Sarah said. "And why is everybody running?" Even a child noticed something was different. She pulled Chaya-Sarah closer to her. This was the first time in a long while that she came here without Jonah. *Jonah*, she thought, *who was on the other side of the world. Is that why Lomza seemed different?* she wondered. Maybe it was also because it was the first time she had ever been here while having no idea when or even if she would ever return home.

Shayna took Chaya-Sarah's hand and they walked the quarter mile to her sister-in-law's house on a street in the Jewish section of town. Shayna knocked on Rivka's door. There was no answer. She knocked again. Feeling more than a little alarmed, she knocked a third time. This time her brother-in-law, Nachman, opened the door. Shayna's relief was palpable. Nachman told her the family was in the back yard and he just came into the house to get something. Otherwise, he would not have heard the front door. He told her that there was plenty of room for them to stay. Two of his cousins were staying with them, but they had no children. He welcomed his sister-in-law into the house. They followed him into a room that served as their living and dining area. "Make yourselves comfortable and I'll go get Rivka. She was just going to come in to make some tea."

A while later, the adults were sitting at the table enjoying sugar cookies fresh from the oven and rugelach that Rivka baked on Friday. It was mid-afternoon and the children raced in to grab a treat, then immediately ran back out to play. Shayna shared her story of the recent events that brought her here to Lomza, and she learned about all of theirs. Like Chaim's family, Nachman's cousins abandoned their home in western Poland when their town was overrun with trucks carrying German soldiers. Unlike the others, though, they had an additional and chilling observation to report which was that the German soldiers were singling out Jewish neighborhoods for the harshest treatment and most vicious attacks. No one was terribly surprised by this, yet the words still seemed to freeze the air and entomb the listeners in ice.

During this time people did not know very much beyond their own immediate experiences and what they heard from other people they chanced to encounter. Even though this information filled everyone with a cold dread, it did not indicate what they needed to do next. There was a sense of urgency crippled by feelings of inertia. It was impossible to know exactly what was happening other than that Germany invaded Poland. Rivka and Nachman had a carved mahogany radio gifted to them by Nachman's parents who lived down the street, but only static came out of its fuzzy cloth speaker. No newspapers were delivered today. It seemed to these frightened people sitting around this table that time had stopped. All they could do was wait for it to begin again. How long they must wait and what form it would take when it did begin was a matter of great concern.

The next day, the adults lingered at the table after breakfast. The women started clearing the dishes and pouring themselves and the men more hot water for another cup of tea. The children were outside playing. That morning Shayna took her satchel of money and tucked it into the undergarments she wore beneath her dress. It was not that she did not trust the people in the house, it was just that she realized that with the uncertainty of the situation they were in and with so many people coming and going, she reasoned it would be a good idea to keep it with her at all times.

"How about a game of cards?" Rivka suggested, trying to be a good hostess. Everyone eagerly agreed, happy to have something to occupy their minds that was not depressing or terrifying. An hour into playing, everyone felt more relaxed. Shayna won several games and her brother-in-law teased her that she must be cheating. Then something happened that would instantly transform the jovial mood in the house into something else entirely. It began with a distant, but distinct buzzing noise. One or two people asked if anyone else heard something unusual. They did not all hear it initially, because few shook their heads. Within a minute the sound became loud enough for everyone to hear. Within another minute the sound became louder than any sound any one of them ever heard before. Then it got louder. They all instinctively rushed to the windows to investigate this strange phenomenon, but Nachman's cousin knew what it was without seeing it.

"The warplanes are here!" he cried out. "We need to take cover!"

What Shayna and most of the people in the quaint city of Lomza did not realize at that moment was that one of the most modern and advanced military powers in the world was about to be unleashed on them. They also did not know that Poland had several days prior been infiltrated by 2,000 Sherman tanks, 400 fighter planes and almost 1.5 million German soldiers. Even without that knowledge, it was clear they were being attacked by forces beyond their comprehension and their instincts would cause them to react with an intense fight or flight response.

On hearing those words, a frantic Shayna flew out the front door. The noise was deafening outside as she began to look frantically for Chaya-Sarah. Calling her name would have been useless with the thunderous sound of the planes overhead. She spotted her in the next door neighbor's yard, surrounded by a half a dozen children. They were all squinting and staring up at the sky. Shayna ran to her and swept her up into her arms so fast the child did not have time to react. As she began to run, she called out to the children, "Go home right now!" Shayna turned to go back to Rivka's house which had a small bomb shelter beneath the house. Just at that moment, her disbelieving eyes rose above her to see a monstrous grey plane coming out of the sky directly over Rivka's house. It seemed as though it was bearing down on them and it was so close she thought she saw the pilot's insect-eye goggles. She almost tripped, but regained her balance, turned and began to run in the opposite direction away from her sister-in-law's house. She ran as fast and as furiously as she believed was possible. As she ran, she became aware of explosions behind her, to the right of her and to her left. She realized that bombs were being dropped everywhere. She could also hear guns firing and it sounded as though the bullets were coming out in rapid succession. Shayna did not know what that was. She had never heard machine gun fire before. The noise and confusion increased the sense of panic in her and everyone around her. People were running at every speed and in every direction. Which way should she go? She experienced the tunnel vision that happens during extreme trauma. Propelled by massive amounts of adrenalin, her breathing came out in hoarse huffing sounds. *Just run*, she thought. Flee in any direction that was away from the flying beasts that are heaving bombs down to earth and shooting bullets at terrified people.

In the next moment, a building directly in her path was hit by a bomb. The explosion sent wood and stone, mortar and debris flying everywhere. She stopped and stared in horror as people close by fell to the ground injured and covered with blood. She quickly crossed the street and began running on the other side. Holding her child close, Shayna kept running. Chaya-Sarah was silent, her face buried in her mother's neck, her eyes closed tight against the nightmare. Everywhere injured or mortally wounded people dropped to the ground while others who were able ducked into buildings in the hopes of finding shelter or catching their breaths. Just as many people seemed to be running out of exploding buildings, their horrified faces caked with white, chalky dust and dripping with blood. A few times she ran into an apartment building to see if there was a basement or a bomb shelter there. Each time she found any kind of shelter, it was full to capacity and she was forced to go back out in the street.

The chaos on the streets was as terrifying as the bombs and the bullets flying at them. People crashed into one another, stepping over the fallen and pushing each other as society's order broke down and disappeared in the pure and primal horror that was thrust upon them. This was something these people never experienced. It was a road untravelled with no map and no signposts. This was a military force of a magnitude people never knew existed and it was being used not against other soldiers, but against civilians. *What kind of war is this where soldiers purposefully target civilians? Surely this is a mistake,* Shayna thought even through the terror. But there was no mistaking that bombs were falling and guns were firing on people who collapsed, bloodied and broken, right before Shayna's eyes. She held on to Chaya-Sarah as tightly as was possible without hurting her and ran and ran and ran.

Shayna's legs seemed to move with a will of their own and her mind was somehow able to formulate thoughts even as the sound of her pounding heart and wheezing lungs became louder than the explosions around her. It began to enter her awareness, like a flickering candle in a dark cave, that she was running toward the edge of town where blue skies were visible beyond the smoke. *Would they be safer there?* she wondered. Even the crowd seemed to thin out a bit. Maybe, even through her panic, her mind was able to function and guide them in the right direction. She slowed to catch her breath and look around. Not too far away on the edge of town was a three-story apartment building that was still standing. It was surrounded by rubble, but it had escaped the bombs. Maybe there they would be safe and could rest a while.

Shayna entered the building and stood in the foyer, breathing in the darkness and trying to catch her breath. Someone had drawn the curtains in an effort to hide from the enemy, so Shayna was only able to see shadowy figures of the people inside with them. She set Chaya-Sarah down gently, her arms stiff and trembling. Staying close to her mother, Chaya-Sarah's round, dark eyes searched her surroundings. She began to tug at her mother's skirt.

"Mama, I don't like it in here," she cried out.

Shayna sighed as her breathing slowed back to normal. "We have to stay here right now," she told her. "Just until the planes go away." When they stopped talking, Shayna became aware of the disturbing sounds in the room, sounds like crying, moaning, gasping and other sounds of suffering. Some people were praying in Hebrew. The iron cold stench of blood along with sweat and fear entered her nostrils.

"Mama, let's go," Chaya-Sarah cried, again.

As their eyes adjusted to the darkness, they saw that the room was filled with people. Men, women and children covered every inch of the floor, the chairs, a couch, a stairway. Some stood, leaning against the wall or an open doorway. Like them, these people sought shelter in this building. Like them, they hoped to find safety from a monster they did not completely understand.

Chaya-Sarah was now able make out more details in the room. What she saw made her stare with pure horror in her eyes. A woman cried as she rocked the lifeless body of a child in her arms. A man sitting on the floor moaned and, with his left hand, he held a dark shapeless form where his right arm should have been. It dripped a steady stream of red liquid onto his legs. A woman held her head and moaned. Chaya-Sarah could see a dark, red gash on the side of her forehead from which rivulets of blood ran down her face.

"Mama, I can't stay in here! We have to leave!" the child cried out as she grabbed her mother's arm and tried to pull her toward the door.

"No, *maidel*, we have to stay. We can't go out there!" Shayna exclaimed.

"Please, mama! We need to go!" Chaya-Sarah kept trying to pull her mother toward the door.

Shayna felt unbalanced, but held her ground, "No, *maidel*."

Chaya-Sarah stopped begging, let go of her mother's arm and bolted toward the door. Before Shayna had time to react, the child opened it, letting in a bright rectangle of sunlight, then she disappeared.

"Chaya-Sari! No! Where are you going?" Shayna yelled as she gathered her strength and followed her daughter. Shayna burst through the door, but did not immediately see Chaya-Sarah. The child did not stop when she got outside. She kept running down the dusty street, passing bombed-out buildings and people lying dead or injured in the street. Shayna spotted her daughter and began running after her yelling out her name. The child heard her mother, but did not stop running.

Shayna grew desperate, "Chaya-Sari, please stop!" The chase went on for several terrifying moments with Shayna wondering if she would have the strength to catch up with her child. Finally, thanks to her longer legs, Shayna reached Chaya-Sarah and grabbed her daughter's arm.

"Don't ever run away from me again!" Shayna cried as she hugged her and looked around. Fearing they were too exposed out on the street, she began immediately leading her back to the building they had been in—the only place she thought would be safe for now.

She begged, "Please, *maidele*. We have to go back. I still hear the planes and bombs are exploding. It's not safe."

"Mama, no! I don't want to go back there . . ." Chaya-Sarah's exclamation was interrupted by the loud buzz of an approaching plane. They both looked up and their eyes opened wide with shock and fear as they saw a warplane flying toward the building they just left. They turned and began running farther away from the building. Just then, a huge, ear-popping explosion filled the air behind them. They instinctively slowed and turned their heads to see what happened. Both mother and daughter stood transfixed in utter horror as they watched the building they had just been in disintegrate into a mountain of rubble, smoke, and dust. They both stared in mute silence. There could not possibly be anyone left alive in there. If Chaya-Sarah had not run out of the building a few minutes ago, that, too, would have been their fate. Shayna looked down at her daughter as if the child were possessed by a spirit. She did not have much more time to dwell on this thought as the sound of a plane was growing louder. Thinking was a luxury now. What was needed was reacting and running, like an animal operating on pure instinct.

Shayna grabbed her daughter's hand and without a word they both continued running away from the bombed building and the sound of the plane. They raced past more destroyed buildings and houses, finally leaving the city and approaching open grassy fields. Shayna took this chance now because staying in the town was not an option. Even though they were easy targets in the fields, the planes seemed to be concentrating on the populated city. There was something else appealing about the open fields. Just beyond those fields were dark, sheltering woods where they might be able to hide from the flying monsters. *If only we could reach those woods*, Shayna thought to herself, *maybe we would have a chance.*

Without looking back, Shayna urged Chaya-Sarah to continue to run. For a short while the buzzing engine of the planes seemed to be getting more distant. Then Shayna thought she heard one growing louder. She prayed as she struggled to keep running that it was her imagination. Suddenly, Chaya-Sarah stumbled and fell. Shayna stopped, lifted her into her arms and started running again. In the distance were the tall trees of the forest. They looked so far away and the growling engines of a plane were getting louder. It was not her imagination. Shayna's mind raced along with her body, trying frantically to find a way to save them.

Suddenly, the flying metal monster seemed to be upon them. There was no more time to think. Chaya-Sarah covered her ears as the roar of the plane was so close, it sounded as if it would swallow her and her mother. Shayna tried to run faster, but the plane was overtaking them and Shayna heard the sound of what must be bullets hitting the ground behind them. *Gut in Himmel* (God in Heaven), *were soldiers really shooting at a defenseless woman and her child?* Shayna was somehow able to wonder through her panic. In the next fraction of a second the plane was directly over them and there was no more time to wonder and no more time to run. Shayna stopped abruptly, pushed her child face down on the ground and threw herself on top of her, covering Chaya-Sarah's entire body with her own. She balanced herself on her elbows to avoid putting her total body weight on her child and put her head down over Chaya-Sarah's and squeezed her eyes shut. The ground around them exploded as a torrent of bullets rained down and sprayed dirt, rocks and grass at them and into the air. The sound was deafening and they both felt the vibrations of the plane as it flew right above them. Shayna screamed for Chaya-Sarah to cover her ears, but she knew it was probably useless. The sound above them was too loud to compete with. This attack lasted just a few terrifying seconds, but it felt like an eternity before the bullets stopped and the plane began rising back into the sky. *Was it over or would there be more?* Shayna cautiously lifted her head and saw the plane bank to the right and head into the eastern sky. No bullets hit either one of them. *Had the soldiers just been playing with them?*

Shayna sat up, caught her breath and helped Chaya-Sarah into a sitting position. She looked up into a blue sky over Lomza filled with rising pillars of thick, black smoke. She watched to make sure the flying beast, the glare of the sun like a sparkling blanket on its metal surface, was getting smaller and farther away and no others were visible in the sky. She was startled as a flock of swifts, undeterred by the human drama unfolding around them, passed overhead on their way to winter in the Mediterranean. *Such beauty amid all the horror, or was it the other way around?* Shayna wondered. Her breath slowed, and she felt some of her strength returning. She swallowed and looked at her daughter who was uncharacteristically quiet. How much time passed since they left Rivka's house. An hour? A day? A month? She had no sense of time. The only things she was able to feel were exhaustion and thirst. The only thing she knew was that she needed to find shelter and food for her child before the sun went down. Shayna pulled herself up, hoisted Chaya-Sarah into her arms and began running, again, away from the city.

Within ten minutes both mother and daughter heard the ominous sound of another plane coming closer. Shayna turned to see it begin to nose dive directly toward them. Shayna, again, threw Chaya-Sarah on the ground and positioned herself on top of her. Shayna squeezed her eyes shut and held onto her child as the thing flew over them and bullets rained down. Chaya-Sarah said not a word. When the sound of the flying beast faded away, Shayna sat up and searched her daughter's face, brushing some blades of grass out of her eyes. She looked up at the sky to make sure it was safe to continue. She saw by the position of the sun they had maybe an hour of daylight left. She needed to get closer to the forest. Once there, they should be able to keep walking west, along the edge of the forest. If more planes came, they would be close enough to run into the forest and hide. She suddenly realized, too, that they had been running in the direction of Lomzatseh where her brother, Shmulke, lived. Maybe they could reach his house before sunset or soon thereafter. Her plan firmly set, Shayna began to get up, but Chaya-Sarah stopped her.

"Mama, look! I see some people over there," she cried with excitement, pointing behind her mother and uttering her first words since their fortuitous escape from the doomed apartment building. "And there's a cow!"

CHAPTER 13

Mid-September 1939
Lomzatseh, Poland

I used to think that we were the ones in charge of our
destinies, but I learned then that, in time of war, normal
citizens were nothing but leaves that would fall in the
thousands or millions in the surge of a single storm.

~Nguyễn Phan Quế Mai, *The Mountains Sing*

The morning of the day the bombing started in Lomza, Mirzsa's house in Nowogrod was quiet until a neighbor banged on her front door. When she and her husband opened it, the man stood there breathlessly announcing that German and Polish soldiers were fighting near the bridge and more soldiers were joining them. He left quickly to tell others. When they heard this, Mirzsa and Chaim, along with many other families in Nowogrod, decided the war was getting too close for comfort. They gathered some sweaters and blankets for the children and headed east toward Lomza. Mirzsa convinced her husband that they should bring the family cow, Simcha, because the children needed milk. The family joined many others walking east on the main road to escape the hostilities. After they had been walking for a few hours, they began to see an ominous sign ahead of them in the distance. Plumes of black smoke were rising from the city of Lomza. Many of the people, including Mirzsa and her family, responded by leaving the main road and walking south toward the outskirts of the city. The sky in that area seemed to be free of the smoke. It gave people some hope that the Germans were not attacking there. Also, like Shayna, Mirzsa thought immediately of Lomzatseh, the neighborhood outside of Lomza where her older brother lived.

As the group from Nowogrod walked through the fields, they became aware of the dark grey, buzzing warplanes circling over the city like wasps around a hive. They nervously watched them, hoping the planes stayed far away, but a few times they appeared to be getting closer. Other times, they appeared to be chasing people on the ground. Chaim told his wife that if one came near them, they needed to stay together, but run toward the forest. The thought of it filled Mirzsa with a cold fear. She was already exhausted from hours of walking and holding her children. She wondered how she would have the energy to protect them from warplanes, and she would not have long to find out.

"Oh my God, it's coming toward us!" a woman cried out in fear as she picked up her child and began running from a plane that appeared in the sky, seemingly out of nowhere.

"Look! I see a person running on the ground just beneath it; I think it's a woman," someone said pointing to the area. "She fell and the plane is right above her!"

Everyone watched in horror as the warplane swooped close to the ground directly over the woman lying face down in the grass. In the next second, the plane rose high into the air and seemed to be coming toward them. The terrified people started to turn and run, but the plane banked and flew in a different direction. They all watched it disappear into the smoke-filled sky over Lomza. Some now turned their attention to the woman on the ground who sat up and revealed that a child had been underneath her. People were shocked. Some, including Mirzsa and her family, began to walk quickly toward the woman and child to see if they were injured and needed help. As they got closer, Mirzsa looked at the woman in the pale blue dress and the girl with dark brown braids with disbelief. *No, it can't be,* she thought to herself. *Is it possible?* She separated from the crowd, keeping her eyes on them, and began running in their direction.

"Oh my God!" Mirzsa cried. "That's my sister and her daughter!" The two of them were both still on the ground and Mirzsa was terrified that they might be hurt.

"Shayna! Chaya-Sarah!" she called out as she ran.

Shayna thought she heard her sister's voice calling her name, but doubted her ears which were just beginning to work again after being assaulted by the loud noise of the plane.

"Mama, it's aunt Mirzsa," Chaya-Sarah yelled out.

Shayna stood up, turned around and could not believe her eyes. "Oh, my God." Shayna took Chaya-Sarah's hand and they began to run toward Mirzsa. They were all running so fast that when they reached one another, they almost collided.

"Are you both alright?" Mirzsa caught her breath and cried out. "We saw the plane attack you!"

"We're okay," Shayna answered breathlessly. "We were heading for Lomzatseh."

"We are, too!" Mirzsa answered. They hugged and cried and Mirzsa kissed Chaya-Sarah. Because there was no time to waste, they immediately began to walk quickly in the direction of their brother's house. Shayna and her sister each held onto one another with one arm and carried a daughter in the other while sharing their stories about what they had each experienced in the last few days. Chaim held his son and kept an ear and an eye open for any planes that might be approaching. When they got closer to the forest, they turned and continued walking along the edge of the woods. The forest in that area was too dense to walk through, but they wanted to stay close by to be able to run there for safety if another warplane attacked.

They continued walking as fast as possible even as exhaustion began to creep into every muscle. At times they were barely able to lift their feet over the rocks and tall grass. A few people, especially older ones, in other parties fell to the ground as they walked and needed to be helped up by family members. Eventually, adult arms ached too much to hold tired children. Mirzsa suddenly had an idea. She spread their red blanket on the cow's back and let the children take turns riding her. Shayna told her sister to put the young ones on first. When it was Chaya-Sarah's turn, Shayna lifted her daughter and set her gently on the blanket. Chaya-Sarah laughed with delight. She loved being around cows, feeding, petting and playing with them, but this was the first time she ever rode one.

"It feels funny, mama, but I like it," she observed as she leaned forward gently on the back of the bovine creature. As they walked, Shayna stayed close by, keeping one hand protectively on her daughter's back.

"Mama, you don't have to hold me," Chaya-Sarah protested. "I'm big enough to ride by myself."

Shayna moved away, but not too far, still keeping an eye on her daughter. They continued walking this way until they heard a familiar and ominous buzzing sound fill the air. The sound grew louder very quickly. Everyone looked skyward fearfully in the direction of the noise and were horrified to see the grey nose of a German warplane coming toward them. Shayna did not waste a second. She grabbed Chaya-Sarah, lifted her off the cow, and ran along with the others toward the forest. When they reached it, everyone squeezed themselves and their children into the spaces between the tall, sheltering trees. Some cried out as the hard surface of the bark scraped knees, shoulders and elbows. When they felt safely hidden, they looked up to see the plane dive near them, almost grazing the trees. They watched in amazement as the flying beast swooped down right over the poor cow. The children covered their ears and shut their eyes. Almost as quickly as it appeared, the plane soared back into the sky and flew away followed by a trail of thick, black smoke. Everyone hesitated, afraid it might return. Chaim walked out first, checked the sky in all directions, then motioned for Shayna and Mirzsa to come out. The sisters both took a deep breath and exhaled a simultaneous sigh of relief as they slowly climbed out of the dense foliage with their children. They reunited with the cow who was standing nonchalantly wearing her red blanket and grazing on a clump of grass. Both Shayna and Mirzsa checked her for any injuries and saw she had none.

"Thank goodness they didn't hurt Simcha!" Mirzsa cried out.

"I guess you're safe from the Germans if *du bist a keyalah* (you are a cow)," Shayna observed with just a hint of irony. She lifted Chaya-Sarah back onto Simcha and they all began walking again.

◆ ◆ ◆

When they arrived at Shmulke's house, they found it packed with people who were also running for their lives from the German invasion. Shmulke's wife, Raisa, and their two teen-aged children were there to welcome them, but Shmulke was not. He was in the Polish Army Reserves and Raisa had not heard from him since a knock at the door several nights ago pulled him out of their bed and into his uniform. He disappeared into the night with his battalion. The family knew he was fighting Germans, but they had no idea where he was. "Maybe Nowogrod or Lomza," Raisa guessed with a look of deep worry on her face mirrored on the faces of her children. "I pray to God the war will be over soon and he'll come home in one piece."

Everyone said "*oluvai* (may it be so)" as Raisa turned to her two children. "Why don't you both take the *klaineh kinder* (small children) into another room and play some games with them? I'm going to prepare dinner."

Raisa's son immediately lifted up his favorite cousin, Chaya-Sarah, stood her on a chair and turned around, giving her his back. "Hop on. I'll give you a ride." Chaya-Sarah was thrilled to oblige. Raisa's daughter followed suit by picking up Chaya-Sarah's three-year old cousin and the two teens marched off to another room bidding the other children to follow.

That night and the next week, everyone tried hard to be pleasant to one another. They all made an effort to conserve space and food in a house that had too little of either. The family's potatoes and other vegetables growing in their modest garden were disappearing as was any food in the cold cellar. They had enough supplies to keep up with the needs of a family of four, but not the demands of this large crowd. Fortunately, Lomzatseh was spared the bombs and physical attacks of the German soldiers and there was still some food available at the local greengrocer. There were, however, no new food deliveries arriving at the store and there were many people to feed, not only in this house. Since the arrival of so many displaced people, the population of the area had grown to well beyond its capacity.

Piled onto the immediate needs of food and water were the fears and the questions about what was going to happen next. After a few days, the bombing stopped and there was hopeful talk that maybe the war was over. Even so, fear was pervasive along with worry over family and friends in other towns. Everyone considered their options. They all knew that Germany and Russia signed a non-aggression pact a week before the invasion. While it obviously did nothing to prevent the German invasion of Poland, it was rumored to contain a secret agreement about dividing Poland between the two countries. Shayna had no doubt that it was better to be on the Russian side, but no one knew exactly where and when the dividing line would be drawn.

As the food supply dwindled and days passed with no more planes in the sky or bombs falling out of them, Shayna started to think about going back home. She wondered if, like this village, maybe Zbojna was spared the air attacks and the destruction. *Would it be safe to assume the Germans did not bother with tiny towns and villages?* She did not know the answer, and thus, did not know what to do. No one did. No newspapers arrived with reports about what was going on nor were any radio stations delivering anything but static for people lucky enough to even have radios. Mail delivery ceased altogether. Shayna and her family were completely cut off from the outside world and fast running out of ideas and resources. They were exhausted and traumatized in a way that was completely beyond anything they ever experienced. Home seemed like the only place to go.

Shayna and Mirzsa along with Jonah's sister Rachel and her husband and two children who they discovered also ran to Lomzatseh all decided to return home. The group left together, saying their good-byes to friends and family and began walking. Their first stop was Nowogrod where Mirzsa and Rachel lived, then Shayna and Chaya-Sarah would continue to Zbojna. After walking almost an hour on the dirt road, the tired families were more than happy to give up a few *zlotys* when a Polish man stopped to ask them if they had money for a ride. He hitched the cow to the wagon as the family climbed aboard. The wagon was afflicted with one broken rear wheel that made it dip slightly with each turn as if it had a limp. Inspite of that, they were all relieved to be sitting. As they made their way slowly to Nowogrod, the driver chatted about his adventures earning his living by transporting people and goods between local cities and towns. He warned them that Nowogrod was in terrible shape. The German bombs completely flattened it. The adults needed to hear what he had to say, but they wanted to cover the ears of their children. They also each secretly hoped that he was prone to exaggeration because his words only added to their misery and their mounting anxieties.

When the wagon dropped them off and unhitched the cow, the five adults stood shoulder-to-shoulder holding their five children and looking out over the disaster that was once their town of Nowogrod. Even with the driver's words of warning none of them imagined the horrifying scene before them. The bombs destroyed literally everything. Very few buildings were left standing. The ones that were left were empty shells with only one or two walls still up and no rooftops. Areas still smoldering sent coils of smoke into the air that left a grey haze over everything. Trees were broken and charred. The landscape was unrecognizable. They were stunned. For a few moments, no one said a word. When they were finally able to react, they decided to go to the spot where their homes once stood to see what they could salvage. First they stopped at the area where Mirzsa's house was. They stood and watched as Chaim sifted through the rubble that had once been their home. It was obvious there was nothing to save. Everything was burned to the ground.

"*Ganovim* (thieves), *khayes* (animals)!" Mirzsa cried out with tears in her eyes. She held Dvayrie and Volf close as she looked out over the charred ground.

"Those names are too good for them," Shayna said. She looked at her daughter, bent down and gently lifted her into her arms. It was frightening for a child to witness such horrible destruction and learn the fragility of things at such an early age, but to see parents breaking down emotionally was even worse. Shayna knew this and was careful not to allow her daughter to see any fear or weakness in her. She would only allow anger to show, anger that provided strength they both needed to fight exhaustion and discouragement.

They all watched Chaim look through the debris one final time to be sure there was nothing of value to save. Their son tried to go and help his father, but his mother held him back. Chaim turned to face his family and shook his head in despair. There was nothing.

"Should I check the root cellar for food?" he asked his wife.

"No, we took it all with us when we left," Mirzsa answered.

They all turned and went to search for Rachel and Mayer's property. It was a few blocks away, but it was difficult to find without the buildings and other landmarks that used to be there, including the house itself. They used the position of the roads and their general sense of direction to figure out where the house once was. When they located the area, they found themselves standing before piles of rocks, dirt and splintered wood. Everything was peppered with signs that people once lived there—tattered clothes, burned shoes, pots and pans, a doll torn in half. But what had been a house was now only rubble. Everyone watched as Mayer searched, but found nothing worth saving.

Suddenly he put his hand up to his forehead. "My sewing machine!" Mayer cried. In the shock of losing his home, he almost forgot that he hid it in the root cellar. Mayer was a tailor and his sewing machine was his most valued possession as well as his livelihood. It was a state-of-the-art machine that he saved his money for years to be able to purchase. Mayer searched in what had been his back yard and found the door to the cellar. The door would normally lay flush with the ground, but it was now at an odd angle, propped open with rocks and other debris. He frowned and took a deep breath when he noticed the lock was broken. He lifted the door and stepped down into the cold, dark space. Within a few minutes, he climbed back out, looked at his wife and held up two empty hands. He shook his head and walked slowly back over the charred debris and rejoined the others.

"It's gone?" Rachel asked. "The sewing machine is gone?"

Mayer shook his head. "Someone must have taken it," he answered.

They just stared at one another. That was the family's sole source of income.

"Is there any food left?" Rachel asked.

"Nothing," her husband said. "Not even a shred of potato peel."

The shock of the destruction that happened here rendered the adults speechless. The world they knew, the lives they created, the homes they built vanished seemingly overnight. How was it possible that the fruit of years of struggle and hard work could become useless garbage in the blink of an eye? They all looked around with an emptiness and a despair none of them ever felt before.

"Let's find a wagon and go to Zbojna," Shayna said, refusing to give in to any feeling even resembling defeat.

The mere suggestion of a possible course of action to take provided some relief to the stunned and grief-stricken people. They each lifted a child or took the hand of one, and began walking toward the main road that led to the bridge that went across the Narew river. They were quiet as they walked, silenced by a shared sense of dread as they each privately worried about what they would find when they got to Zbojna.

CHAPTER 14

Late September 1939
Zbojna, Poland

There is nothing a man will not do to another,
nothing a man will not do for another.

~Anne Michaels, *Fugitive Pieces*

When the weary travelers arrived in Zbojna, they were relieved to find it outwardly unchanged. Homes were intact and people were physically unharmed. Miraculously, no bombs had fallen here. Trees and wildflowers, birds and other wildlife were carrying on with their lives just as they did when Shayna and Chaya-Sarah left a few weeks ago. As in the previous war, this *shtetl* seemed to be an oasis in a desert of destruction. Shayna wondered, as she trudged home, if the oasis was a mirage that might disappear at any moment or worse, a trap with their enemies just biding their time outside its tree-lined borders. It looked like the same place she left, but it did not feel like home to her anymore. Home was a place where Jonah was. Home was a place where she felt safe. This was not that place anymore, but it was familiar and there were family and friends here and Shayna did not know where else to go.

The party from Nowogrod was greeted by family and friends with great relief and enthusiasm like Ulysses returning to Ithaca from his mythical journey. They were all hungry for information about what the travelers saw and experienced and if they encountered any of their friends or relatives. Shayna and Mirzsa discovered with great relief that Edke and her family were here. They had, in fact, never left Zbojna. By the time her husband and son got home, it was too late to travel, and the next day, a kind of inertia set in or maybe it was fear. They stayed home and worried over the fates of their family members in other towns as they listened to faraway explosions and watched the snaking plumes of smoke spread out on the blue horizon like black watercolor paint. Yudke and his family also went east to Lomzatseh and returned several days ago. Shayna was surprised and happy to see her brother Sholem's family here in Zbojna. They lived in Lomza, but his wife Etta and their three children left when the bombing started. Shayna's tall, handsome brother was in the Polish army somewhere fighting Germans. Shayna could see the hard lines of fear and worry etched on her sister-in-law's face. Etta was ten years older, but it made Shayna wonder if she, too, had developed worry lines on her face in the last few weeks. That concern disappeared immediately beneath a mountain of far more pressing issues.

Since the Germans invaded Poland, food was in short supply. Markets were closed. People had to rely on their vegetable gardens and whatever dwindling stocks they had in their pantries and cold cellars. Shayna could see desperation in the eyes of the people around her, and the children looked too thin. If food was an important expression of love, and in the Eastern European Jewish culture it most definitely was, then love was going to have to find another avenue to travel. Food was just not available. At one point, Shayna resorted to visiting a local farmer who owed her family money for bicycles. With Chaya-Sarah by her side she knocked on their door. The woman who opened it was curt and eyed Shayna with suspicion. Shayna did not ask for the money that was owed her. Instead, she only asked for its value in food—potatoes, bread, an egg, anything. The woman only gave her narrowed eyes and an admonishment that sent chills through Shayna's body. "If you come, again, we will go to the Germans and report you." Shayna visibly recoiled from those words and their implication. What was even more painful was the exposure of her child to such hatred, such ugliness. It was not the way she and Jonah taught her to treat people. Shayna took Chaya-Sarah's hand and they hurried home.

◆　◆　◆

Despite the fears and shortages they now were forced to live with, the people in the Jewish section of Zbojna tried to create some semblance of normalcy in their everyday lives. Chaya-Sarah returned to her classes at the Yiddish day school. Shayna spent her days trying to figure out how to find food and answer the bigger questions. What should they do now and will they be able to get to America? She already ran and came back once. *Now what?* She wondered. She needed information, even in the form of a mere hint, to help her make an informed decision about what to do next. In the meantime, she could only wait.

One Thursday afternoon at the end of September, Chaya-Sarah came home from school to find her mother in the kitchen cutting up an apple. It was one of the many tricks she employed in an effort to make what little food they had more appealing to her daughter. She smiled as she watched Chaya-Sarah crunch into her afternoon snack. While she was eating, Shayna took out her sewing kit, placed it on the table and began to mend some worn socks. Keeping busy was the only way she knew how to combat the rising tide of anxiety she felt every day. Talking about normal things helped, too, so they chatted casually about what Chaya-Sarah learned at school today and her plans for playing with her friends and cousins this afternoon.

"Mama, can I go outside now?" Chaya-Sarah asked as she quickly finished all she wanted of the apple and wiped her hands on her mother's apron.

"Can you please finish your apple?" Shayna asked looking down at the browning slices left in her daughter's plate. "And don't you have lessons to do for school tomorrow?"

Before Chaya-Sarah could protest and beg her mother to let her finish her lessons later, something made her stop. That something caught her mother's attention, too. They both heard and felt a sudden and deep rumble in the air. Within seconds the wood floor of their house began vibrating. Then they heard a thundering, rhythmic beat that seemed to be growing louder as if whatever was causing it was getting closer.

Chaya-Sarah looked at her mother. "What's that?"

Shayna was unable to answer that question. She had no idea what it was, but her instincts told her it was not going to turn out to be anything good. She stood up and walked briskly from the kitchen to the front door with Chaya-Sarah following right behind her. She opened the door and looked out. The sight outside her house made her breathing stop as if a rock just lodged itself in her throat. Before her astonished eyes were rows and rows and rows of black-uniformed German soldiers. They were goose stepping down the main street not more than six feet from her doorstep. Chaya-Sarah walked out in front of her mother, but stood close by and stared in amazement, too. Shayna looked down at her daughter and immediately bent down, scooped her up and held her protectively in her arms. Shayna had seen soldiers before, but never anything like this. Mother and child both watched in silence the alarming display of military power, the mother with a cold and knowing apprehension and the child with a naïve curiosity.

The high-stepping, stiff legs of the soldiers moved in perfect and chilling synchrony. Their eyes looked straight ahead as if being controlled by something at a fixed point directly in front of them. Their rigid bodies were lined up in even rows with bayonets hanging on their shoulders just like the toy soldiers Chaya-Sarah once saw in a shop window in Warsaw. Shayna wondered how many there were—*one hundred, two hundred, more?* The sight and the sound of this parade would be impressive if it were not so utterly terrifying. Shayna turned to her left and then to her right. She saw her sister and brother and other neighbors on their front doorsteps watching, too, in stunned silence. It was as if they were all unwillingly and unwittingly standing at attention.

Very suddenly, an irregular movement in one of the lines caught Shayna's eye. To her shock and amazement, one soldier shifted his gaze slightly and glanced in her direction. She did not believe what she was seeing. She continued to watch, more fascinated than afraid, as he broke away from his comrades and began walking toward her and her daughter. He stepped quickly and with purpose. She did not have time to react before he was standing right in front of them. "*Gutten tag, Frau,*" he said as he removed his black helmet. "May I please have a drink of water?"

Shayna did not understand every word of German he spoke, but being a Yiddish speaker, she understood enough. She blinked and paused momentarily more from the shock of this surreal moment than anything else. She nodded and disappeared into the house. Within minutes she reappeared at the front door with a full glass of water, still holding Chaya-Sarah in the other arm. The girl watched with fascination as the soldier took the glass from her mother and drank it in its entirety without even stopping to breathe. "*Danke*," he said as he wiped his mouth with the back of his hand. He handed the glass back to her and gave them both a tentative, almost sad, smile. To Shayna's surprise he did not turn immediately and walk away. Instead, he reached into his jacket pocket and brought out a package wrapped in newspaper.

"Please take this piece of bread," he said as he held it out in front of her. She just looked at it without moving, but he held his hand there.

"*Danke*," she said, finally, and she handed Chaya-Sarah the empty glass, then reached for the bread. She was not going to be proud when her child was hungry.

As he started to leave, he paused, glancing for a moment at the mezuzah on the outer frame of the front door then back at Shayna. "You are Jewish?" he asked.

"Yes," Shayna answered with an unblinking gaze that met his while she involuntarily squeezed her daughter tighter.

"*Frau*, take your child and leave right away. Tomorrow Poland will be divided at the river."

Shayna listened intently, not realizing that she was holding her breath as he spoke. The soldier pointed east and continued, "You will be better off on the Russian side. Do you understand?"

Shayna nodded and the soldier turned to go. She watched him return to his row in the procession of marching soldiers. When she was able to breathe again, Shayna went back into her house. By the time she walked through the door, she already formulated a plan. Remarkably, the soldier told her exactly what she needed to know at the precise moment she needed to know it. The Narew river was going to be the closest demarcation line where the Germans and Russians partitioned Poland and it was to be divided tomorrow. She did not know why he told her, but she did not have time to ponder that. She only knew she must pay heed to his words. She and Chaya-Sarah needed to leave Zbojna and go back across the river as quickly as possible. As her mind raced, she also knew that she needed to tell her family and friends what the soldier told her. Before she could take a step to do that, her thoughts were interrupted by a frenetic knocking at her front door. She ran to open it. Standing outside were Edke and Mirzsa and their husbands along with Yudke, his wife and their youngest son, and running behind them were a few neighbors and friends. They had all seen the German soldier approach Shayna and bombarded her with many questions.

"Why did the soldier approach you?"

"What did he say?"

"Were you afraid?"

"What did he want?"

"What did he give you?"

Shayna told everyone to come in and take a seat, then she proceeded to tell them of her entire exchange with the German soldier. She concluded her discourse with these emphatic words: "We all need to leave right away, go across the river and get to the Russian side." There was a moment when no one spoke. They were sitting quietly and digesting the words they just heard and what those words meant.

"Yes, I believe we should all go," Yudke looked at his wife and she nodded in agreement. "Be very careful, though. Everyone knows that the bridge to Nowogrod is down, right?" Some did and some did not know, but everyone wanted more information. Yudke had a friend, a Polish engineer, who told him the whole story. In anticipation of a war with Germany, Polish engineers tried to protect Nowogrod by rigging the bridge so that when the Germans invaded, the Poles could pull a series of switches and levers to damage the bridge and cause water from the river to overflow on the Germans. Unfortunately, one of the engineers was a German spy and he sabotaged the project so that it worked the opposite way. When the switches were flipped, just a few days ago, the bridge was destroyed and low-lying areas in Nowogrod were flooded. It served to keep Germans from entering Nowogrod using the bridge, but it also prevented people from escaping, too.

"We will need to find a boat to get across the river and after getting across, we must look for high ground to reach Nowogrod," Yudke concluded.

"But Nowogrod is completely destroyed," Mirzsa's husband sounded dubious, like he was not convinced that leaving was the right thing to do.

"Yes, it is," Shayna answered. "But from there, you can walk or take a wagon to wherever you want to go." Chaya-Sarah who was sitting on her mother's lap, listening intently, shifted positions slightly and leaned back against Shayna. Sitting among adults having a boring conversation for this long would have normally sent her flying outside to play, but after seeing the soldiers and sensing the fear all around her, she wanted to stay near her mother.

"You can get to Lomza from there or Lomzatseh or wherever you want to go. The most important thing is that you will be on the Russian side," Yudke added. "Listen, we are lucky that we have a choice between the Russians and the Germans. Neither of them are a bargain, but, trust me, you want the Russians."

Everyone was quiet, again, stunned over the stark reality facing them. There were only two choices and neither was appealing. They could stay here at home and deal with German soldiers or they could leave, become homeless, and deal with Russian soldiers. Shayna and her brother knew that, even though they must abandon their homes, being on the Russian side was the lesser of two evils. Shayna's sisters looked at their husbands who were silent, but whose furrowed brows spoke of deep and worrying thoughts. Edke turned to Shayna and broke the silence, "Where is Rachel and her family? Weren't they staying here with you?"

"Yes, but they left a few days ago—I don't know where they are," Shayna answered.

The neighbors stood up, thanked Shayna and Yudke, wished them all well and left to go home. Yudke followed them saying he was going to spread the word, then pack some things and leave with his wife and family. He hugged his sisters and shook hands with his brothers-in-law. "*Zay gezunts*" flew around the room as they all tried hard to push away overwhelming feelings of fear and uncertainty. When he hugged Shayna, he said, "You'll come with us to Shmulke's." Then he added quietly, "Please talk to our sisters before you go. I don't think their husbands understand we need to leave."

Shayna nodded. "Yes, of course, but don't wait for us. I'll convince them to go with me and we'll meet you at Shmulke's."

After he left, she tried to make her sisters and brothers-in-law understand that they must not stay, that there really was no choice. They shook their heads and held their ground. They were not going to leave. They were either too afraid or just unable to see that it was the right thing to do. Shayna realized that there were no magic words. Nothing she said would convince them to go. They did not want her to go, either, but Shayna made it clear that she and Chaya-Sarah were leaving. She reminded them that a German soldier—the enemy, himself—told her that as Jewish people they would be better off on the Russian side. They listened, but did not want to budge. Shayna finally gave up trying to convince them. She needed to leave. They all hugged and wished each other well. With a worried look on her face, Shayna watched her sisters return home with their husbands. Then she got busy. There was no time to waste.

She turned to Chaya-Sarah. She kept her voice far more calm and steady than she felt. "*Maidel*, I know you heard that we need to go away again and that we're going back to uncle Shmulke's house. First, I have to prepare some things we need to take with us. You can bring one thing with you. It can be whatever you want, but it has to be something you can carry easily." She watched her child lift her sweet chin and glance upward, pondering this challenge.

"Okay, mama."

"Now," Shayna continued. "And this is very important. I need you to stay with me. You cannot go out and play. We have to stay together. Okay? Do you understand what mama is saying?"

Chaya-Sarah, her sweet, beautiful mischief-maker who demonstrated that she was perfectly capable of willfully defying her mother, now sensed the gravity in the tone of Shayna's voice and to her mother's great relief responded with a simple "Yes, mama."

"Good," Shayna said. "Now, please bring me your high-topped leather shoes."

This time there would be no suitcase, only a bag with some clothing. Nor would the money be placed in a satchel. She was concerned not only with desperate people on the road with them, but also soldiers who could easily find the money and take it. To protect their money, Shayna planned to carefully tear open the lining of her daughter's shoes, place the money inside and sew it back up for safe keeping. When Chaya-Sarah brought her shoes into the kitchen, Shayna opened her sewing basket and prepared the lining of the shoes to carry the money. She kept some of the money with her that they might need in the next few days and carefully sewed the rest into the lining of her daughter's shoes and placed them on her feet. She looked out the window and from the position of the sun reasoned that they had a few hours left of daylight. There was no time to waste as her mind raced through what she still needed to do. She remembered the bicycles. There were four remaining in the shop. As she thought the first time she left, they were inventory and that meant money that she and Chaya-Sarah needed. She should protect them somehow, but only if she and her daughter were returning to Zbojna. She did not believe they would, but how could she know for sure? She wondered what Jonah would tell her to do. She thought of putting them in the cold cellar, but then she remembered what happened to her brother-in-law's sewing machine.

With Chaya-Sarah standing and watching her mother, Shayna moved the bicycles to the back yard. She then took a shovel and dug four shallow holes in the soft part of the ground. When she finished, she laid each one inside each depression and covered them with dirt so they could not be seen. She stood back and was pleased to see that the bicycles fit perfectly in the underground spaces. She brushed off her hands and looked at her daughter. "We're almost ready to go," she said.

Back in the house, Shayna began filling a sack with some clothing, mostly sweaters since the days were getting colder. As she looked for appropriate clothes to take, she found Jonah's fur-lined leather jacket and picked it up tenderly. He bought it to replace the one Chaya-Sarah destroyed when the family was in Ostroleka. *Had that incident happened just a few months ago?* Shayna mused. *It seemed like a million years ago.* When he was packing for his transatlantic journey, Jonah insisted on leaving the jacket for her and Chaya-Sarah. She had been so angry at him, wanting him to take it for himself. They argued, then she uncharacteristically gave in.

"What, you think it doesn't get cold in America?" Shayna remembered yelling at him.

"I'm going to find a job and I will buy another one—probably two more," Jonah reasoned calmly, smiling at his wife.

She held the jacket for a moment, then folded it neatly into the sack. Then she changed her mind. She knew from experience that the sack and anything in it, like the suitcase she took last time, could easily be lost or stolen. She had to assume that the only things that were safe were what they carried on their backs or was sewn in their shoes and even those were not guaranteed. She took a few sweaters out of the bag and began putting them on Chaya-Sarah.

"Why do I have to wear all these sweaters, mama?" Chaya-Sarah wanted to know. The days were getting colder, but it was not cold enough to warrant wearing so many sweaters.

"We could lose the *peckele* (little sack) and I want to make sure you have warm clothes with you," Shayna answered. "I'm going to wear more clothes, too." Shayna put on one more sweater than she needed, then put on Jonah's leather jacket. Chaya-Sarah just shrugged, thinking how strange adults were at times.

In the kitchen, Shayna put what little food they had, two apples and two pieces of bread, into the bag. As she did, she asked her daughter if she decided what she wanted to bring. Chaya-Sarah nodded and walked over to the shelf where Shayna kept the pots and pans. She took one of Shayna's smaller cooking pots and held it up to show her mother.

"I want to bring this," she said.

"You want to bring a *tepeleh* (little pot) with you?" Shayna asked, somewhat surprised. "Not one of your dolls or a book, maybe?"

"No, I want this," Chaya-Sarah said confidently.

"Why do you want to bring a *tepeleh*?" Shayna wanted to know.

"So you can cook my food in it and make sure everything I eat is Kosher," said Chaya-Sarah, looking very adult and very serious.

Shayna looked at her daughter. She was filled with so much love and so much fear for her child at this moment, she did not know whether to hug her or to cry. She decided that she had time for neither. "Let's go," Shayna said as she took one last look around the house. She was overcome with a feeling that this was the last time she would be in this home that she and Jonah built. She noticed all the things around her that people often stop noticing in their daily lives—things that if she were moving in a less dramatic and sudden way, might be coming with her. The silver filigree picture frame that held an image of her and Jonah just after they married stood on a table near the couch they bought in Ostroleka. That couch was probably the most expensive item they ever purchased. When they decided to buy it, they looked at each other and giggled like naughty children. Shayna smiled inwardly at the memory until she glanced at the carved wooden box that held all the family pictures. It was next to the *Shabbes* candlesticks that were her mother's. They stood on a delicate white doily that Shayna made for her mother. Years later, after her mother passed away, it came back to her as things have a way of doing. *What will happen to all these artifacts of my life?* Shayna wondered. *Will they fall into the hands of friends or enemies?* It would have been easy to give in to a feeling of melancholy at that moment, but she fought it off in the best way she knew how. She decided to pay one last visit to a friend.

Shayna left the house with Chaya-Sarah and walked quickly toward the farmhouses behind the Jewish section of town. She knocked when they reached the door of her Polish friend, a woman she was fond of who was always kind to Shayna and her family. As a frequent visitor to their dry goods store, the woman often stayed and chatted with Shayna, offering to help with various tasks around the house, especially after Jonah left. She brought Chaya-Sarah treats of baked goods and homemade candies, and she and her family were among the first people to purchase bicycles from the shop.

The woman was both surprised and happy to see Shayna and Chaya-Sarah standing in her doorway. She invited them to come in, but Shayna thanked her and explained that they were in a rush and could not. Her purpose for visiting was just to tell her friend that she was leaving and if she did not return, which she did not expect to, she wanted her friend to know that she and her family were welcome to anything in her home. The woman looked confused and said she was sad that they were leaving so suddenly. Shayna was not sure if the woman understood why, as Jewish people, they needed to leave, but she did not have time to explain. The two women hugged, said good-bye and wished each other well. Standing in her doorway, the woman continued to watch as Shayna and Chaya-Sarah walked quickly toward the main road and disappeared.

CHAPTER 15

Late September 1939
Narew River

Our lives are fashioned by our choices.
First we make our choices. Then our choices make us.

~Anne Frank

Shayna and Chaya-Sarah walked along the main road going east toward the Narew river. Other groups of people were walking, too, but no one Shayna recognized. An occasional horse-drawn wagon went by, but only a few. As the wide, meandering river came into view, Shayna was reminded of all the times she crossed it, playing nearby as a child or picnicking on its grassy, tree-lined banks with her husband and child. She watched the light of the afternoon sun dancing on the river's choppy waves. The natural beauty of the area did not escape her notice, but it did nothing to soften the edges of the extreme situation she now found herself and her daughter in. Shayna knew that the bridge was down so she needed to find a boat or a raft to take them across. As they got closer, an autumn breeze cooled by the surface of the water chilled their skin portending the colder weather to come. Shayna was glad for all the sweaters she put on her daughter and that she brought Jonah's leather jacket even if she did not need it right now.

When they reached the river near the destroyed bridge, Shayna saw several boats moving down the river and one large raft. They all seemed packed with people. She waved, but they either did not see her or were too full to bother to respond. *Should we just stand here and wait for a boat to come along?* Shayna wondered. That did not seem like a promising idea. She began walking along the river's bank. As she did Shayna remembered a Polish family that lived not too far away. They owed money to Jonah's lumber business. *Would they possibly help?* Shayna asked herself. *I must at least try.* She took Chaya-Sarah's hand and they began walking faster along the river bank. Chaya-Sarah was uncharacteristically quiet, not even stopping along the way to pick flowers or point out different bird species.

"Let's go a little faster," Shayna said as she looked at her daughter. "Are you okay, *maidel?*"

Chaya-Sarah looked up at her mother and said, "I'm so tired, mama, and thirsty."

Shayna stopped, bent down and picked up her daughter. "I know. I'm sorry. We don't have much farther to go," Shayna tried to sound more reassuring than she felt. She berated herself for not stopping to have a drink of water before they left. It occurred to her, with an accompanying pang of anxiety in the pit of her stomach, that if they did not reach Nowogrod before twilight descended on that broken village, she would likely not be able to find a wagon to take them to Lomzatseh.

They finally reached the home of the people who owed Shayna and Jonah money. Their cottage was nestled between the river and the tall trees at the edge of the forest. A man and a woman both greeted her at the door, and she introduced herself and told them of her predicament. They turned to each other, had a short conversation, then turned back to Shayna. They agreed to give her a row boat in lieu of payment. *Thank goodness for kind, reasonable people*, Shayna thought. The woman also gave them a drink of water and the man helped them into the boat, giving Shayna a quick lesson on how to row against the current. The river currents were strong this time of the year and Shayna never captained a boat before so she felt nervous even with its compact size. She and Chaya-Sarah climbed in carefully and each sat down on the two benches facing one another. Shayna noticed that even being tethered to the dock, the boat bounced around in the choppy water. She made sure that Chaya-Sarah was secure in her seat and that she understood clearly that she was not, under any circumstances, to stand up. Shayna gripped an oar in each hand and got a feel for controlling them as the man untied the boat. He threw the end of the rope back into the boat and she thanked him.

As the boat moved away from the shore, Shayna felt the pull of the river's current and smelled the damp, fishy air that hung over the water. A soaring feeling, part exhilaration and part terror, grabbed her just below the sternum. With one eye on the shore she wanted to reach and the other on Chaya-Sarah who was smiling with delight at being out on the water, she rowed as fast and as hard as her body allowed. Her arms quickly grew tired, but as the boat responded to the angle and the pressure of the oars, she began to enjoy a feeling of confidence. *I think I'm going to be able to do this*, she thought to herself. She felt some of the tension leave her body and almost enjoyed the rocking motion of the boat. Chaya-Sarah, too, seemed to like being on the water. Giving her mother a sly, sidelong glance, she carefully slid her hand over the side of the boat and began to stand.

"Don't you dare," Shayna said. "*Vey iz mere.*" As much as she really wanted to put her hand in the water, she expected her mother's response and immediately snapped her hand back and sat down.

Shayna's sense of control over the boat did not last long when she realized they were getting closer to the opposite bank and she needed to figure out how to moor the vessel. She began to row more slowly and guide the boat parallel to the river bank. She searched for docks that she could grab onto and then tie the boat to as the man had told her. He warned her not to try and come ashore on the grassy bank because it would be too slippery and difficult to hold the boat steady as they disembarked. She saw the parts of the bank that were flooded, so she kept an eye out for higher ground. After searching for a while, Shayna spied a grassy slope rising high over the river bank. She stopped rowing and looked toward the top of the hill. She saw a Jewish cemetery up there with its many six-pointed Stars of David carved into the headstones. At the bottom of the hill, slightly behind her and to the right, was a wooden dock with one boat already tied to it. Shayna breathed a sigh of relief, then began to contemplate how to maneuver the boat to the wooden dock.

"*Maidel*, I don't want you to move until I tell you to," Shayna commanded. Then she added, "*Farshteyst* (understand)?" for good measure.

"Yes, mama," Chaya-Sarah answered dutifully.

"Okay, hold on," Shayna said as she struggled with the oars to guide the boat slowly toward the dock. When they got closer, the boat bumped the dock too hard and the force moved it away. Shayna tried again and the same thing happened. After a few more tries, she was finally able to get close enough to grab the wooden post of the dock and tie the rope to it. She sighed with relief and leaned over to take Chaya-Sarah's hand. "Let's go," she said as she carefully helped her daughter first, then she stepped out of the unsteady boat and onto the solid dock. Shayna looked up the steep slope and took a deep breath. She could not help thinking, *I hope my daughter does not want to be carried.* Fortunately, her rambunctious girl was eager to climb after sitting in the boat. She ran ahead of her mother as they walked up the incline, careful to avoid the burial plots and looking back periodically to make sure Shayna was not too far behind.

When they finally reached the top, Shayna looked around. Maybe an eighth of a mile to their right, near a bend in the river, stood a house and a gristmill that had miraculously escaped the bombing. She saw groups of people walking towards the buildings and others standing outside. Shayna turned to look at the position of the sun on the horizon. *Maybe it's getting too close to sunset to walk into Nowogrod to find transportation to Lomzatseh,* she thought. *In no time, it will be too dark to be on the road.* She made up her mind right there to walk toward the house and the mill on the edge of the river.

"Let's go this way," Shayna said as she began to walk toward the mill.

When they got to the mill, Shayna discovered that the Jewish family who owned it opened their grain storehouse to everyone who was running from the German invasion. She was pleased to see there was also a well, although many people were standing in line waiting their turn for a drink. Shayna took her daughter's hand and they walked into the large storehouse. As her eyes adjusted to the darkness, she realized the room was filled with people of every size and every age. She guessed there were thirty or forty people in there. They clustered in family groups on the dirt floor around sacks of grain and flour and bales of hay. She sighed. It was a sight, like so many she had seen recently, that Shayna never imagined she would see. As she began to look for a suitable place for them to rest, she became aware of a slight tugging on the skirt of her dress.

"Mama, can we go to uncle Shmulke's house now?" Chaya-Sarah wanted to know.

"We can't go tonight, *maidel*," Shayna hugged her daughter to her as she answered. "It's getting too dark to travel. We'll go there tomorrow." Chaya-Sarah looked out the window and noticed the streaks of purple and pink in the darkening sky. She turned back to her mother and held onto her as they walked around and Shayna searched for a place for them to settle for the night. She found a spot against the wall among some sacks of grain that looked, while not exactly inviting, like something Shayna could work with. At least they would be off the dirt floor.

"Let's rest here," Shayna said to her daughter as she led her to the spot she found and tried to make them both comfortable. Once they were sitting, Shayna took an apple and one piece of bread out of her pocket. That was to be their dinner tonight. She saved the other apple and piece of bread for breakfast. It was the only thing she had to fortify them for the trip to Lomzatseh in the morning. After that was eaten, there would be no more food. Once at Shmulke's house, she hoped to find other sources of food. *Maybe with the Russians in charge, some of the food markets will be open*, Shayna thought to herself in an effort to calm her fears about securing nourishment for her child. *The Russians would not want to starve people they can use for free labor.*

After they finished dinner, Shayna removed Jonah's jacket so she could use it as a blanket for Chaya-Sarah, if necessary. Then she stretched out on the sacks of grain. They were hard and the outside was rough, but she was glad to be able to put her head down. She opened her arms for her daughter to join her. Chaya-Sarah happily snuggled into her mother's body. Shayna's shoulder was to be her daughter's pillow this night and her body would serve as a cushion against the harsh sacks. Chaya-Sarah was so exhausted, she did not ask for a bedtime song and soon fell asleep in her mother's arms. Shayna had been too tired to remove her daughter's braids or brush her hair. One of the braids lay across Shayna's neck, tickling her skin, but she dared not move it for fear of waking her child.

Shayna did not get much sleep that night. She spent most of those dark hours listening to the cries of babies, the snores of old men, and the whispered conversations emanating from different corners of the dark warehouse. She also discerned the soulful hoots of owls coming from outside the building and, through the window, she watched the crescent moon arc its way across the night sky. It was not, however, the constant noises punctuating the air or the gritty feel of the sacks that kept her awake late into the night. What kept her up were incessant thoughts and worries parading through her mind like a marching band that will not leave. Added to that deluge were the question marks that came at the end of every one of those thoughts making sleep virtually impossible. Shayna tried to focus on getting to her brother's house in Lomzatseh. She had no idea what she would do after that. The future seemed like a winding, treacherous road full of hidden dangers and obstacles. A solid plan was needed, but right now she did not have one. That made her more uncomfortable than the sacks of grain beneath her. Although her mind fought it, her eyes closed as her body began to acquiesce to sheer exhaustion. She reminded herself that she may not have a plan, but she had a goal and that goal needed to be her sole focus and her main source of strength. Her last thought as she fell into a fitful slumber was of finding Jonah.

◆ ◆ ◆

At the break of day, Shayna opened her eyes to see streaks of white light beaming into the warehouse. Dust particles from the bags of grain rose high into the air and sparkled in the sunlight like dancing fireflies. She propped herself up on one elbow. The warehouse bustled with activity. Many people were up and moving around. Some, like her, were just opening their eyes to the new day. Just a few were still sleeping. She was amazed that she fell asleep at all.

Shayna's eyes immediately found her daughter who was sitting up next to her, making funny faces at a scruffy, but sweet-looking boy just a few feet away. Except for a few strands of burlap in her hair, Chaya-Sarah looked none the worse for having spent the night sleeping half on her mother and half on a sack of grain. *Thank goodness children are resilient*, Shayna thought, but the realization did not make her worry less about her child.

"Mama, you're up!" Chaya-Sarah said, hugging her mother. "I tried to be quiet and not wake you."

Shayna plucked the debris out of Chaya-Sarah's hair and kissed her daughter on the head. She felt pangs of hunger in her stomach which in her mind translated to *my child must be hungry*, so she took the remaining food out of her pockets. "Let's have breakfast, then we'll go to Lomzatseh." Just as they finished their meager meal and got up to stretch, they both noticed a commotion near the door of the warehouse. They looked in that direction. Several people were talking excitedly and seemed to be the cause of a crowd gathering.

"Let's go over there and see what's going on," Shayna said as she put Jonah's coat on in an effort not to lose it. She took Chaya-Sarah's hand and walked closer to better hear what was being said. The people were saying something about German soldiers. Did she also hear something about Zbojna? Shayna thought that was what she heard, but she was not sure. As Shayna got closer, she saw that some of the people were dripping wet as if they had been in the water. She picked up Chaya-Sarah and made her way through the crowd. Shayna listened as they told a frightening story of what happened across the river. German soldiers arrived at dawn and immediately started to terrorize the people who lived in the Jewish part of town. They broke into homes, kicking people out of bed and forcing them out on the street. The crowd of people listening all looked at each other with horror in their eyes. And it was in Zbojna. Shayna thought about her family and felt sick to her stomach.

"Edkelkee!" Chaya-Sarah cried as she suddenly recognized her friend. "Mama, look, it's Edkelkee!"

Shayna saw her, too, and joined her daughter in waving and calling out her friend's name. Edkelkee looked up when she heard her name and searched the crowd. Suddenly, she spotted Chaya-Sarah and began to run toward her. Shayna gently lowered her daughter to the ground and within minutes the happy children and their parents were hugging one another. The joy of seeing people they knew quickly dissipated when their story continued.

"It was horrible," Edkelkee's mother said. "They chased us to the river and forced people to jump in or they would shoot them. We were lucky. We found a boat." Suddenly, she turned to Shayna. "I saw your sisters!"

"Where?" Shayna asked with panic rising in her voice. "Did they get across the river?"

"They were running south along the river," the woman answered. "They wanted to get across, but they were trapped." For a moment, there was silence and Shayna just stared at her. Her mind quickly processed the information and translated it to the rest of her body.

"Sorry, I have to go," Shayna cried. "I have to try to help my family!" She picked up her daughter, moved through the crowd and began running. She had no idea if she could help them, but knowing that her sisters and their families might be trapped, she needed to do something. Maybe she could bring them a boat? She decided to go back to the dock where she tied the boat the day before.

"Mama, why are you running?" Chaya-Sarah asked as she held on tight, sensing the fear and desperation in her mother's movements.

"We need to bring your aunts a boat," Shayna yelled out as she ran toward the river.

When they got closer to the dock, Shayna suddenly stopped. Her hopes of saving her family were dashed. The boat was gone, and so was the other one that had been there. *No boats,* Shayna moaned to herself. *What can I do? I must find a boat.* Through her panic, she seemed to remember something that might offer a solution. *Wasn't there a Polish man who lived near here who did some work for Jonah's lumber business? Yes,* she thought to herself. *He's a builder and he lives on the river. But where exactly?* She recalled that he maybe lived in Nowogrod near the bridge. She took her daughter's hand and they began moving quickly in that direction. They raced through the tall grasses on the river bank with Shayna hoping that her memory was correct and that his home was outside the flooded areas. Finally, she saw a clearing in the grass and there it was—the cottage by the water just as she envisioned it. Shayna was thrilled. They made their way to the door and Shayna knocked hard. "Let's pray he will help us," she cried out just as the man opened the door. His eyes grew wide as he recognized Shayna, but was surprised to see her standing in his doorway without her husband.

"Where is Jonah?" the man asked. Still out of breath, Shayna told him he was not here, but there was no time to explain. She needed a boat. He told her that he had a boat, but he was sorry it was not for sale.

"I don't want to buy it," Shayna explained. "I just need someone to take us across the river to find my sisters."

"How many people are we talking about?" the man wanted to know.

"Four adults and five children," Shayna answered. "I have money. I can pay you."

The man hesitated. He began scratching his chin and looking like he was not sure about this. Shayna became alarmed. She needed this man's help to at least attempt to save her family. Then she noticed he was looking at Jonah's leather jacket. She began to remove it. "Do you want this? It's a beautiful jacket, lined with fur. It was my husband's. Here, take it," Shayna said as she handed it to him. "Just please help me find my sisters."

When they reached the man's boat, Shayna was pleased that it was much larger than the one they crossed the river in the first time. It would clearly have enough room for her sisters and their families. She only hoped they could find them. The man rowed across the river with the ease of one who has done it thousands of times, but Shayna still felt a rising tide of anxiety in her gut. She held Chaya-Sarah tightly in her lap as her eyes searched the opposite shoreline. When they got closer, Shayna was able to see all the people gathered at the water's edge. She noticed that some were jumping into the frigid water. She knew that no one in her family, except Jonah, was a strong enough swimmer to get across the river with no boat or raft. She frantically combed the bank for her sisters or anyone in their families, but saw no one. It was at that moment that a horrified Shayna saw something that made her blood run ice cold. Some of the people who appeared to be swimming by their boat were actually bodies floating in the river. At first she assumed they must have drowned. Then she noticed the bodies with gaping gunshot wounds and red water surrounding them. Shayna tried to cover her daughter's eyes, but Chaya-Sarah pulled her mother's hands off her face.

"No, mama, I want to help find our family," Chaya-Sarah cried.

"Where do you think your sisters might be?" the man asked.

"I'm not sure," Shayna answered. "Can we get closer to the river bank?"

"I can't get much closer," the man said. "Do you see those soldiers over there?" Shayna saw them. They were pushing and prodding people into the water. No wonder she had seen so many bodies. The air was filled with the unbearable sounds of people screaming and guns firing. Shayna saw an old man stumble and fall into the water. Someone tried to enter the water to help him, but a nearby soldier took aim and shot them both. Even though their boat was some distance away, Shayna immediately moved a protesting Chaya-Sarah to the floor. Then she put her hand on her daughter's head to lower it below the height of the sides of the boat.

"I don't want to sit on the floor, mama!" Chaya-Sarah cried.

"Please, *maidel*, stay there and keep your head down." Shayna begged. "The German soldiers are shooting people." There was no point keeping her daughter from the truth anymore. Not when it could save her life.

"This is as close as we should get over here," the man said. "We can get closer to the bank farther downstream and see if they went that way."

As the man rowed them in a southerly direction, Shayna kept her eyes trained on the bank hoping for a glimpse of someone in her family. She looked closely for two couples and their children running along the grassy bank as she tried hard to avoid looking at the bodies floating in the water. It was impossible not to see them even if only out of the corners of her eyes.

"*Vey iz mir*," Shayna cried. "This is a nightmare."

"There's another group running over there," the man said, pointing in the distance ahead of them. Shayna searched the area and then she saw them. They were a large group of people—men, women and children—moving quickly near the edge of the water. Shayna took a deep and hopeful breath, staring intently at the group as the boat got closer. She saw Mirzsa first.

"Oh my God, that's them! That's my family!" Shayna shouted. "Mirzsa! Edke!"

"They probably can't hear you," the man said. "Wait until I get us closer."

When the boat caught up with Shayna's family, Chaim saw the boat first and urged his family to stop running. He pointed to the impossible sight of a boat approaching them. Then they saw Shayna in the boat. They did not believe their eyes. The exhausted and terrified group stared at the boat as if it were a fantasy that would disappear into thin air if they looked away.

"I can't stop here, there is no dock," the man yelled to them as he pointed to an area downstream. "There is a dock about twenty yards ahead. Meet us there." Shayna's family ran with relief and excitement to the dock. When the family arrived a short while later, the boat was waiting for them. Shayna's two sisters, their husbands and children climbed aboard, filling the boat almost to capacity. The three sisters kissed and hugged, laughed and cried, then quickly took their seats. They held on to their children as the boat began to take them to safety.

"I can't believe it. I can't believe you're here," Edke cried out.

"It's a *nes* (miracle)," Mirzsa echoed her sentiment.

Shayna introduced them to the man who was rowing and they all thanked him profusely. Then Shayna turned to her family and said, "Tell me what happened." They all shook their heads and simultaneously told her how horrible it had been as the women all hugged their children.

"It started when the German soldiers came back, but this time they were not marching," Chaim said.

They knocked on our doors and demanded to come in or they would break the door down!" Edke cried.

"When I opened the door, they pushed their way into the house barking orders at us to leave immediately," Meerche added.

"They told us to go to the river or we would be shot," Edke said with tears in her eyes. "In my whole life, I never felt so afraid."

"We grabbed the kids and started running. Everyone started running toward the river," Chaim continued.

"We saw people jumping in the river or maybe the soldiers were pushing them," Edke cried. "I can't imagine anyone made it across. Only the strongest swimmers could make it. If you hadn't come back . . . I don't know what would have happened to us."

"How did you get away from the soldiers?" Shayna asked.

"We knew the bridge was out so we didn't stay on the main road. We ran into the fields toward the clearing near the river where we used to picnic sometimes," Edke said.

"We were lucky because they didn't follow us into the woods," Meerche added.

"A lot of the people didn't know the bridge was out or maybe they were just confused so they stayed on the main road. We tried to tell them, but some were too far away to hear us and everyone was panicking," Chaim told them. "The soldiers were running after them and we could hear gunfire."

"When we got to the river, we didn't know what to do," Edke cried. "We hoped we would find a boat. There was no way we could swim across with the children."

"We were trapped. Thank God you came back for us," Mirzsa said.

"*Vey iz mir*," Shayna said as she stared wide-eyed at the faces of her family. Just at that moment, another floating body appeared in the water. Shayna and her sisters shielded their children's eyes just as the boat collided with it and the man pushed it away with the oar. Edke put her face in her hands and they all said silent prayers.

"Forgive me. In a million years, I never thought I would ever say it," Edke moaned. "But thank God our parents are not here to see this."

❧ CHAPTER 16 ❧

October 1939
Russian Side of Poland

*This is my soul and the world unwinding, this is my heart
in the still winter air. Finally whispering the same two words
over and over: Keep walking. Keep walking. Keep walking.*

~Emily St. John Mandel, *Station Eleven*

When the boat docked on the Russian side of Poland, Shayna and her family took turns climbing out as the man held the boat steady. They thanked the man very gratefully for his help.

"What is the fastest way to Nowogrod?" Shayna asked the man.

"Follow this path," he said as he pointed to a narrow dirt road between the trees that led away from the river. "It's about a ten-minute walk."

Shayna took one last look at Jonah's leather jacket which she inwardly acknowledged the man wore well, and they all went on their way. To the dazed and exhausted family, the uphill walk to Nowogrod seemed more like an hour rather than ten minutes. Everyone was absorbed in their thoughts and the shock of what was happening. They were homeless. They were refugees. Even the children were quiet and did not voice their usual pleas of "I'm tired" or "I'm hungry." When they reached the main road, they barely noticed the other groups of bedraggled people moving in the same direction, some still in nightclothes, others struggling to hold each other up as they hobbled along.

"It looks like there are some wagons and horses up ahead," Chaim observed.

They approached a Polish peasant who was leaning on a large wagon and smoking a cigarette. He agreed, for a reasonable amount, to take the group to Lomzatseh. They all quietly piled into the wagon and made themselves as comfortable as possible on the wooden benches. As the two grey horses began to pull the wagon forward, Volf decided that the floor of the wagon looked more inviting than the bench he sat on. He jumped down and, before any parents could intervene, all the children followed him and began to wrestle on the floor and tease one another. The adults seemed to reach a tacit agreement simultaneously to let them have some fun. This moment of childish play, however fleeting, made life seem almost normal. Shayna sat between her two sisters who each took one of her hands. They all silently wondered the same thing, *What will we find when we get to Lomzatseh and what will we do when we get there?"*

As if in an answer to the unspoken question, Mirzsa said, "At least we got away from those German monsters."

"Now, we'll have to deal with the Soviets," Chaim said. They all nodded and sighed anxiously.

"The leaves are so beautiful now," Edke remarked, her voice soft and far away.

Shayna looked at her sister then beyond her at the breathtaking display of brilliant red, orange, and gold leaves dancing in the autumn breeze, but she did not really see them. Her mind was on the new landscape of her political world. She used to live in Poland, but Poland did not exist anymore. Where it had been was now Germany on the west side and Soviet Russia on the east side. She was grateful to be on the Russian side, but she wondered what new rules would be established by the Soviets. She frowned when she realized that her goal of getting to America might be even more distant now. The city of Warsaw was on the German side, so there was no American Embassy anymore from which to get a visa. In any case, traveling west was closed to her so going to Warsaw was not an option. Nor was going to Danzig. In fact, leaving the way Jonah did or the way she left from Hamburg so many years ago was impossible now. She must find another path to lead her and her child not only safely out of here, but also to Jonah. She could not envision such a path at this moment and that troubled her.

Shayna's thoughts were interrupted by the sound of a child crying out in pain. In the rough and tumble play on the floor of the wagon, Volf got a splinter in the palm of his hand. In tears, he immediately went to his mother to show her his injured hand. Mirzsa studied the injury and expertly pulled out the offending piece of wood that was lodged in his palm. She then stopped the bleeding with the inside of her sweater and his tears with a hug. The other children watched this operation carefully and decided the floor was too dangerous a place to hang out and the wooden benches might be, too, so they all clambered onto their parents' laps for the remainder of the trip.

"Mama, when will we get to Shmulke's house?" Chaya-Sarah asked her mother with a yawn.

"We'll get there when we get there, *maidel*," Shayna answered, absent-mindedly, her mind still far away. "Put your *kepele* (head) on my shoulder." The response did not answer the question, but it satisfied Chaya-Sarah. She made herself comfortable on her mother's lap, leaned her head back and listened to the steady percussion of the horses' hooves hitting the ground as she studied the fall scenery that passed by their wagon.

In the few short weeks since Shayna and her sisters left, they found the world completely changed in the suburb of Lomzatseh. The town was still overrun with Jewish refugees who were forced by the Germans to flee from their cities, towns and villages, but now the Russians were in charge. They came in and took over everything, including all business enterprises no matter how small. Tailors, seamstresses, butchers, clockmakers, shoemakers, greengrocers and so many more now found themselves working in Sovietized businesses that they were no longer in charge of. The state not only owned their businesses, it would also collect a large portion, if not all, of the proceeds of any sales, leaving them virtually penniless.

Russian soldiers with their long, double-breasted black coats and shiny black boots were everywhere, patrolling the streets alone or in groups. They took over an old farmhouse on the edge of town and made it their local headquarters. None of the villagers knew what became of the people who lived there. Others, mostly men, disappeared from their homes on a daily basis, taken by Russian soldiers to labor camps that were established in the surrounding areas. Shayna's older brother, Shmulke, had only just returned from fighting the Germans when four soldiers knocked on the family's front door, pushed their way in and searched the house. They forced him along with his son to leave with them. He and his wife begged them not to take their seventeen-year-old son so he could help take care of his mother, but the soldiers ignored their pleas. They left Raisa collapsed and crying in the front yard as they carried off her husband and son.

A week after that incident, the wagon carrying Shayna and her family pulled up in front of Raisa's house. The homeless group was cautiously thrilled to reach an intact home where they were welcome. Raisa was relieved to see them. "Thank God you're all safe," she cried as she and her daughter helped the children out of the wagon and everyone hugged. After they all went into the house and drank some water, they sat down and took a breath. Raisa tearfully told them what happened to their brother and nephew.

"Where did they take them?" Shayna asked first.

"I don't know," Raisa said, shaking her head and looking miserable. "But people told us the Russians established work camps everywhere, so who knows where they are?"

◆　◆　◆

The next few days were difficult for everyone. Just like the town, the house was overrun with people who were homeless, desperate and starving. What limited food was available had to be acquired with money and only after standing for hours on bread lines. Shayna was grateful for one thing. She and Chaya-Sarah were given their own modest room with a single bed in Raisa's house. It was a narrow bed, but fine for the mother and daughter. Having a private room gave Shayna a much needed place to rest and to think. At least it gave her a sense of relative safety in the midst of the chaos around her.

One day, Shayna and Chaya-Sarah ventured out of the house to look for food. All that was available to them was bread. And getting that bread was going to be a challenge. Standing between the bread and Shayna was a long line of hungry people that seemed to go on for miles. Holding hands, mother and daughter took their place in the line and did their best to pass the time. After waiting for hours, Shayna was rewarded with one small loaf of bread. As they left the bread line, Shayna held the package close to her, guarding it as if it were gold bullion. It was all they had. She also knew she needed to make it last. Who knew how often she would be able to procure this sustenance? When they arrived back in their room, Shayna set down the bread and collapsed on the bed. She had not been sleeping well and the hours standing on line sapped whatever energy she woke up with that morning.

"Let me just sleep for a little while, *maidele*, okay?" Shayna implored as she pressed her head into the pillow and closed her eyes.

"Okay, mama," Chaya-Sarah answered.

Shayna was asleep before Chaya-Sarah finished answering. The child sat in the bed next to her mother and happily played with one of her cousin's dolls. A few peaceful minutes passed this way when, very suddenly, a man appeared in the doorway, startling Chaya-Sarah. She looked up from the doll. She recognized him as someone she had seen in the house, but he was not one of her relatives. He smiled and waved at her, but she just stared at him with wide, serious eyes and pursed kewpie doll lips. Then he put a finger to his lips as if they were playing a game in which she needed to be quiet. She continued to stare at him as he began tiptoeing silently into the room. Chaya-Sarah blinked at this strange behavior, which now alarmed her. She started to shake her sleeping mother even as she kept her eyes on the man.

"Mama, get up!" she cried.

"Darling, I asked you to let me sleep," Shayna said with her head on the pillow and her eyes still closed.

Chaya-Sarah continued shaking her mother as she watched the man creep slowly into the room, getting closer and closer.

"Mama! Mama!" she cried, beginning to panic when she realized that he was reaching for their bread.

"Chaya-Sari, please," Shayna answered, annoyed with her daughter for not letting her take even a short nap.

"Mama, the man is taking our bread!" Chaya-Sarah finally blurted out.

Shayna's eyes flew open and she jumped out of bed. She grabbed the bread just as the hand of the would-be thief was an inch away from snatching it. The man jumped back in shock and looked at Shayna. She did not say a word, but her eyes pierced him like daggers. He held up his hands, sheepishly backed out of the room and left quietly. Shayna immediately got up and closed the door, placing a chair in front of it. She put the loaf of bread under her pillow and took a deep breath to calm herself. She put her head back down on the pillow, but was reluctant to close her eyes anymore that afternoon.

◆　◆　◆

A few days later, Shayna and her sisters returned to the house after another long day of waiting on bread lines only to make a horrific discovery. Mirzsa's husband, Chaim, was gone.

"Russian soldiers came into the house and took him away," Raisa cried.

"Oh, no!" Mirzsa responded. "When? Where did they take him?"

"It was about an hour ago, but I don't know where," Raisa responded. "I only saw them forcing him to walk down the road with them." The women looked at each other, overcome with feelings of horror and helplessness.

"They only just took him, so maybe we can get him back," Shayna offered as she began walking toward the door.

"Do you really think so?" Mirzsa asked.

"We need to try," Shayna said as she took Chaya-Sarah's hand and looked at Mirzsa who was in tears. "Get one of your kids and let's go."

The two women and two children walked down the dirt road toward the old farmhouse, passing villagers and Russian soldiers who were milling around the streets of the town. When they got closer to the farmhouse,

Shayna saw a large fenced-in area to the right of it with a rectangular table set up in front and a line of civilian men standing in front of that. There were some Russian soldiers sitting at the table, speaking to the first man in line, then writing something on a piece of paper before the man was taken away behind the wire fence.

Shayna marched over to the soldiers with Chaya-Sarah by her side and Mirzsa and Dvayrie trailing behind. Two soldiers sat at the table. One was a large, red-faced man with black hair and a black mustache and the other man of slight build with hair the color of straw and brown freckles on his cheeks and nose. They both looked up and stared at her. The thin one greeted Shayna politely in Russian. Shayna nodded, then got right to the point.

"There has been a mistake," Shayna said in her slightly broken Russian. "My sister's husband, Chaim Ladowicz, was just brought here, but he is needed at home. As you can see, his wife has a child and more at home to take care of."

The soldiers both looked at her with their mouths open, seeming to lose their ability to speak. They turned to each other and the big one mumbled something to his diminutive comrade, then turned back to Shayna, squinting his eyes slightly. "What's your name?" he asked.

"My name doesn't matter," Shayna answered. "What matters is that my brother-in-law be returned to his family immediately."

The big, black-mustached soldier looked a bit taken aback, then he seemed to recover. He tilted his head slightly to one side, gave her a broad, disingenuous smile, and asked, "Where is your husband, pretty lady?"

"Never mind where he is. He's not here," she answered sharply, then softened. "What about my brother-in-law? We are begging you. Please let him come home. His wife needs him to protect his family."

The big soldier laughed. It was an ugly sound of derision. "It turns out that we need him more than you do, so he is staying with us," he said with a smirk. Shayna met his dark gaze, then looked over at the light-haired soldier who was looking down. He coughed and almost seemed embarrassed. He began to apologize to her, but the big one interrupted.

"What my comrade is trying to say is that you better go home, pretty lady, unless you want to sign up for work duty, too."

◆　◆　◆

Aside from dealing with dramatic moments when Russian soldiers absconded with husbands and sons or people tried to steal their food, most of Shayna's time was spent talking to people and gathering as much information as she could about their current situation. She listened carefully and learned well from all she heard. Many Jewish people, including most of her family, felt that they were relatively safe on the Russian side. They did not want to leave their homes or the homes of family members and venture into the frightening abyss of homelessness. Shayna listened to their arguments, but also realized that they did not have the same motivation or opportunity to attempt getting to America. Their families were all here with them and they did not have siblings or a spouse in America as she did. Some were also trapped because they had a spouse or a child in a Soviet labor camp whom they did not want to leave.

Shayna listened and thought and listened and thought some more. It was clear to her what her two objectives needed to be and that they were inextricably tied to one another. The first was to escape from where she was and the second was to make sure that it somehow opened a path to America. Because those goals were intertwined, she had to make sure that the solution for one supported the solution for the other. She did not want to escape from here and then get stuck somewhere else. That was an important reason that she did not accept a proposal by the Russian military. They were offering any refugee safe passage to wherever they wanted to go in the world. The refugees only needed to sign up and the Russians promised to help them get there. It sounded too farfetched to Shayna who knew that the Russians would never help Jewish people. If anything, they planned to take them somewhere, probably Siberia, and use them for free labor. As a result, she did not add her name to any of the Russian lists. Her brother, Yudke, signed up, believing that it was a way for him and his family to get away from here. Shortly after he did, he, his wife and three of his children said their good-byes to their family and friends and disappeared. When Shayna asked a Russian soldier what the plans were for these refugees, he volunteered only that they were going to be taken to Minsk. He would say no more.

Some people who wanted to leave told Shayna they were going south to Romania because they believed, or hoped, that the country would remain neutral. Shayna considered this, but did not feel certain that she could get to America from there. One thing she noticed in talking to people was that if she said she wanted to get to America, people laughed. "Sure, who doesn't want to go to America?" some asked in response. "In our dreams," others responded. Even when she told them her husband was there, they had the same response. She began to remain silent about her second goal and only allowed herself to reveal the first one of wanting to leave Poland. Then she ran into one of Jonah's friends.

The man was a childhood friend from Ostroleka who also came to Lomzatseh to escape the German onslaught. He was a very smart business-man whose family imported merchandise from other countries. He was well traveled and knew people who lived all over Europe. He and Jonah had recently lost touch and he did not know that Jonah was in America. Shayna told him everything, including her desire to reach America.

"Of course you want to go to your husband," Jonah's friend told her. "And you should."

"But how can I?" Shayna asked. "I've just been trying to get informa-tion about how I can do that."

The man looked down, stroked his beard and pondered this for a few minutes, then he picked up his head. "If you can, go to Vilna in Lithua-nia," he said brightly. "From there you will be able to communicate with Jonah and from there you might be able to get to America." That was all Shayna needed to hear. She thanked Jonah's friend and wished him well. Now, all she needed was to figure out how to get to Lithuania. She did not know how that was going to happen, but she was prepared to travel through fire and ice to get there.

◆ ◆ ◆

That afternoon, when they got home, Shayna told Chaya-Sarah to go and play with her cousins whom she heard in another room of the house. No children were allowed outside anymore unsupervised. Shayna found her sisters and her sister-in-law and asked them to please gather in the kitchen. Feeling the weight of emotion behind her request, they looked at each other and quickly took seats at the kitchen table. Shayna did not waste any time. She told them everything that Jonah's friend told her. She told them that she was going to act on that information and leave immediately for Lithuania. Everyone was silent at first, but then began to discuss the ramifications of going or staying.

Edke began to cry, "It's too dangerous!"

"I have to go," Shayna explained gently.

"Are you sure about this?" Mirzsa asked, her brow furrowed with consternation over her sister's announcement.

"My darlings, I don't feel I have a choice," Shayna continued. "I have to try to go to Jonah. I can't do that from here. I can't even communicate with him from here. From Lithuania, I will be able to write to him and possibly get to America."

Shayna sounded so decisive, they did not know what else to say. They also knew their sister very well. When she made up her mind, there was nothing anyone could say to change it. Edke got up, walked behind her sister's chair and put her arms around her shoulders and neck and rested her head lightly on Shayna's head.

"I'm so afraid," Edke said overcome with emotion and love for her sister. "I wish we could all stay together."

Shayna reached up and placed her hand on her sister's arm. "I know. I wish so, too." Everyone sat quietly lost in their own pain and fear.

"How will you get to Lithuania?" Mirzsa asked, breaking the silence.

"I need to figure that out. People told me to go to Bialystok and then from there I will find a way to the Lithuanian border. Jonah's friend, Itche, lives in Bialystok with his wife. Maybe I can find them and they will be able to help me."

Raisa looked at her with frightened eyes, but her words were strong. "Yes, I believe you should go to Bialystok first. You can take the train from Lomza. It will take about two hours."

"Good. We'll leave in the morning," Shayna said, feeling like there was no point in wasting any more time.

◆ ◆ ◆

The train station in Lomza was the noisiest, most crowded and most smoke-filled Shayna ever experienced. The sounds of talking, yelling, crying and coughing coming from the mass of people surrounding her could barely be heard over the screeching brakes and the screams of escaping steam as the train pulled into the station. *Where is the line to get tickets?* Shayna wondered as she frantically searched the crowded platform, worried that it might be too late to get on this train.

"Do you know where we get tickets?" Shayna asked the people in front of her.

"I think we're on the line," a woman turned around and answered her.

Shayna stood in the crowd feeling more miserable than she ever imagined was possible. Next to saying good-bye to Jonah at the train station in Warsaw, leaving her family this morning was the most painful thing she ever needed to do. Even though she thoroughly believed that it was the right thing to do, it was terrifying to be taking this step alone with her child. She also worried for the safety of her family, but she understood why they did not want to go with her. Raisa and Mirzsa were not willing to leave their husbands who were somewhere in Russian labor camps and Edke's husband, Meerche, had no relatives in America to sponsor him or help pay for their passage. They all thought, too, they would be reasonably safe under the Russians. She prayed they were right.

Shayna lifted Chaya-Sarah into her arms as the force of the crowd pushing in every direction made her feel they were being crushed. Even though the temperature outside was a brisk forty degrees, the heat of the train and all the human bodies pressed together made Shayna feel she was in an oven. She brushed the moisture from her glistening brow with the back of her free hand.

"Mama, I've never seen so many people mushed together in one place," Chaya-Sarah observed.

"I know, *maidel*. Let's hope we get on the train soon," Shayna answered, her voice sounding distant and strained.

"We will, mama," Chaya-Sarah said as she laid her head on her mother's shoulder. The typically rambunctious child had an instinct for knowing when her mother was stressed and needed her to be quiet and cooperative.

Finally, Shayna was at the head of the line. She got two tickets for the train bound for Bialystok. "Will we make it on this train?" Shayna asked, worried about the crowd of people gathered between her and the train.

"You should," the young ticket agent said as he thought about her question. "This train doesn't leave for about thirty minutes."

Shayna thanked him then joined the crush of people waiting for the doors of the train to open. Shayna took a deep breath and prepared herself for another unpleasant wait in the ever-growing crowd of people. By the time the doors opened fifteen minutes later, Shayna found herself in an avalanche of people falling toward the inside of the train. Shayna thought that it would be a miracle if no one fell and got trampled. She held on tightly to her daughter as she fought to keep her balance. When she reached the door, she climbed aboard the train being careful not to trip with her precious cargo. Inside the train was not any better. The crowd outside continued to push the people who were already on the train in a desperate attempt to get on. Shayna looked around her. She frantically searched for vacant seats so they could escape the overwhelming sea of people, but there were none. On every seat, people were piled high on one another's laps. Others began sitting down or standing in the aisle that was fast running out of space, too. It did not take long for Shayna to realize that she was going to be standing with Chaya-Sarah in her arms for the two-hour ride to Bialystok. It was either that or sit on the floor and risk being stepped on and she was not prepared to let that happen to her child. She searched to find a place where she could stand securely and was somehow able to find the edge of a seat to lean against. She then set her feet somewhat apart and braced herself for the journey. As the doors closed, she felt compassion for the people who were not able to get on and was grateful to be standing.

It was during this ride that she was able to formulate the plan that had been brewing in her mind for the last few days. Shayna was fully aware that it was vital that she be shrewd when dealing with people who might be able to help her. There was an overabundance of desperate people, but a dearth of resources. In some cases, money might be enough to provide incentive to anyone to help them, but what if it was not? She remembered how people laughed when she said she wanted to get to America. She must not tell people anything that seemed like an impossible dream for many. She wanted to inspire sympathy, not incredulity. Toward that end, she decided to make up a story that her husband was a Polish soldier who was wounded and in a Lithuanian hospital. She would play the wife trying desperately to reach him. She turned the idea over a few times in her mind and, as she did, she liked it more and more. It was not so far from the truth and who would not help a young woman, traveling with a child, reunite with her soldier husband?

An ache in her arm and shoulder brought her attention back to the crowded train. Chaya-Sarah was asleep with her head on her mother's shoulder, so Shayna dared not move. *Let her sleep through this miserable train ride*, Shayna thought. Shayna noticed there was no conductor coming to collect tickets. Looking over the mass of people on the seats and in the aisles, Shayna realized it would be impossible for anyone to get through this crowd for any reason. *I could have saved the money I spent on the tickets*, she silently lamented.

Shayna was able to peer out of a section of window that was not blocked by people's heads. She watched as the rural images going by were eventually replaced by the houses and buildings, streets and signage of a city. She sensed the speed of the train begin to slow. In spite of the challenges that lay ahead, knowing this excruciating ride was nearing its end gave Shayna the tiniest sense of elation, but one she needed. Her arms ached. Her legs felt wobbly. Nevertheless, she felt herself ready for action. Ten minutes later, when the train screeched to a halt in the station, the relief in the train car was palpable. People moaned and stretched, took deep breaths and sighed out loud. Chaya-Sarah sensed the change in the atmosphere, picked up her head and looked around.

"Did you have a nice nap, *tokhter* (daughter)?" Shayna asked. Chaya-Sarah blinked and nodded a groggy affirmative response.

"When we get off the train, I'll find us something to eat," Shayna said as Chaya-Sarah put her head back down on her mother's shoulder.

Before the war, roughly 107,000 people lived in Białystok proper. With over 50,000 Jewish inhabitants, it was one of the most ethnically diverse cities in Poland. The Jewish population of the city that Shayna encountered when she stepped off the train had swelled by the tens of thousands. It was a metropolis of refugees from all over Poland. Shayna found that many desperately wanted to get to America. The fiction she created about her husband being in Lithuania came in handy. As they walked among the throngs of people, Shayna told Chaya-Sarah of the plan to tell people that her father was a wounded soldier in a Lithuanian hospital so they would be more sympathetic and more likely to want to help.

"It's like a game," Shayna told her. "Okay, *maidel*?" Shayna needed confirmation that her child understood. She wanted to make sure Chaya-Sarah did not contradict the story she heard her mother telling people.

"Yes, mama," Chaya-Sarah liked games and this one even more so because it involved her father whom she missed so dearly.

◆ ◆ ◆

As soon as she and Chaya-Sarah arrived in Bialystok, Shayna began searching for three things: food, Itche, and someone with a wagon to take them to the Lithuanian border. By necessity, the pursuit of food came first. While standing on a bread line for almost two hours, Shayna spoke to as many people as she could for information about the other two items on her list. After securing some bread and fruit, they walked the streets of

Bialystok while they ate and Shayna continued talking to people. Everyone she encountered sympathized with her need to reach her husband in Lithuania, but the only thing they were able to offer her was advice. They themselves were either refugees like her or they lived in Bialystok, but no matter—neither group had any resources or power to help her. One person knew of Itche, but did not know where he lived although he offered to make inquiries for her and try to get a message to him.

In the meantime, Shayna continued to ask questions and listen carefully. A clear picture began to emerge. The Lithuanian border was roughly twenty miles northeast of Bialystok. It would involve an almost two-hour wagon ride. The problem was that the border was closed on both the Polish side and the Lithuanian side. Any effort to cross it was going to be thwarted by both Russian and Lithuanian soldiers. Shayna knew there were Polish people with wagons who were offering to take refugees to the border for a price. Some even claimed they knew how to get around the guards and sneak people into Lithuania. The latter group wanted a steep price to do this, but Shayna could not be sure what they were saying was true. Shayna encountered one Jewish man who came back from the border having tried unsuccessfully to cross it. He reported that he saw many others turned away from the border by the Russian guards, but they were now stuck there with no place to go. Shayna was becoming exhausted with all the information she was trying to absorb as well as the realization that there was no straightforward solution to this problem. She knew that she needed to take her time and plan wisely and carefully.

"Let's sit down for a minute," Shayna said as she found a cluster of trees on the side of a main street to sit near. She took an apple out of her pocket and offered it to Chaya-Sarah who, as usual, was not interested. Shayna was so relieved she was sitting, she did not fight with her daughter to take even a few bites of the apple.

"Mama, is someone going to help us go to Lithuania so we can see *tati*?" Chaya-Sarah asked.

Before Shayna could remind her daughter that her father was not in Lithuania, but was really in America, she thought she heard the sound of someone calling her name. *Maybe I didn't hear it right or it must be another Shayna*, she thought. Then she heard it again, but closer this time. Shayna looked up and saw a man holding a bag running toward her. She stood up when she realized it was Jonah's friend, Itche, waving at her.

"Shayna, is that you?" he yelled as he got closer. Shayna waved back even while she could not believe her eyes. When he reached her, they embraced, then he turned to greet Chaya-Sarah, "Someone is getting so big! I can't believe I'm seeing you both. What are you doing in Bialystok?"

"I can't believe I found you," Shayna cried happily. "I've been asking everyone in Bialystok if they know you."

Shayna explained everything they had been through, and Itche invited them to stay in his home. He and his wife were renting a one-bedroom house. They also left their Polish *shtetl* and ran here when the war started. When they got there, his wife apologized to Shayna and Chaya-Sarah that they needed to sleep on the floor.

"We only have one bed and we have no couches," she said. "Only these four chairs." They both offered to make the floor more comfortable for them by spreading some blankets down.

"Please, we'll be fine," Shayna told them. "We're so grateful to have friends to stay with."

The following days passed uneventfully with Shayna going out daily to continue gathering information about the border situation. Some days she accompanied Itche or his wife to the market for food. She always kept Chaya-Sarah by her side. Only when Shayna closed her eyes to sleep did she let her child out of her sight. Food was still scarce, but Shayna made a delicious soup with the vegetables Itche and his wife grew in a tiny garden in the back of the house. They talked about Jonah and everyone wondered how he was and what he knew about the war. They sympathized with Shayna about how difficult it must be to have no communication with him. Itche and his wife knew the truth of where Jonah was, but they both agreed that the story of his being a wounded soldier in Lithuania was a good idea to tell strangers.

Shayna appreciated the hospitality and the company of Itche and his wife, but all she thought about, day and night, was getting to Lithuania. She wanted to leave right away, but the precarious border situation made her more cautious. She spent time carefully searching for suitable people to give them a ride there. She knew she needed to bide her time and find the right moment to go. That moment came after about two weeks and it arrived in the form of an unexpected rumor from the border. There was talk going around that because of the growing number of Jewish immigrants trapped at the border, the Russians might open it to release them into Lithuania, but only for a few days. That was just what Shayna needed to hear. She wasted no time. Although she did not know exactly when and if that was going to happen, she could not take a chance and miss the opportunity.

Shayna quickly resewed their remaining money back into Chaya-Sarah's shoes, keeping some out for immediate needs. She once again dressed her daughter and herself in all their sweaters. She thanked Itche and his wife who handed Shayna some fruit for the road, and they left. She and Chaya-Sarah found the Polish couple Shayna spoke to previously about a ride to the border. They seemed kind and sympathetic to her story about finding her husband. They agreed on a price and Shayna and Chaya-Sarah climbed into the wagon that was pulled by two horses. Mother and child settled back for the two-hour ride on the dirt road through unfamiliar fields and forests to the Lithuanian border.

❧ CHAPTER 17 ❧

November 1939
Lithuanian Border

There comes a time in a man's life when to get where he has to
go—if there are no doors or windows—he walks through a wall.

~Bernard Malamud

"W hy are we stopping here?" Shayna asked the people driving the
wagon. Chaya-Sarah was playing with her braids and Shayna's
mind was a million miles away when the wagon came to a halt in front
of a large home with many windows and a gable-shaped canopy over the
front door. As the horses stomped their feet and snorted, Shayna leaned
forward to address the couple, again, as it seemed they did not hear her
the first time.

"Why are we stopping here?" Shayna repeated.

The two people turned to look at her. "This is as far as we can go,"
the man said. "The border is just up ahead a few miles, but the Russians
are not letting anyone through."

Shayna was about to indicate that she heard otherwise and that she
thought they agreed to take her all the way to the border, when the front
door of the home opened. An elegantly dressed older woman stepped
out and approached the wagon. Streaks of grey ran through her dark
hair that was piled high on her head and she wore heavy make-up that
made her look like a clown Chaya-Sarah saw performing on the street in
Warsaw. The woman greeted the couple warmly as if she knew them well.
They introduced her to Shayna and Chaya-Sarah then repeated to Shayna
that this was as far as they will take them. They added that their friend
would be happy to offer them refreshment and a place to stay. Shayna
thought for a minute, then realized that she did not have a choice. She

and Chaya-Sarah will have to find other transportation or walk the rest of the way to the border. In the meantime, she thought it wise to accept the offer of food and drink to help strengthen them for the challenges ahead.

"Come, *maidel*, we're getting off here," Shayna said to Chaya-Sarah as she stepped down from the wagon, lifted her daughter out, and paid the couple. The woman smiled at them and gestured toward her home. They followed her down the cobblestone path to her door, and stepped in while the woman held it open for them. Chaya-Sarah's eyes grew wide as she walked through the door and beheld the wonders of this woman's home. There were dolls everywhere—on couches, on tables, on chairs, on bookshelves. They all wore lace dresses engorged with multi-layered, white petticoats. Most were sitting, but some were standing, and one was laying in a cradle covered by a delicate lace blanket. Except for the one sleeping in her cradle, they all looked back at Chaya-Sarah with big, blue eyes framed by cascading honey-yellow curls. Even Shayna was impressed. Beyond the dolls, almost every square inch of the woman's home was covered in lace. There were lace tablecloths, lace pillows and cushions, lace doilies and lace curtains. The woman's home was a lace palace.

"Do you like my dolls?" the woman asked as she watched Chaya-Sarah feasting her eyes on them.

"She hasn't learned Polish yet," Shayna responded. "She only speaks Yiddish."

"Oh," the woman said with a powdery smile. "No matter." She gently removed an elegant doll from a shelf and handed it to Chaya-Sarah with bony hands. The girl looked at her mother for approval. When she saw her mother nod, she gingerly wrapped her hand around the doll and politely thanked the woman. It had braids like her, except the doll's were blonde instead of dark brown. The woman pulled out a chair at her formal dining table for Chaya-Sarah to sit on and gestured for Shayna to take another one.

"Please make yourselves comfortable while I prepare some tea," she said as she walked out of the room.

"Mama, there's so much lace everywhere!" Chaya-Sarah exclaimed in a soft voice. "And look at all these dolls!"

"Yes, it's amazing, like something in a fairytale," Shayna said in a soft voice.

The woman soon returned carrying an ornate silver tray that held a china teapot with a lavender floral design and cups and saucers to match. She sat down, delicately poured three cups of tea, then removed two plates of cookies and pastries from the tray and put them on the table before them.

"Please help yourselves to these treats and here are some sugar cubes for your tea, if you'd like," the woman said as she lifted the matching sugar bowl.

"Thank you very much," Shayna said. "We appreciate your kindness and generosity." Even as Shayna said those words and meant them, she wondered privately what ulterior motives this woman might have. The people who gave them the ride clearly meant to bring them here instead of going all the way to the border. *This was too tidy a package. What kind of arrangement do they have with this woman,* Shayna wondered as she sipped her tea. It did not take long for her to find out.

"My friends tell me that your husband is in a Lithuanian hospital. He is a wounded soldier?" the woman said, sounding partly like she was making a statement and partly as if she was asking a question.

"Yes," Shayna answered.

"Times are so difficult," the woman said sympathetically, shaking her head. "And they seem particularly hard for Jewish people right now." She paused, seemingly waiting for a response from Shayna.

"Yes," Shayna said, sipping her tea and putting a piece of cake and some cookies in front of Chaya-Sarah who was playing with the doll. Both women gazed at the child lovingly.

"Your daughter is a beautiful child," the woman interrupted Shayna who was about to tell her daughter to have something to eat and drink.

"Yes, thank you," Shayna responded.

The woman took the affirmative response as an invitation to launch into a speech that sounded somewhat rehearsed to Shayna. It started with some heartwarming stories about people, particularly Jewish people, who suffered through extreme adversity, but found a way to help their children. She did not say immediately how they accomplished this. In any case, Shayna was more interested in seeing Chaya-Sarah bite into a piece of cake and sip some tea. By the time the woman got to the part about how the answer for these people was to send their children to live in Catholic homes, Chaya-Sarah was eating her second cookie and Shayna was thrilled.

"That the children are raised Catholic is not a repudiation of Judaism, mind you," the woman said shaking her head. "No, I would never even suggest that. Conversion is more a logical extension of Judaism and, beyond the spiritual benefits of which there are many, it will also keep your child safe from harm in this very dangerous world." She looked at Shayna and patted Chaya-Sarah on the head.

Shayna paused for a moment. "Listen, dear, you are kind and we appreciate the refreshments," Shayna said politely, "but there will be no converting."

"Maybe it's something you need to think more about . . ." the woman began to clarify further why it was a good idea when Shayna's hand went up in the air.

"Please, we need to go," Shayna said firmly. "We have to get to the border before dark." Shayna stood and thanked her again for her hospitality, then turned to her daughter. "Chaya-Sari, let's go."

As they walked to the door, the woman followed close behind and continued talking to Shayna, but this time with an added note of urgency in her voice. "Please listen to me. I can take very good care of her." Shayna turned to the woman who stopped talking for a moment when she saw Shayna's face. Shayna looked at her as if she were completely out of her mind as she held Chaya-Sarah closer to her.

"You don't understand," the woman continued anyway, but stuttered a bit. "Your child will be safer with me and I can give her a good life . . . a very good . . ."

Shayna took Chaya-Sarah's hand and they were both out the door before the woman even finished her sentence. They followed the main road the wagon had been on when it stopped at the woman's house. Even though the area seemed to be remote, Shayna was able to tell by the wagon ruts in the dirt that it was a well traveled road. Still, she did not know where they were. She was not sure if the road led directly to the border. She watched and listened carefully for signs and sounds of refugees and soldiers.

"Mama, what was that woman saying that upset you so much?" Chaya-Sarah asked as they trudged along the side of the dirt road.

"That lady wanted us to change our religion," Shayna explained leaving out the part about the woman suggesting Chaya-Sarah stay with her. She thought that idea might be too terrifying to Chaya-Sarah.

"You mean she didn't want us to be Jewish anymore?" Chaya-Sarah asked.

"Yes, *maidel*," Shayna answered. "That's right."

"Why, mama?" Chaya Sarah asked. "Why doesn't she want us to be Jewish?"

Shayna thought for a moment before answering. "Because some people think their religion is better than someone else's and they think they are doing them a favor."

"That wouldn't do us a favor," Chaya-Sarah thought out loud. "We love being Jewish."

"Yes, *maidel*," Shayna smiled at her child. "Yes, we do."

After walking for over an hour, Shayna thought she saw some movement in the distance. Then she heard human voices. There was another dirt road that led in the direction of the sounds. She took Chaya-Sarah's hand and they began walking down the other road. Soon the sound of talking grew louder and Shayna saw a large crowd of people. Many looked very much like refugees, but there were also dozens of soldiers in Russian uniforms. The people all stood between a cluster of wooden buildings. A tall, barbed wire fence rose from the ground behind the buildings and spread to the left and the right deep into the forest, so deep that Shayna was not able to see where it ended. When they got closer, she noticed that there was an opening in the fence. That area was guarded by a handful of soldiers. *This must be the Russian checkpoint for the Lithuanian border*, Shayna reasoned. She held her breath as they slowly approached the area. Her senses became attuned to her surroundings, including the mood of the people. Beyond the checkpoint there were more soldiers and more wooden buildings. All of that was surrounded by dense forest as far as her eyes could see. Shayna picked up Chaya-Sarah and joined the line of refugees waiting in front of the checkpoint. She immediately began talking to the people around her. Just as she had learned in Bialystok, these people confirmed that the Russians issued an edict and opened the border for the last two days. Shayna breathed a sigh of relief. They reached the border at the perfect time. She watched with excitement as the Russian soldiers let small groups of refugees, maybe six at a time, pass through the checkpoint and just walk into Lithuania. She felt her spirits lift even as she worried about what she would find on the other side.

By the time Shayna and Chaya-Sarah got through the Russian checkpoint, fine threads of late afternoon sunlight were streaming through the tall trees. *It will soon be twilight and then it will be dark*, Shayna thought as she held Chaya-Sarah and walked with the other refugees. *One step at a time . . . One step at a time*, she repeated to comfort herself. Soon the refugees found themselves in front of another checkpoint. This one, Shayna learned, was guarded by Lithuanian soldiers, but they did not seem to be letting people through. There was no line, just a mass of people standing around and some sitting on the ground. Shayna walked closer to the checkpoint and started asking people what was happening.

"They let some people in earlier, but now they stopped," two people told her. "We don't know what's going on."

"They won't let us through," someone else said.

Shayna stood with the other refugees, watching the Lithuanian sentries and wondering what to do. As the number of refugees standing around waiting grew so did Shayna's impatience. *They let some people go through, so maybe they just needed a little inducement?* Shayna thought. Shayna began walking slowly toward the sentry standing nearest to her in front of the checkpoint. She stopped when he saw her and put his hand up to signal her to halt. She continued looking directly at him.

"Please, let me and my child pass through," she pleaded in Polish. "My husband is a soldier in the hospital in Vilna. I need to go to him."

The young soldier continued to hold up his hand as he shook his head from side-to-side. Shayna was not going to be deterred. She reached into her sweater pocket and pulled out something she was saving for just this type of situation. It was an American ten dollar bill that Jonah sent her just before the war started. The soldier's eyes widened in surprise when he saw the money. He kept his hand up, but he began to walk toward her. When he reached her, he studied the bill in her hand. Suddenly, he snatched it from her and stuffed it into his jacket pocket.

"Wait here one minute," he said and he turned and walked over to another soldier who was standing closer to the checkpoint area.

The refugees had all been staring at Shayna and now they watched the soldier with great interest. They all wondered if it was possible for this woman to successfully negotiate with these soldiers. If it were possible, then there might be hope for them and their families, too. They held their collective breaths. After a brief conversation with the other soldier, he turned and walked back slowly to where Shayna stood holding her daughter. They both stared at the soldier coming toward them with more curiosity than fear in their eyes.

"I can let you go, but up ahead there are more soldiers who will stop you," he said. "So, there is no point in letting you go through. They will just send you back." With that he turned around and walked away.

Shayna stood there for one moment watching him walk away with her money. She and her child needed that money. Did she dare demand her money back? She realized that the soldier could easily shoot her. She thought she heard gasps and murmurs in the crowd as she began to follow the soldier. With her child in her arms, she stepped over debris and pieces of barbed wire fencing, finally making her way to where the soldier stood. Shayna stopped in front of him. He tried not to look shocked, but it was obvious in his eyes that he was amazed by her courage. Shayna looked him directly in the eye and held out her hand. The air was so still, not even a breath was heard in the crowd of refugees. The soldier stared back at her. In the tension of the moment, a winter bird sang out a territorial warning to other birds. The soldier seemed to be thinking, then he slowly reached into his pocket. He took out the ten dollar bill and handed it to Shayna who took it, turned and walked back into the stunned crowd.

The refugees, Shayna included, did not know what to do next or where to go. They all realized that if the soldiers did not let a woman and child in for money, they would not let anyone in. They also realized that they were nowhere—they were not in Lithuania and they were not in Poland. The Russian soldiers had merely let them into a no man's land between two countries. As the sun began to fade in the sky, the refugees decided to walk back to Poland, through the Russian checkpoint. They did not know where else to go.

The Russian soldiers watched the exhausted refugees return to their checkpoint. The soldiers looked frustrated and began speaking among themselves. One man called out to the soldiers in Russian, explaining to them that the Lithuanians would not let them in. Shayna was not able to hear the soldier's response, but she became aware that they were opening the gate to the checkpoint and were letting the refugees back into Poland. She followed the group of people back through the open gate. Once the large group of refugees returned to the Russian checkpoint, they began speaking nervously to one another in Yiddish. They were all hungry, exhausted, and frightened. The sun was disappearing fast and no one had any idea of what they should do next. Shayna buttoned up Chaya-Sarah's coat against the encroaching cold, night air.

Suddenly, the soldiers began to surround the refugees. Next, they were barking out orders in Russian as they pushed everyone in the direction of a large wooden building.

"Where are we going, mama?" Chaya-Sarah asked. Shayna felt a pang when she realized how good her child was being, not complaining once through this long and exhausting day.

"I don't know, *maidel*," Shayna answered honestly. She inched closer to one of the soldiers and quietly asked him where they were going, but he did not respond.

As they got closer to the building, Shayna realized from the bars in the windows that it looked like a prison. *Are we being arrested?* she wondered. When they got in, Shayna looked around. It was obvious that the authorities were locking up as many people as fit into each cell. There was no one protesting or fighting the soldiers. People were too exhausted. And with night fast approaching, they were relieved to be inside, even in a prison. Shayna and Chaya-Sarah found themselves locked in a cell with a group of people who all began to sit down on the dirt floor. Shayna sat down in a corner, put Chaya-Sarah on her lap and watched as the prison guard locked the cell.

"Why are you putting us in here?" Shayna asked him.

"Yes, what is going on?" other people wanted to know.

The soldier looked at them almost apologetically. "We tried to let you go, but the Lithuanians won't let you in," he explained. "Basically, we don't know what to do with you." A great murmur arose in the crowd as everyone in the cell began to talk at once. Shayna's head fell back against the wall and she closed her eyes. Being locked up in prison was not in her plan, but here they were, in a cell with four bunk beds for what seemed to be over twenty men, women and children.

"We saw what you did at the Lithuanian checkpoint—It was amazing." Shayna turned to the voice that came from her left. She saw two young women sitting on the floor next to her, looking at her and smiling.

"Yes it was. You are so brave," the other young woman said.

"Listen, that money was mine; I need it for my child," Shayna said as if it were obvious that she just did what was necessary. "And the nerve of him to take it when he didn't let me go across."

The two women laughed and continued to sound impressed as they both indicated that neither of them would have been brave enough to do that. If they were in that situation, their money would be gone. The three women took turns introducing themselves, grateful to have a slight distraction from their unpleasant circumstances. One of them, Gittel, was trying to get to Lithuania to reunite with her father who was a rabbi. She was young, only nineteen. Gittel carried with her a Waterman fountain pen with a gold tip that she held onto like a talisman although she never spoke about it or its significance. The other, Meryl, hoped to get to America. Like Shayna, her husband went to America before the war. In addition, their ten-year-old son was with him so she was especially anxious to reunite with them. These two women, each traveling alone, met in Bialystok and decided to stay together on the journey to Vilna.

Everyone in the cell tried hard to cooperate with one another. They spent the night taking turns between the beds and the floors as judiciously as was possible. Very few adults slept, but were happy if their children did. When it was their turn to give up a bed, Shayna held Chaya-Sarah on her lap to keep her off the cold floor. It was as miserable a night as Shayna had ever known, but the long hours of discomfort, while they were exhausting, did not weaken her. Instead, they only strengthened her resolve to get across the border. The question was how. As the night dragged on, her thoughts were focussed on getting to Vilna and writing to Jonah. Her poor husband had not heard from her in months. She could not bear to think of him alone and wondering if his wife and daughter were even alive. She was determined to find a way to get around those guards.

◆　◆　◆

The next day, the Russian soldiers unlocked the prison cells and opened the doors. Shayna got up slowly from her cramped position in one of the beds. She did not remember falling asleep, but she must have because she had a dream about Jonah. In the dream, she heard his voice calling her name, but she was unable to see him. She found herself in a strange house with many rooms and she looked for him everywhere, but she could not find him. Shayna shook away the memory of the dream, holding on only to the sweet sound of her husband's voice as she took Chaya-Sarah's hand and walked outside. Overnight, the checkpoint area appeared to have turned into a refugee camp. The place was teeming with people—refugees, soldiers, local peasants and farmers. Apparently, many vendors came to sell food and other supplies to the refugees. Bread lines were set up in a few places and the soldiers allowed people to get water from a well. Shayna looked over the scene and assessed the situation.

"Let's go get some food and water," she said as she found a line to stand on and the women followed her.

After waiting on line for hours, the women found a place to sit and eat the bread and fruit they bought. Chaya-Sarah sat on the grass next to her mother. They all chatted while they were eating, trying to relax and distract themselves from their present situation, but not Shayna. Her mind was working overtime, trying to think of a way to sneak past the guards. *There must be an opening in the barbed-wire fence or it must end at some point*, Shayna thought. *It could not cover the entire border between the two countries*. Shayna watched the Russian soldiers, but she knew they were not the problem. It was the Lithuanian guards who were not letting them in. They were the ones to get around.

Just then Shayna noticed a soldier walking by. She waved and motioned for him to come over and join them. He walked over, greeted the women politely and squatted near Shayna. The two women stopped their conversation and watched Shayna and the soldier. She offered him a piece of her apple, but he declined. She exchanged some pleasantries with him, in Russian, which the women did not understand. He smiled and seemed flattered so she felt emboldened to continue. She did not want to waste anymore time and decided to get to the point. Shayna told him she wanted to know how long the fences were and the feasibility of anyone sneaking around the Lithuanian soldiers. He thought carefully about her questions and looked around as if to see who else was listening before he spoke.

"All I can tell you is this," he began, still looking around. "The fences are not very wide—maybe fifty yards, but if you go around them during the day, you would be seen by the Lithuanian guards. It is best to go under cover of darkness. We won't stop you. Not tonight."

Shayna nodded and thanked him. He stood up and was gone. The women immediately turned to Shayna with their eyes wide, wanting to know about the exchange she just had with the soldier. While Shayna and the women huddled together exchanging information, they did not notice a Polish man in his thirties with dark hair walking through the crowd. He was observing the refugees. He stopped periodically, struck up a brief conversation with a group of refugees, then he moved on. He wore a cap that restrained his hair which seemed to want to fly out in every direction and a dusty jacket that hung unevenly on him as if it were too big or belonged to someone else. He noticed Shayna speaking with the Russian soldier, and now he came over to speak to her. He smiled at the women and child. It was a broad, friendly smile that displayed two front teeth that were chipped at a funny angle, making them look sharp. Chaya-Sarah thought it made him look like a beaver. Other than that, he did not have an unpleasant face. The women all thought it was almost boyish. He exchanged pleasantries with them, then he looked at Shayna.

"I would like to offer you my services," he announced as he removed his cap, releasing a mass of tousled hair. "I can help you get into Lithuania. I know how to get around the guards and I know my way through the forest." The women all looked at each other, then back at the man.

"Tell us more," Shayna said as she eyed him suspiciously. He took that as an invitation to get closer.

"May I?" he asked as he started to sit down. Shayna nodded and he joined their circle. "It is best to go at night," he explained. "That way you are less likely to be seen by the Lithuanian guards. But because it is dark, you will need a guide who knows the terrain. There are all kinds of dangers in the forest—fast-moving streams, wild animals, fallen trees and hidden depressions that might be covered by leaves and other debris." He looked at all their faces which looked back at him in rapt attention, so he continued. "I've grown up right here in these woods. I have been playing in this forest since I was a young boy. I know the entire forest between here and Lithuania and could even walk through it blindfolded," he said as he smiled. "I can help you get to Lithuania." He stopped and looked at Shayna. Everyone was quiet. Shayna was thinking.

"You make a strong argument for hiring a guide, but I have not decided yet. If I say yes," Shayna asked. "What is your price?" Shayna's instincts told her that they needed this man to get them out of Poland and into Lithuania. When the man told her his price, they haggled a bit and finally decided on an amount that seemed agreeable to both of them. The man offered his hand to Shayna. She shook it.

"Meet me at the Russian checkpoint just before sunset," he added. "I will also need ten percent of the money up front . . . you know, as an assurance of our arrangement."

"I will give you all the money we agreed on when you get us safely into Lithuania," Shayna said.

◆ ◆ ◆

Later that day, the sun was a dying shimmer of light hovering over the floor of the darkening forest as the three women and one child followed their guide through the no-man's-land between Poland and Lithuania. Holding Chaya-Sarah's hand, Shayna walked behind the man while Gittel and Meryl walked behind them. As the soldier told Shayna, they had no trouble getting past the Russian guards. The Russians were still letting refugees go, hoping to get them off their hands and give the refugee problem to someone else. The group stepped slowly and carefully as they made their way through the forest which was carpeted with crunchy brown leaves, twigs, fallen branches and the exposed roots of trees. Every so often they passed a mossy area where, under other circumstances, Shayna would have stopped to collect the succulent mushrooms growing underneath to make soup for dinner.

The man wended his way around a grassy hummock, then squatted down behind it and bade the women do the same. "We're close to the point where the Lithuanian fence ends. A sentry walks by this area every hour or two, especially at night. We're going to wait here until it is completely dark. After the sentry checks the area and leaves, we will cross. For now, just stay down, and keep very quiet."

Shayna and the women all settled down, happy to have some rest.

Chaya-Sarah found a comfortable spot on her mother's lap while she played with some moss that grew near her feet. With the sun setting, the dropping temperature made them all shiver with cold. Shayna buttoned up Chaya-Sarah's sweaters to her neck and took her hands in her own to warm them. Chaya-Sarah leaned her head back on her mother's chest. "I miss *tati*," she sighed.

"I do, too, *maidel*," Shayna whispered as she hugged her a bit tighter.

"Shhh, I think I hear guards approaching," the man said suddenly and they all got quiet and very still. "Do not make a sound." The man put his finger up to his lips. He smiled and winked at Chaya-Sarah when he saw her looking his way and aping him with her forefinger.

At least two sentries approached the area. The group heard the voices of the men along with the crunching of crisp leaves and snapping of dry twigs under their feet. They stayed quiet as the two soldiers continued to walk to the edge of the fence. When they got there, the soldiers stopped and put their guns down. One sat down on the ground while the other leaned against a tree. The one who was sitting removed a cigarette from a pack in his front pocket, lit it and took a long drag. He took one more deep drag, then passed the cigarette to the standing soldier. They both took turns sucking on the cigarette and did not appear to be eager to leave anytime soon.

The soldiers continued relaxing and smoking for what seemed like hours, but was probably just twenty minutes as everyone stayed quiet and did not move. They said not a word, nor did they sneeze or cough as they continued to listen to the soldiers voices and their occasional laughter. They were close enough to smell the pungent odor of the cigarette smoke. When the soldiers finally decided to leave, they all breathed a sigh of relief, but waited until the sounds of the crunching leaves and their voices were completely gone before anyone spoke or moved.

"We're going to leave now. Follow very close behind me," the man said as he stood up. "I'm going to make some twists and turns to avoid some dangerous areas. Step carefully. We will have to walk through some water, but they are just streams, not very deep, and I will take you to the shallowest parts. No talking while we we are crossing the border. Okay? Everyone ready?"

Shayna translated his words into Yiddish for Chaya-Sarah and the women whose Polish was not as good as hers, and everyone nodded in agreement. They stood up and turned to follow the man as their eyes adjusted to the shadowy world of the forest at night. Shayna, again, held Chaya-Sarah's hand and the two women followed close behind them. They made their way as quietly and as stealthily as they could, stepping carefully. They held onto trees when they felt unbalanced to avoid falling. The sound of dry, dead leaves crackling under their feet was magnified in the stillness of the cold air, making them feel like they were announcing their presence for miles. They were too frightened of the Lithuanian soldiers to be aware of the bitter cold. It nipped at their ears and noses and chilled them through clothes that were inadequate for a winter night in the woods.

As they approached a stream, the man stopped suddenly. "Be careful," he whispered. "We're going to be walking through some water here."

Shayna quickly motioned for one of the women to help her put Chaya-Sarah on her back. Gittel lifted the girl as Chaya-Sarah reached for her mother, wrapping her arms around her mother's neck and her legs around her waist. Shayna bent over slightly to accommodate the weight of her child as they all began walking. Soon the crisp, dry leaves gave way to slippery and soggy ground. Before too long, they found themselves ankle deep in water. They all sucked in shocked breaths when the icy water reached their bare skin. Their thin leather shoes were no match for even a shallow stream. Shayna was so glad she was carrying Chaya-Sarah as the frigid water got deeper and at times reached their knees.

After almost an hour of trudging over both dry land and through cold streams, the refugees found themselves deep in the forest. Believing they were a safe distance from the guards, the man located a clearing where they could stop and rest. He took out a cigarette and offered one to the women who each declined. After he took a few puffs, he motioned to Shayna that he wanted to talk to her privately. Shayna looked at the women and shrugged. She had no idea what he was going to say to her. She followed him to where he walked a few yards ahead of her, bringing Chaya-Sarah with her. He stopped and found a place for them to sit. Shayna waited for him to speak.

The man cleared his throat and said, "We are in Lithuania now and away from the border sentries."

"That's true," Shayna responded, "but we are still deep in the woods."

"Yes, well, I will take you and your daughter the rest of the way," the man said as he looked at Shayna.

Shayna nodded still unsure of the man's point, "That was our agreement . . . that you would navigate us through the woods to safety."

"But only you two," he added, "Not the others."

Shayna studied him, then glanced back at the two women who were looking at them with worried faces. "What are you saying? We should go with you and leave those two girls here in the middle of the woods, in the middle of the night?"

"The thing is, Shayna, I like you," he stammered while trying to take her hand. Shayna quickly took her hand from him.

"You agreed to take all of us," Shayna demanded. "I am paying you to take all of us."

"I want to help you . . . Please come with me," the man begged. "I will take good care of you and your daughter."

Shayna felt outraged and let it show. "I'm not going to leave those two women. Do you want more money? I will pay you more money, if that's what you want, but you need to help all of us," she stated the last three words emphatically.

"No," the man shook his head. "I don't want more money. I'm only interested in helping you and your daughter," he said.

"And if my daughter and I don't go with you?" Shayna asked.

"My offer is only for you and your child," he said as he smiled his crooked smile and took another drag of his cigarette.

Shayna stared at him with venom in her eyes. "Please, I beg you. I have a child here."

The man just shook his head and threw his cigarette to the ground. Shayna looked at him with daggers in her eyes and took her daughter's hand. They trudged back to where Gittel and Meryl were standing. She explained to them what the man told her. The women were shocked. How could this man leave three young women and a child to fend for themselves in a dark forest? They all turned their heads simultaneously to look at him. He was already gone.

The women, now alone with no guide to show them the way, looked at the trees of the forest as if they were seeing them for the first time. In the grey light of the quarter moon high above them all color was gone from the once vibrant forest. Everything seemed to be shrouded in a pallid, ghostly mist. This was not the magical place where Chaya-Sarah used to enjoy the wonders of nature and pick mushrooms and berries. The forest Chaya-Sarah loved so much was now a dark and foreboding place full of shadows and strange shapes that she did not recognize. One tree looked like a giant old man hunched over at the waist, towering ominously over them. Another was like a scary witch who was reaching out to grab them with gnarled fingers. And where were the sounds of birds singing and frogs calling to one another? The night creatures made very different sounds. There were odd screeches and growls and a mysterious rustling sound not far away. The forest had suddenly become a frightening place.

"Mama, I just saw two yellow eyes looking at me," Chaya-Sarah cried as she sensed the fear in the adults around her. "They were so big!"

"It was probably an owl," Shayna said.

"I'm scared," Chaya-Sarah declared. "Pick me up! Please, pick me up!"

"You love owls," Shayna said as she lifted her daughter into her arms.

"Mama, where are we going?" Chaya-Sarah was in the mood for questions even though Shayna was not.

"Not now, *maidel*," Shayna said, her anxiety showing. "Let me think."

"I just asked where we're going," Chaya-Sarah said with a slight pout.

"We're going to *Uchpatchuch*," Shayna said sounding more irritated than she meant to.

"*Uchpatchuch?*" Chayna-Sarah answered. "That's a pretend place you and *tati* say to be silly." The seven-year-old knew sarcasm when she heard it.

Shayna took a deep breath to calm herself. "Right now, we have to get out of the woods and we have to find some people who can help us. That's where we're going . . . we're going to find help."

"Are we lost?" Gittel asked. Everyone looked around. Gittel's question made them huddle closer together as they shivered in the cold. They looked out into the darkness as the crisp, pine scented air they breathed escaped from their mouths in a white, powdery mist.

"No," Shayna said so loudly it almost startled everyone. "We are not lost." Shayna remembered the general vicinity of the path they took to get to this clearing. She knew that they must continue in the same relative direction. She also knew from reading adventure and travel books that sailors used the North star, the brightest star in the northern hemisphere, to guide them when they were out at sea. Shayna looked up now and found that star. She pointed it out to everyone. Chaya-Sarah knew that star, too. Her father showed it to her when they went for walks on bright, moonlit summer nights.

"That is our beacon," Shayna said. "Let's go."

Shayna led the way as she and Chaya-Sarah and their two companions trudged through field and forest and stream. They continued for hours in the cold, dark woods. At times they found themselves in water up to their ankles and sometimes up to their knees. Their shoes were soaked with water and caked with mud, making it difficult not to slip even when they walked on dry leaves. Shayna tried to keep Chaya-Sarah on her back as much as her strength would allow. They moved as quickly as possible, trying not to think about how cold their bodies felt or how numb their feet and hands were. Shayna stopped periodically and looked upward, then continued on the path or adjusted it slightly if she thought it was necessary. Chaya-Sarah lifted her eyes up along with her mother.

"Are we still on the right path, mama?" Chaya-Sarah asked with the reflection of the starlight dancing in her wide, brown eyes.

"Yes, *maidel*, we are," Shayna answered. "God-willing, we are." It comforted her as much as her child to hear herself sound so positive. The torturous journey seemed to go on forever and the women struggled to keep putting one foot in front of the other. As they pushed themselves, each one silently prayed that they were moving in the right direction and would soon find someone, anyone, who could help them.

Then they saw a light.

✑ CHAPTER 18 ✎

Winter/Spring 1940 Lithuania

The common humanity of people, not the power of governments, is the only real protector of human rights.

~Jan Karski

The light seen by the weary refugees was still too far away for them to know with any certainty exactly what it was. They each fervently hoped that it was not a trick of the eye, like a reflection of moonlight or starlight in a body of water. Their trembling legs felt weak and rubbery and they neither knew nor cared whether that was from the cold or the exhaustion. They just knew those legs could not carry their freezing bodies much longer or much farther.

"It looks like it might be a lantern," Gittel said with a bit of hope in her voice as she squinted to get a better look at the light that was getting closer and brighter with each step.

Please, they all cried quietly to themselves. *Please be a lantern*. Their prayers gave way to cautious optimism when it seemed more and more that it was a flickering, human-generated light. Their cold bodies barely had enough energy to keep moving, but hope released a bolt of hot adrenaline into their veins. They picked up their pace with little regard for how exhausted or out of breath they were. They could not reach that light fast enough. Finally, they saw what it was and, more importantly, what was around it. The light was coming from a window in a farmhouse. The women felt overcome with excitement and relief. Suddenly, Gittel fell over onto her hands and knees and let out an involuntary yell. They all stopped to help her.

"Are you okay?" Shayna asked.

"Yes, I'm fine," Gittel responded, standing up and regaining her balance and composure. "I just got so excited, I think I tripped over a rock."

"We're so close now," Meryl cried out. "We're almost there."

"Yes, but where?" Gittel said, expressing a concern that tempered the exhilaration and relief they were beginning to feel. They realized that this remote house probably belonged to Lithuanian farmers. It was no secret that the Jewish and the Lithuanian people were uneasy neighbors. The thought was like an injection of fear laced with a tincture of trepidation. When they resumed walking, it was at a slower pace. *How willing would these people be to help four bedraggled, Jewish refugees who showed up uninvited at their door in the middle of the night?* They each kept their fears to themselves, but they did not have to be telepathic to know what each one was thinking.

When they reached the house, they stopped. Shayna approached the window illuminated by the lantern light. She stood on the tip of her toes to peer in, but saw no one inside. She knocked softly on the glass. At first, there was no response, so she knocked again. This time two child-like eyes peered out over the bottom of the window. They were immediately followed by four larger eyes that appeared higher in the window. A man, a woman and a child stared out at them. Shayna and the others smiled cautiously and waved. The man and woman did not react, but seemed to be speaking to one another. After what seemed like a very long time to the weary refugees, the man motioned for them to go to the front door. They all trudged toward the entry of the house where they found the man standing in his doorway. He looked at them and asked, in Lithuanian, what he could do for them.

"Sorry to disturb you and your family, but we're running from the war in Poland," Shayna said. "All we need is to be taken to the nearest home of Jewish people. Can you help us?" Between his knowledge of Polish and Shayna's of Lithuanian, Shayna was able to get her message across.

The man looked at the three women and one child who were wet and shivering with cold. "Is it just the four of you?" he asked.

Shayna nodded as the man held up his hand for them to wait. He stepped back into the house. He came out a few minutes later wearing a hat and coat, and motioned for them to follow him toward a large wooden building that stood near his house. When he slid open the wide door to the building, they saw a table and work area with all kinds of metal tools both on the table and hanging on the wall. The tools were unfamiliar to them and Chaya-Sarah and the women were fascinated. The man disappeared into the barn for a few minutes, then reappeared with two shiny brown horses that walked calmly on either side of him. They smelled of warmth and hay. The women watched as he brought them out and hitched them to his wagon. He motioned for the refugees to climb in, and stood nearby to offer them a hand before he got into the driver's seat and took the reins.

The man chatted amiably as the horses pulled the wagon over the cold, dirt road. Shayna translated his words to the other women who did not speak Lithuanian. They found out that the man was a blacksmith, which explained all the strange tools he had. He told them that he was taking them to a Lithuanian town on the border of Belarus that had a large population of Jewish people. The Lithuanians called the town Eisiskes, but to Yiddish speakers it was known as Eishyshok. It was about thirty minutes away. He knew one family in particular who might be able to help them. The refugees were all so relieved to be sitting and getting a ride somewhere, they almost did not care what he was saying or where they were going.

◆ ◆ ◆

The Jewish family in Eishyshok took pity on the cold, exhausted people. They offered them dry clothes to wear, warm food to eat and comfortable beds to sleep in. *Let me not take these things for granted ever again,* Shayna thought to herself. When she removed Chaya-Sarah's muddied shoes she found that the water they slogged through had made its way into the lining, leaving their money soaking wet. She removed the soggy paper bills, squeezed the water out taking care not to tear them. She then laid the bills over the chairs to dry along with their shoes and wet clothes. As the day wore on, the women felt their energy and optimism returning. They were in a free country that was not occupied by either Germany or Russia. Shayna felt a rush of excitement when she learned that this town was only forty miles from Vilna. She was closer to contacting Jonah than she had been for months. Over a relaxed dinner of hot chicken soup followed by stuffed cabbage and a sweet potato *tsimmes* (stew), the women learned that this family did not have the resources for them to stay beyond another day. That suited the women who were ready to continue on their journey. They decided to go to Gittel's brother's home, which was in a *shtetl* closer to Vilna. The generous family offered to help them find transportation there the next day.

When the women awoke the next morning, their muscles were a bit stiff and sore, but they were surprised to feel so rested and refreshed after the ordeal of getting across the border. Their clothes and shoes were dry and they were eager to be on their way. After thanking their hosts profusely and wishing them well they boarded a rickety wagon pulled by two grey horses. As the wagon began to move, the mood on board was considerably lighter than it had been at any point since the women first met. They all admitted it was hard to believe that had happened just three nights ago. It seemed to them that weeks had passed since that awful night they spent on a prison floor. They watched the activity of the bustling town of Eishyshok go by the wagon as the driver snapped the reins lightly and clicked his tongue to coax the horses into a canter. The taste of freedom was sweet and almost made them believe that life was returning to normal. Of course, they all knew that nothing could be further from the truth. They had seen too much in the last few months to believe that life would be normal again anytime soon.

A cold breeze made Shayna shiver and reminded her of the challenges that lay ahead for them. She closed the top button of Chaya-Sarah's sweater to cover her neck, then returned to her thoughts. America was still a distant dream, and although they might be in a democratic country at the moment, there were hungry fascists and communists salivating at the borders and ready to pounce. She knew that it was only a matter of time before either Germany or Russia marched in to claim this country as their own. In the meantime, she wanted to contact Jonah and get her hands on whatever documents she needed to get to America. Nothing meant anything without the documents.

Chaya-Sarah put her head on her mother's arm and sighed. "Mama, where are we going?" she asked. There was a pause and then Chaya-Sarah continued, "I know, we're going to *Uchpatchuch,* right? But when will we get there?"

Shayna took a deep breath and started to speak, but Chaya-Sarah interrupted her, "Wait, I know that, too. We'll get there when we get there." She laughed and her mother joined her.

"My clever *maidel,*" Shayna said as she wrapped her arms around her sweet girl and kissed the top of her head.

◆　◆　◆

They arrived at Gittel's brother's house in the early afternoon. Like Gittel's father, her brother was a rabbi. He and his wife were very warm and generous people and their house was a full one occupied every moment with family, friends and lots of children for Chaya-Sarah to play with. Shayna learned a lot about the current political state of Lithuania from talking to the people there, especially Gittel's brother. When the Soviets allowed Lithuania to become an independent republic in October, life improved for the many Jewish people who lived there. As a result, Shayna and her traveling companions were not alone in seeking asylum in that country. In the last few months, tens of thousands of Jewish people fled here from German- and Soviet-occupied Poland. While the country was a safe haven for them at the moment, Gittel's brother warned that the Soviets were clearly not finished with this country. They still had army bases established in many locations, including one right on the outskirts of Vilna, the city where Shayna and her friends wanted to go.

"What they are planning is anyone's guess, but whatever it is will not be good for us," the rabbi told her. "The other thing you all need to be aware of is that only Lithuanian citizens can get jobs. Polish refugees are not allowed to work here. They must receive assistance from their families or the Jewish organizations that are helping refugees find food, shelter and clothing."

The rabbi gave Shayna the names of people he knew in one of the Jewish organizations in Vilna. Shayna was not looking for financial assistance. She still had some money sewn in the lining of Chaya-Sarah's shoes and hoped that soon Jonah would be sending more, but she knew that she could use a hand getting settled and finding her way around. So, she was happy for his help.

"They will take good care of you," he told her. Shayna was grateful for these wonderful people. She stayed there for two nights and when it was time to go she hugged all the new friends she made along with her traveling companions, Gittel and Meryl. They planned to stay on longer with Gittel's brother.

"Make sure the organization knows where you settle so we can find you when we get there," Gittel said and Meryl nodded in agreement.

In late December of 1939, near the end of what had been a turbulent five months for Shayna and Chaya-Sarah, they boarded a train for the hour-long ride to Vilna. As hard as it was to leave this comfortable family setting, Shayna felt a thrill knowing she might soon be able to communicate with Jonah.

◆　◆　◆

The city of Vilna, with its population of 200,000 of which a quarter were Jewish, did not surprise Shayna, but it was different from any Eastern European city she ever visited. She was familiar with its reputation among the Jewish people of Europe as the Jerusalem of Lithuania and now she could see why. There were many synagogues. They were handsome stone and brick buildings, not at all like the modest wooden structures of Poland. Yiddish and Hebrew schools flourished here, too. They were elementary, middle and high schools as well as *yeshivas* (Jewish colleges) and rabbinical schools. It was no wonder that she had seen the wagon of rabbinical students and rabbis fleeing here to escape from Poland when the Germans invaded. She saw many of them here now, young men with their long, black coats and *payes* (sidelocks) walking the streets in large groups, animatedly discussing Talmudic issues or racing hurriedly to their classes. *It's so comfortable,* Shayna thought, *so haimish (homey).* She enjoyed the feeling of being in a place where *Yidishe mentshn* (Jewish people) were able to worship freely and live without constant fear, yet she harbored no illusions. *This place appears to be a safe island in a hostile ocean,* Shayna thought, *but for how long will it be so?*

Shayna took Chaya-Sarah's hand as they left the train station and crossed the busy street. There was no snow on the ground, but the icy air nipped at their cheeks and noses and Shayna was grateful that they were bundled up in all the clothes they owned. In her sweater pocket, Shayna carried a piece of paper the rabbi gave her with the names of the people he knew at the Jewish organization. She stopped to ask a friendly-looking woman for directions to that building. "*Antshuldik mir* (excuse me), I'm looking for the Hebrew Immigrant Aid Society," Shayna said. "Can you tell me where they are located?"

The woman paused as if she did not hear her or maybe, Shayna worried, she did not speak Yiddish. Then the woman's face lit up. "Oh, HIAS," the woman said brightly, indicating that she both knew the name and spoke Yiddish. Fortunately, she also knew exactly where it was. "Keep walking in the direction you're going. It will be about four blocks down and on your right."

The people at HIAS were a lifeline for Shayna. They helped her find a room to rent in the home of a Jewish family with children whose youngest was the same age as Chaya-Sarah. With the money Shayna had, she was able to pay the family some rent money. After getting settled in their room, Shayna sat down to finish her letter to Jonah. She started it in Gittel's brother's house with pen and paper the rabbi gave her. She told Jonah everything they went through and, most importantly, that they were well and missed him very much. On this, their first afternoon in the room in Vilna, Shayna added the address of the house where they were now renting a room. She felt a rush of excitement as she completed it and sealed it. Finally, she allowed herself the luxury of anticipating that she might hear from Jonah soon.

"Let's go mail this letter to your father," Shayna said as she checked herself in the mirror and adjusted her dress. *I need to buy some lipstick*, she thought to herself as she stared at the pale reflection looking back at her. She did not like this unpolished look at all. She turned to her daughter from whom she had not received a response. Chaya-Sarah who was on the bed happily playing with a doll the family's little girl let her borrow, suddenly appeared gloomy.

"Why are you mailing him a letter? Aren't we going to see him now? Isn't he in the hospital?" Chaya-Sarah hit her mother with a barrage of questions that made it very clear that she was confused.

Shayna sat down on the bed next to her daughter and allowed herself a deep sigh, one that brought more air into her lungs than had been there in a long, long time. She realized that her child heard the story so often of her father being in Vilna that, now that they were here, she forgot or did not want to remember that it was fiction. Gazing out the window, Shayna gathered her thoughts.

"Do you remember that I had to make up the story that your father was in a hospital in Lithuania?" she asked her daughter gently. "I had to do that so people would sympathize with us and help us get across the border." Chaya-Sarah was quiet so her mother continued, "Remember that *tati* went to America and he is waiting there for us?"

Chaya-Sarah sat quietly, mulling over her mother's words. Of course she knew her father went to America. She heard her parents speak of that magical place hundreds of times, but America was just the name of some faraway place in her imagination. What did she know about distances or directions? She knew that back in her *shtetl*, her neighbor's well was twenty steps from her house. She knew that if she ran very fast, she reached her best friend Edkelkee's house by the time she counted to ten. She knew that some of her cousins lived in neighboring towns and it took a long ride in a horse-drawn wagon to reach them. She also knew that she and her mother had just traveled farther than she had ever gone in her life.

It was so far, in fact, this could even be America. It made sense that her father was here. In a child's mind, the line between fantasy and reality was a soft one at best. The story of her father lying in a hospital bed in Vilna became so real to her, she was counting on it to be true. She wanted it so much to be true.

Chaya-Sarah toyed with the strands of hair knit tightly into her left braid which for some reason was her favorite one to bother with when she was upset. The cold, hard truth of her mother's words began to work their way into her consciousness replacing the warm dream of her father being here. With the sudden realization came tears of frustration and sadness.

"I want *tati*," she cried.

"I want him, too," Shayna said gently. "But he's in America."

"You made him leave us and go to America!" Chaya-Sarah barked, angry at her mother now.

"*Maidel*, no," Shayna was at a loss for words after her daughter's harsh accusation.

"Yes, it's your fault that he went away!" Chaya-Sarah continued. Shayna blinked slowly and collected her thoughts. She wondered how to explain the vagaries of the adult world of warfare and immigration to her seven-year-old child when she herself could barely grasp them.

"Darling, he had to go to America when he got his visa," Shayna pleaded with her daughter, then waited a moment for that to sink in. "We will join him soon. That's why we came here to Vilna, so we can get visas, too."

"When, mama? When will we see him?" the child demanded through her tears. Having nowhere else to place her anguish and frustration, she laid the intense emotions on her mother.

"I don't know exactly. We have to be patient," Shayna struggled to find the right words. "Soon, God-willing, we will get the papers we need and your father will send us money for the tickets, then we will be able to go to him . . ." her voice trailed off as her mind tried to grasp the daunting task before her. There was so much distance and so many potential obstacles between the two of them and Jonah. It felt as though he were at the center of an intricate maze that was filled with riddles and traps that she had to figure out a way through. Chaya-Sarah felt it, too, and dropped her head as her slight shoulders began to tremble with great sobs.

"We have to be strong," Shayna said as much to herself as to her daughter as she held back her own tears and tried to pull Chaya-Sarah toward her. Her daughter resisted at first, then relaxed and gave in to the comfort of her mother's arms. She sat like that for a while, not saying anything, just crying until Shayna broke the silence.

"*Mayn zis kind* (my sweet child)," Shayna said. "Please don't cry." Then Shayna heard something she had not heard her daughter say in what seemed like a very long time.

"I'm not crying, mama," Chaya-Sarah lifted her head, wiping the tears from her left cheek and sniffing. "My heart is crying."

◆　◆　◆

Two weeks later the letter that Shayna mailed from Vilna was sitting on the kitchen table of Esther and Izzy's house in the Bronx. Esther, who had been staring at it as she waited for her brother to get home, jumped up like a released Jack-in-the-box as soon as she heard the knob on the front door turn. "He's here . . . Jonah's home!" Esther cried. Izzy came running out of the bedroom. He wore pants with no belt and a ribbed, cotton undershirt that revealed the curly, grey hairs on his chest and arms.

The door opened slowly and a tired Jonah, still wearing the cold air of the wintry January evening, walked into the apartment. He looked startled to see his sister and half-dressed brother-in-law staring at him like excited children hoping he had candy for them. Smiling from ear to ear, Esther handed him the envelope before he even closed the door behind him. He looked at her face, then at the envelope. Jonah recognized the handwriting before he even saw the Lithuanian postmark. His legs suddenly felt weak. After four long and harrowing months of not hearing from Shayna, here was his name on an envelope in her handwriting. He sat down and began to struggle with the obstinate adhesive.

"How can a simple paper envelope be so difficult to open?" Jonah said with uncharacteristic frustration in his voice, his strong hands trembling.

Esther, beyond anxious herself, reached over to try to help just as he got it open. Izzy stood by her as they listened to Jonah read the letter, tears of emotion leaving shiny tracks on her cheeks. Jonah began to cry, too, in great, joyful sobs as he struggled to read Shayna's letter through water-logged eyes. When he got to the end, he put the letter down and looked at his sister and brother-in-law.

"It's a *nes* (miracle) from God," Jonah said as his sister brought him some tissues.

"A *nes*," Esther repeated blowing her nose into one of the tissues.

Jonah spent the rest of the night writing a letter back to his wife and daughter, but not before he read Shayna's letter over and over and over again.

◆ ◆ ◆

Transatlantic travel being what it was, by the time Shayna received a letter back from Jonah, one full month passed. Chaya-Sarah's eighth birthday came and went. Shayna baked a sweet, rhubarb pie which was her daughter's favorite. She enrolled her in a Yiddish elementary school which Chaya-Sarah started immediately. Shayna wanted to make sure that her daughter's education did not suffer so she also sent her to a rabbi for private Yiddish reading and writing lessons to make up for the months of school she missed. She was grateful that the principal of Chaya-Sarah's school, Regina Weinreich, was helpful, too, giving Chaya-Sarah special attention to help her catch up with her lessons. Besides taking an instant liking to one another, Shayna and Regina bonded over similar life situations. They were both separated from their husbands who were in New York City and they both had a child in Vilna with them. At twelve, Regina's son Gabriel was a bit older than Chaya-Sarah. Regina also had an older son, Uriel, who was with his father, Max, in America. The women's friendship would prove to be a positive one for both of them and an important one for Shayna.

One afternoon Shayna returned to the home where she was renting a room and there on a table in the foyer nestled in a pile of mail was a letter from Jonah. Shayna's eyes lit up. She reached for it greedily as she cried out, "It's from America—from my husband!" She ran into her room, threw her purse on the bed and tore open the envelope. When she took out the letter, she pressed it to her cheek even before she read the words. She breathed in the smell of ink from Jonah's pen that permeated the air near the crinkly paper as she began to read his words slowly and methodically. She did not want to miss anything he wrote. She studied each word, striving to read between and beyond them. Would he tell her the truth about how he really was, how he suffered these last few months without a word from his family trapped in a war zone? *Of course not*, she thought. *He would not want to upset her. He would coat his words with honey.* Just as she expected, she read how he was the happiest man in the world to hear from her and to know that his precious girls were safe. He admitted that he cried when he got her letter and read it at least twelve times before he picked up a pen to write back. She knew her husband well so the tears did not surprise her nor did the admission. Of course he would have been overcome with emotion when he got her letter, the first indication that his family was alive and well. He told her he was pleased with his new job as a salesman in a successful line of men's, women's and children's clothing. She sensed the excitement and the pride in his words and wanted to hear more detail, but he immediately went on to discuss the important business of their immigration papers and how the job will enable him to send her money.

In the months after he first arrived in America, he and his older brothers, Irving and Abe, completed the sponsorship papers she and Chaya-Sarah were required to submit to get an American visa. Even though Jonah was gainfully employed and could easily have supported his family, he was not yet a citizen so he did not qualify to be one of the two required sponsors. Ensuring those documents were ready had been one of the few things that kept him going during those long, harrowing months of only bad news of war coming out of Europe with no word from Shayna or anyone in Poland. He also told her that it was too risky to send money in the mail anymore. Instead, he would wire the money to her through the telegraphic offices of the Thomas Cooke Travel Agency. The money will have already arrived there when she reads this letter, he wrote. She laughed at his next sentence which addressed the question that had immediately popped into her head. He wrote that the agency was charging roughly thirty-three cents on the dollar to wire money. Even as far away as he was, he read her mind. It was expensive, he added, but there was no amount too much to spend on bringing his girls to America.

Shayna put down Jonah's letter and immediately sprang into action. She asked around and found out that the nearest Thomas Cooke Travel Agency office was in Kovno, the capital city of Lithuania. She already knew that Kovno was also home to all the foreign consulates. The city was slightly over an hour train ride away. Her next step was clearly a trip to Kovno to retrieve the money that Jonah sent and fill out visa applications at the American Embassy. She had enough money left for the train fare with just a little to spare. Shayna brought Chaya-Sarah with her because school was closed that day late in January for *Tu BiShvat*, the Jewish Arbor day.

On what was to be the first of many train rides to Kovno, Shayna and Chaya-Sarah sat watching the bare deciduous trees and evergreen conifers fly by the train window. Chaya-Sarah told her mother the story of how they planted several trees on the grounds of the school yesterday. She was in a chatty mood so Shayna sat back and enjoyed the distraction of her daughter's voice. She told her mother that the trees were a gift of some wealthy Jewish people who supported the school. She was one of the kids who helped put the dirt back in the holes after some of the older boys dug them and another group placed the baby trees carefully inside. Next, Chaya-Sarah, still on the subject of trees, began reminiscing about the pine sapling she helped her father plant in their back yard in Zbojna just a few years ago.

"Remember, mama?" Chaya-Sarah asked. "It was when I was a little girl." Shayna smiled partly at the memory and partly at her child talking about herself when she was a little girl as if she were not one still.

"Yes, I remember," Shayna said, feeling like it was a century ago. "One of your father's customers gave it to us as a gift. The tree was the same height as you were. We were going to watch every year to see which one of you grew taller first."

"I beat it the first year, but then the tree started to get ahead of me!" Chaya-Sarah cried out in glee.

"Yes," Shayna said, still smiling at the memory.

"I loved that tree, mama." Chaya-Sarah's happy voice took on a more serious tone.

"I know you did, *maidel*," Shayna said aware of a sudden stabbing ache in her chest. *What is that?* Shayna wondered to herself. *I could not possibly be homesick for Poland.* Then she realized that it was not the home she left that she missed. It was a longing for the concept of home and the man who belonged in that home with them.

"Will we ever go back so I can see the tree?" Chaya-Sarah asked. "*Tati* said that one day it would be taller than all of us!"

"I don't think so, *maidel*," Shayna said. "But, God-willing, you will plant many more trees."

"Anyway," Chaya-Sarah mused. "My favorite are the lilacs. I love how they look and smell, mama."

"Yes, *maidel*," Shayna said. "They are beautiful."

Chaya-Sarah suddenly became quiet. She lowered her head onto her mother's shoulder and closed her eyes. Shayna, on the other hand, was wide awake. Anyone who glanced her way would have seen a calm and lovely young woman out for a train ride with her daughter. They would have been wrong. She was anything but calm. She even had a sudden urge to check her purse for the papers that Jonah sent. She knew they were there, but anxiety made her look just the same. She clicked open the metal clasp on her purse, took the papers out and carefully unfolded them. Even though the writing was in English and she was unable to read even one word, the papers somehow comforted her. She looked them over for a while then folded and tucked them neatly back into her handbag.

She closed the metal clasp, patted the bag on her lap, looked out the train window and sighed.

The first stop after they got off the train was the Thomas Cooke Travel Agency. Shayna asked people on the street for directions and found out it was just a few blocks away. She closed the top button on Chaya-Sarah's coat against the cold and they carefully made their way through the bustling city. The streets teemed with horses pulling all sizes and shapes of wagons, and there was an occasional military-looking vehicle which she later learned were Russian jeeps. Shayna held Chaya-Sarah's hand as they crossed the busy street and arrived at the building that housed the travel agency on the first floor. The line was long. It snaked out the door and down to the corner of the block. As they took their places on line, Shayna was relieved to see that it was advancing at a steady pace. After standing for almost an hour, a yawning Chaya-Sarah by her side, Shayna found herself at a window covered with iron bars. It had an opening at the bottom for passing papers. The structure reminded her of the prison cell where she recently spent the night. Just as Jonah wrote in his letter, the money was waiting for her. She thanked the agent and walked away relieved that they now had plenty of money to pay for food and rent in the coming weeks.

Their next stop was the American embassy. As they made their way to the street where the embassies were located, Shayna felt grateful to be in a place where they were still open and she was free to apply for visas. Nevertheless, she felt anxious about what difficulties she might face trying to get them. As she approached, she was immediately made aware of one of those difficulties. Hordes of people were trying to do exactly the same thing she was. All the foreign consulate buildings they passed were surrounded by masses of desperate refugees crowding or lining up outside their front doors and spilling onto the streets. The American embassy was no exception. As she approached it, she saw the large building was surrounded by an imposing iron gate. A crowd of people were gathered inside the gate and a line spilled outside through an arched entryway. So, in addition to getting around the obstacles of the American immigration policy, she would also have to deal with interminable lines. *There must be hundreds of refugees here all trying to get somewhere else*, Shayna thought anxiously to herself as she watched people collect behind her creating an even longer line.

They waited all afternoon on that line that moved inch by inch, hour by hour. When they finally made it into the building, they found themselves in a large waiting room with mahogany chairs upholstered in an elaborate red and gold striped satin fabric. *At least we can sit now*, Shayna thought as she turned and continued talking to the people who were behind her in the line. Chaya-Sarah entertained herself by playing with the fabric on her chair, first tracing the patterns of red with her forefinger then the shapes of gold. As she played, she kept flicking away a loose hairpin that was dangling over her forehead and tickling her skin. She finally reached up and pulled it out, smoothing back the hair that fell in her face. She now began to study the pin in her hand. She never noticed that one side of it was shorter and sharper on the end than the other side which had a slightly rounded tip. She forced the two sides open, taking time to try and smooth out the bend in the middle. When she was not able to do that, she began to move the sharp end of the partially open pin against the arm of the chair, lightly tracing over the circular carvings already there. She inadvertently pushed too hard in one place and nicked the dark-stained wood, revealing the lighter tone underneath. She stared at it for a minute, then rubbed it with her finger. *It's so easy to put a scratch in this chair*, she thought. She glanced quickly at her mother to see if Shayna saw what happened, but Shayna was still looking the other way, deep in conversation.

Years ago, before Chaya-Sarah started first grade, her father taught her to write her name using Hebrew letters. She always enjoyed practicing her penmanship as her father watched her beaming with pride and love. She imagined writing those letters now in the arm of the chair. She decided to try, but she would just write her initials. Holding the pin as steady as she could, she slowly and methodically began carving the letter *Chet* into the yielding wood. She brushed off the loosened crumbs of wood and looked at her work. She was very pleased with herself, so she followed that by carving the letter *Shin*. She was just beginning the letter *Kaf* when she was startled by her mother's voice.

"What are you doing?" Shayna asked in an urgent whisper. "Stop that, young lady! Stop that right now." Chaya-Sarah pulled her hand onto her lap and sat quietly, her eyes looking downward, her face contrite. "We don't deface property," Shayna continued. When she saw that her daughter stopped, she calmed herself and turned back to the people with whom she was conversing. She laughed and made a comment about the unpredictable nature of juvenile behavior and they all nodded in agreement. When her mother seemed to be safely distracted by the renewed conversation, Chaya-Sarah went back to her project, taking the pin and quickly completing the *Kaf.* She sat back, ran her fingers over the once smooth arm of the chair and admired her handiwork.

When it was almost five o'clock, embassy officials cut off the line just two people after Shayna. She breathed in a silent prayer as she realized they just made it. The people right behind her were amazed by their luck as well. The many people who stood after them on line were told to come back another day. Shayna felt terrible when she saw the dejected faces of the people who were sent away.

When it was finally Shayna's turn, a woman held the door to an office open and motioned for her to step inside. The American diplomat, looking formal in a crisp white shirt and thin black tie, sat behind a polished dark walnut desk and nodded as Shayna and Chaya-Sarah walked in. On the left side of the desk sat a middle-aged man in simple clothes. The man greeted Shayna in Yiddish and bid them sit in the chairs in front of the desk. Chaya-Sarah noticed that the chairs boasted the same satiny finish as the chairs in the waiting room. The men looked at Shayna and she back at them. *They were not unfriendly*, she thought. They just seemed a trifle business-like and more than a little tired. The diplomat sat quietly as the man asked Shayna questions in Yiddish about her immigration goals.

After telling her story of wanting to complete an application with the goal of joining her husband who was already in America, she pulled out the sponsorship papers that Jonah sent and handed them to the diplomat. The diplomat took them as the Yiddish speaker turned to the diplomat and spoke to him in English. The diplomat nodded as he set the papers down without looking at them, and began answering the translator in English. Shayna stared at the diplomat, choked by the anxiety of one whose life depended on what he said and the decisions he made. When the translator turned back to Shayna, he looked conciliatory. He explained that she did not need to fill out an application today. Since there were strict quotas regarding how many people can immigrate to America annually from each country, she was able only to add her name to the waiting list and leave her address. If she made it into the quota, she would be notified by mail. Then she would need to come back with the required sponsorship and identification papers and complete an application. If she was approved at that time, she would receive a visa stamp on her passport that would allow her and her daughter to enter the United States of America.

Shayna stared back at the man, then at the diplomat. They saw her beautiful brown eyes, but they did not see her soul crying. A waiting list stood between her and her husband. The distance between them seemed to be increasing instead of shrinking.

"Okay, where do I add my name and address?" Shayna asked.

◆　◆　◆

Shayna and Chaya-Sarah were quiet on the train ride back to Vilna. They were both tired and hungry. Chaya-Sarah leaned back on her mother and played with the end of her left braid. Shayna gazed out the window at the bare trees that stood like silent sentries against the darkening sky. She wondered what Jonah was doing, but was unable to conjure him in her mind's eye. She did not like that feeling. She felt like he was hidden somewhere behind huge closed doors. *Would those doors ever open for her and her child?* Shayna wondered silently. All she had right now was her name on a waiting list. She saw the man write it, along with her address, in a ledger that was presumably filled with many other names and addresses. When she asked, he said he was not able to offer her a time frame for when she might expect to hear from the embassy. Apparently, this immigration process was a mystery to everyone, including the people running it. She patted her purse where Jonah's papers were tucked safely with two change-of-address forms. The diplomat gave her those extra forms when he handed back her other papers because, as the Yiddish translator explained, refugees changed addresses frequently.

◆ ◆ ◆

With the money Jonah wired to them, Shayna was able to buy Chaya-Sarah some new clothes which included a winter coat and a new pair of shoes to replace the ones damaged when they slogged through the mud and icy water at the border. She also decided to find them a new apartment. The family whose room they rented were lovely people. Shayna was grateful to them and everyone who helped them get to this point, but she had no idea how long they were going to be stuck in Lithuania. As long as they had money to afford it, she wanted them to have their own place.

The apartment she found was one room with an efficiency kitchen on the second floor of a building with a courtyard and a catwalk that faced the courtyard. The apartment was modestly furnished, but it was comfortable and pleasing to the eye. Tall sash windows dressed in cheerful lace curtains allowed the room to be filled with sunshine for most of the afternoon. Chaya-Sarah loved the apartment's balcony overlooking the main street which she was allowed go out on only when her mother was with her. Just as Shayna imagined, it was wonderful for her and her daughter to have their own place. It allowed Shayna to have a few brief moments each day when she almost forgot she was a refugee. *I feel like a mentsh (person), again,* Shayna thought, as she started cooking in her own kitchen and inviting guests over for dinner.

Shayna's friends, Meryl and Gittel, were in Vilna now, too, with Meryl living in a room in someone's house and Gittel living with her father. Neither lived very far away. The three women stayed close since their time at the border and continued to spend many hours together, enjoying *Shabbes* dinners and shopping trips and long conversations. They were each grateful for the emotional support and camaraderie they provided for each other. It gave them a safe place to share their deepest worries and fears at this challenging time in their lives.

◆ ◆ ◆

The spring of 1940 passed quietly for Shayna and Chaya-Sarah, but it was an uneasy quiet. There was only silence from the American Embassy. Shayna still had no idea when or even if she would make it through the United States immigration quota restrictions. News from the outside world did not help, either. Newspapers only provided horror stories and images of a world at war. In April, the German army invaded Norway and Denmark. In May, Germany began the invasions of the Netherlands, Belgium, Luxembourg and France. Shayna, along with the other Jewish refugees in Lithuania, were left to wonder how much longer this country was going to remain free. Unsettling questions plagued both waking and sleeping hours. How long was the window of opportunity she had to escape? What path was the smartest and safest one to take?

Troubling thoughts and worries about the family she left in Poland were never far from her mind. She wanted very badly to communicate with them, but she learned that the mail was not getting through. The border between Poland and Lithuania was completely closed now. It had been sealed just a day or two after she and Chaya-Sarah and their friends were allowed through by the Russian guards. Now, anyone hoping to get into Lithuania from Poland was only able to do so illegally by sneaking through the forest and getting around both Russian and Lithuanian guards. Even so, she wrote letters to her brothers and sisters and dropped them in post boxes just in case, by some miracle, a letter were to reach one of them.

Shayna continued to exchange letters with Jonah, writing as often as was possible and devouring every word he wrote. Chaya-Sarah attended school and caught up with her Yiddish reading and writing lessons. She made new friends and attended many birthday parties. She and her mother took the train a few more times to Kovno to collect money wired by Jonah and to exchange telegrams with him which were much faster than the mail. They also returned to the line at the American embassy twice—once to submit a change-of-address form after they moved into the new apartment and another time in the hope of finding out more information about their status on the quota waiting list. Chaya-Sarah took both opportunities during the long waits on the embassy line to decorate another mahogany armchair with her initials and one with just 'Sarah' in Hebrew letters. Both times Shayna saw her doing this and simply shrugged. She had more pressing issues than protecting the arms of embassy chairs. During both visits, Shayna received the devastating news that there was no change in the status of her visa.

"Sorry," they told her. "You have to wait." Shayna never imagined how painful five simple words could be.

Shayna and Jonah Kaufman in Montevideo, Uraguay, 1930

Chaya-Sarah Kaufman at eight months in Zbojna, Poland, October 1932

On left—Jonah, Shayna and Chaya-Sarah Kaufman; on right—Jonah's cousin
(son of Fivel Finkelstein), his wife and daughter in Zbojna, Poland, 1934

From left—Chaya-Sarah Kaufman with a cousin, Ostroleka, Poland, 1936

Standing are Shayna Kaufman (third from left) with two unidentified women (on left) and Jonah's cousin's wife (on right); seated are Chaya-Sarah Kaufman (third from left) with cousins or friends in Zbojna, Poland, 1937

Chaya-Sarah Kaufman, Polish forest, 1938

Chaya-Sarah Kaufman (seated at table on left) at a school birthday party, Vilna, Lithuania, 1940. This photo is also in the book *Flight and Rescue,* United States Holocaust Memorial Museum

CHAPTER 19

Summer/Fall 1940
Lithuania

It is a fantastic commentary on the inhumanity of our times
that for thousands and thousands of people a piece of paper
with a stamp on it is the difference between life and death.

~Dorothy Thompson

For Shayna and many of the refugees stuck in Lithuania, the days turned into weeks and the weeks to months. Although waiting became Shayna's main occupation, she was not idle. She asked questions of everyone around her and read every Yiddish paper she could get her hands on. She was determined to arm herself with as much information as possible about her current predicament. By mid-June, there was still no word from the embassy. School was over for the year, and Shayna enrolled Chaya-Sarah in a sleepaway camp that started the next week. The camp was founded by Regina Weinreich's father, physician and philanthropist Tsemach Shabad, to address the enrichment needs of refugees and other Jewish children over the summer. Shayna felt apprehensive about her daughter being away from her, but the camp had a wonderful reputation as did the people who ran it and Shayna planned to send her for just one session which was only two weeks long.

One June afternoon, mother and daughter sat at their kitchen table discussing what clothes Chaya-Sarah needed for camp. Shayna was making a list of the items she needed to buy her daughter. "Tomorrow, we'll find you a bathing suit and a new nightgown," Shayna said, jotting down notes on a piece of paper. A summer breeze blew in through the open windows, animating the curtains that leapt like dancers on a stage. The warm air also brought in the sounds of a bustling city—shouts of children playing, voices of people haggling with street vendors and the percussive beat of horses walking on cobblestone mixed with the occasional roar of a car engine. Shayna and Chaya-Sarah did not take notice of the sounds. They were too busy. But they did notice when the sounds suddenly disappeared. Chaya-Sarah looked up as a strange silence filled the air. It seemed as if everything and everyone on the street vanished. Shayna lifted her head, too, just as a distant rumbling sound replaced the silence. It was an all too familiar sound, and it grew louder like an approaching thunderstorm.

"What is that?" Chaya-Sarah asked with some alarm in her voice. Shayna looked at her daughter without seeing her. She stood up and began running toward the balcony. Chaya-Sarah followed her. The two of them walked out and stood behind the white iron rail. They both stared in shock at the scene before them. Hundreds of uniformed soldiers marched down the main street. They were moving in rows as far down the road as the human eye could see. The men looked almost identical in moss-green uniforms with matching green helmets on their heads. Shayna recognized them immediately. They were Russian soldiers. They each hugged a rifle to their bodies at a forty-five degree angle with the butt of the rifle in the right hand held just below the waist and the barrel grasped by the left hand up near the shoulder. Like the German soldiers, their boots were black. Unlike the German soldiers, these soldiers were singing. Their voices rang out like an army of giant buzzing ants. The effect was a rousing sound that somehow managed to be both rhapsodic and forceful. In spite of the warmth in the air, Shayna felt a sudden chill. She did not understand all the words they sang, but she did not have to. She knew an invasion when she saw one.

Shayna stood transfixed by the sight and the sound of the procession moving slowly down the street. As she watched and listened, terror gripped Shayna by the throat. This was not her first invasion, but like the first one, it cast a dark shadow over them and portended many new obstacles on the road to Jonah. *Will the Soviet rules get in my way?* Shayna wondered. *Will I be able to figure out a way around them?* Until she suddenly gasped for air, she did not realize she was holding her breath for the last two minutes or that her daughter was dancing.

"Wow, isn't this great?" Chaya-Sarah cried. "They're singing, mama!" Moved by the soaring music and sound of the soldiers' voices, Chaya-Sarah clapped, stamping her feet and marching in place. Normally, Shayna understood that her eight-year-old was unaware of the many dangerous implications of what they were witnessing. She could even forgive her for getting swept up in the excitement of the music and the marching. But nothing was normal now.

"What are you so happy about?" Shayna snapped at her daughter. "Don't be so happy. This is not good for us."

◆　◆　◆

In the following days, Shayna watched and listened carefully for the changes that the Soviets were making to the social and political climate in Lithuania. She now felt even more uncomfortable sending Chaya-Sarah off to sleepaway camp. *It is only for two weeks*, she reminded herself. Her trust in the people running the camp helped to calm her frayed nerves. She felt confident that her child was in good hands. To get through the two weeks, she was able to convince herself that her daughter was having a much better time than she was stuck in their apartment. In the meantime, the Yiddish dailies were full of alarming stories of the increased Soviet presence in Lithuania and its neighbors on the Baltic Sea—Latvia and Estonia. Groups of Russian soldiers were everywhere and huge tanks roaring down the main street became a common sight. The talk in Jewish homes and on the street was that this must be the Russian response to the recent German invasions of the countries to the west. People who did not take their freedom for granted now truly understood what it felt like to be a helpless doll caught between two giant, greedy toddlers. The tension in the air was palpable.

At the end of the two weeks, Shayna welcomed Chaya-Sarah back from camp with nonstop hugging. Chaya-Sarah held on to her mother, too. Shayna could not imagine two people happier to see one another.

After they let go of each other, Chaya-Sarah sat down at the kitchen table as Shayna put out a plate of cookies and made tea. The child regaled her mother with camp stories. She learned to weave. She ran team relay races. She made an apple green clay pot that she brought home for her mother. She even enjoyed conspiring with her roommates to end another camper's constant snoring. Yet, despite these happy tales, Chaya-Sarah made it clear that she did not want to go back for another session.

"Why not?" Shayna wanted to know. "It sounds like you had fun."

"It was fun, but I had scary dreams at night," Chaya-Sarah said, her brown eyes growing wide.

"What kind of scary dreams?" Shayna asked concerned that recent traumatic events were having a negative effect on her child.

"I dreamed every night that someone at camp was trying to cut off my braids!" Chaya-Sarah cried.

"Oy," Shayna exclaimed as she took Chaya-Sarah into her arms. "I'll give them *tsu zingen un tsu zogen* (something to sing and talk about). No one is going to cut off my Chaya-Sari's *tsepelach!*"

That was the end of sleepaway camp for her daughter, but Shayna thought it was important for Chaya-Sarah to attend some form of camp. She still had no idea how long they were going to stay trapped in Lithuania. Their apartment building was on a busy city street and Shayna wanted Chaya-Sarah to be able to play outside safely with her friends over the summer. She found a day camp, called Big Hill, that was just a short walk through the woods. The camp was created by some philanthropic people for the children of refugees. They visited the camp to check it out and they both liked it very much. Chaya-Sarah also told her mother that she wanted her best friend, Rivka, to accompany her to camp. Rivka lived in an apartment down the hall and the two had become inseparable. Shayna was thrilled until she remembered that Rivka was not the child of refugees.

"Darling, Rivka cannot go there," Shayna explained, "The camp is only for refugees."

Chaya-Sarah thought about this for a minute, then said, "I'm not going if Rivka can't go."

Shayna looked at her daughter. The child was the picture of defiance with a dark, intense stare and two arms folded tightly in front of her. Shayna knew that when Chaya-Sarah assumed this position trying to reason with her was going to be futile. Instead, Shayna decided that she needed to do what she always did when she was faced with two immovable forces. She would need to move one of them.

The next day, Shayna and Chaya-Sarah made their way down the wooded path to Camp Big Hill. When they arrived, Shayna found the main office which was in a shack-like building nestled in the tall trees. She politely told the young receptionist that she needed to please speak with the person who ran the camp. After being asked to have a seat and wait just a few minutes, she and Chaya-Sarah were ushered into a cramped office where a man with greying temples sat behind a desk, shuffling papers. He looked up, greeted them and asked how he could be of service. Shayna introduced herself and Chaya-Sarah and told him that she knew how busy he must be so she would be brief. In the next few minutes, she proceeded to convince the man that it was important for her daughter, who had been through so much and whose father was so far away in America, that her best friend, Rivka, who was not a refugee, be allowed to go to camp with her.

"I only have one request," he said. "The camp runs on donations and does not have the resources to accept everyone, so please keep quiet about Rivka not coming from a refugee family." He held his index finger to his lips as he smiled and winked at Chaya-Sarah. She smiled back, mimicking him with her forefinger and making an attempt at winking.

◆　◆　◆

With Chaya-Sarah safely occupied at camp during the day, Shayna spent her days talking to people and gathering vital information about getting out of there. Even as she did so, the shifting political and social landscape kept dropping new obstacles in front of her. The Soviets announced that no Lithuanian nationals were allowed to leave the country. Jewish Lithuanians, like Regina Weinreich and her son, were effectively trapped there. The impact to Shayna, who was not a Lithuanian national, was that she was required to provide evidence that she and her daughter were from Poland. Otherwise, she and Chaya-Sarah would not be able to leave. Shayna had Polish identification papers for herself, but not for Chaya-Sarah. Shayna spent most of July frantically making inquiries to find a way around this dilemma. She learned that the Russian authorities were likely to accept the word of at least two Lithuanian witnesses who swore that Chaya-Sarah was born in Poland on such and such a date. Now, she just needed to find two such people.

Shayna and her friend, Regina Weinreich, spoke frequently and shared the information they were both gathering. They realized around the same time what the best, and probably only, route to America was. Because all western borders were blocked by the Germans, they needed to try and travel east through Russia and Japan. Japan was not at war and they heard that some people were already going that way. They reasoned that the Japanese might offer them an opportunity to board a ship to America. It seemed like a solid plan, but a large part of the plan's success still rested as much on hope as on actual facts. Shayna knew that she would also need money for train and ship tickets as well as visas for safe passage through the foreign destinations. She wrote Jonah to notify him of her current plan.

As the summer wore on, everyone in Lithuania was aware of the impact of the new regime. The Soviets nationalized large businesses, froze bank deposits and transferred privately-owned land to the state. Many Jewish institutions disappeared overnight. HIAS, the organization that helped Shayna when she first arrived in Vilna, was closed. In August, the Soviets annexed all of Lithuania into the Soviet Union and Lithuania officially became the Lithuanian Soviet Socialist Republic. The Soviet secret police (NKVD) was put in place to target political enemies. Anyone considered a threat to the state was arrested and taken away in the middle of the night. The pressure for people to leave was mounting, but the difficulties of doing that were growing, too. Anyone wanting to leave discovered they needed an exit visa to get out of Lithuania. Then the Soviets announced their most devastating decision of all. The foreign consulates in Kovno were going to officially close their doors on August 25 and move to Moscow. Shayna stopped breathing when she heard the news. *How am I going to get our American visas now?* she wondered. *We're going to be trapped here.* She tried to keep calm. She reminded herself that she was still able to correspond with Jonah and receive money from the Thomas Cooke Travel Agency. She told herself that there had to be a solution.

By the middle of August and with a brilliant stroke of determination and luck, Shayna was able to find two people willing to serve as witnesses to Chaya-Sarah's birth in Poland. They accompanied her and Chaya-Sarah to the Lithuanian Ministry of Justice where a notary accepted the word of the witnesses and created a signed affidavit that could be used in lieu of Chaya-Sarah's birth certificate. Shayna breathed a deep sigh of relief. One problem was solved, but she still had no American visa or a Lithuanian exit visa and the consulates would be closing in days. Shayna and Chaya-Sarah made one final summer trip to Kovno in August to see if there was money and to check the status of her visa at the embassy. The Thomas Cooke agent had no money for her and the American Embassy had no visa. A frustrated Shayna returned to Vilna empty-handed. The summer was ending, the embassies were closing and she did not have the papers she needed.

◆ ◆ ◆

In early September, Chaya-Sarah was back at school. The Soviets closed many Jewish schools of higher education over the summer, such as yeshivas and rabbinical schools, but the elementary school where Regina was principal quietly remained open. That morning, Shayna accompanied her daughter so she could meet with Regina. As Shayna approached her office, Regina was standing outside the door, speaking to two teachers. As soon as she saw Shayna, she finished her conversation quickly and told them they would continue later. She beckoned Shayna into the room and closed the door. Regina looked flushed with excitement. The two women started talking at the same time, then both stopped and laughed. They quickly realized that they both knew the same important facts.

The foreign consulates moved to Moscow so there was no question now regarding where they needed to go. They also realized they needed exit visas. Shayna told Regina that she was able to get a Polish birth certificate for Chaya-Sarah.

"Perfect . . . that's perfect. Now, listen . . . I have great news," Regina said. "I found a way for us to get out of Lithuania."

"I'm listening," Shayna said her eyes growing wide.

"Remember I told you that my family had connections in the government?" Regina asked.

"Yes," responded Shayna eager for her to go on.

"Well," Regina continued. "That connection gave me the name of the man who is the Chief of Russian Military Police in Lithuania. That man will get exit visas for us. Can you believe it? We're going to get out of here!"

"That is amazing!" Shayna cried out as she placed her hand on her forehead. The room began spinning slightly. She realized she should not have skipped breakfast this morning.

"Are you alright?" Regina asked.

"Yes, yes. This is wonderful!" Shayna answered. Regina smiled as they began to hug each other in a spontaneous expression of joy. Regina started to speak when a knock at the door startled them both. They turned to see the door open and the face of Regina's secretary peering in and looking apologetic.

"Excuse me, Mrs. Weinreich, the rabbi is here to see you," she said.

"Oh, yes, of course," Regina responded. "Please tell him I'll be right there." The girl nodded and left as Regina turned back to face Shayna. She handed Shayna a piece of paper with the name and the address of the Russian official who she needed to contact for an exit visa.

"Go to Kovno as soon as you can to get the visa," Regina said.

◆　◆　◆

Later that afternoon, an excited Shayna sat at her kitchen table opening a letter from Jonah. After picking up Chaya-Sarah from school, they stopped at the market to buy a chicken and some vegetables for dinner. Now, the bags of food from the market sat on the countertop. They would need to wait. Both Shayna and Chaya-Sarah who was also sitting at the table, were anxious to hear Jonah's words.

"Mama, read it," Chaya-Sarah could not contain her excitement. "What does *tati* say?"

Shayna carefully tore open the letter and began to read out loud. She sensed immediately that something was wrong and stopped. Jonah always started his letters with "*Mayne Tayere Maidelach* (My Dearest Girls)," but this one was addressed to only her. It was as if Jonah was warning her from an ocean away to protect their daughter. Her eyes reflexively jumped ahead and she shivered at the words she saw. Jonah's brother, Irving, passed away suddenly and unexpectedly. Shayna let out an involuntary gasp. Her brother-in-law was only in his late forties. The doctor said it was probably a heart attack. Shayna was fond of the brother-in-law she knew as Srolke. She remembered his sweet and charming nature and how everyone loved him, but how some family members disapproved when he married Nettie. They did not think she was kind enough for him, but he was in love. The two did not have any children and were married for almost twenty years.

"Read it, mama!" Chaya-Sarah cried out. "What does *tati* say?"

"Just a minute," Shayna answered as she continued reading, worrying about how Jonah must feel. Another brother gone and so young. She felt terrible for him. His next words reminded her of yet another reason to worry. His brother was one of the sponsors she needed to get an American visa. Now, the sponsorship papers Jonah sent her were null and void. Jonah needed to find someone else who was qualified and was also willing to sign papers and provide bank statements.

"Mama, why aren't you reading?" Chaya-Sarah asked taking a nibble of apple.

Shayna hesitated. She did not want to tell her daughter about her uncle's passing. Why upset her about someone she never met? "It's nothing," Shayna said. "Just some business about our visas." Shayna looked at her daughter and, as much as she tried to prevent it, her eyes filled with salty tears. It pained her that Chaya-Sarah never knew her grandmothers or Jonah's brother Shlemke, who died in America before Jonah even got there. Now, she will never meet yet another uncle. Each of these people would have adored her daughter and she would have loved them so. Chaya-Sarah caught her mother looking at her instead of the letter and saw the excess water in her eyes.

"What's wrong, mama?" she asked with concern in her voice. "Is *tati* okay?"

"Yes, your father is fine," Shayna said quickly, sniffing and wiping away the tears. "I just miss him, that's all."

"I miss him, too, mama," Chaya-Sarah accepted Shayna's answer, then stood up. She walked over and wrapped her thin arms around her mother and put her head on her shoulder. "I miss him so much."

"*Mayn zis kind* (my sweet child)," Shayna said as she held on to Chaya-Sarah. She thought about her husband and his poor brother. At thirty, Shayna was already acutely aware of how swiftly time moves and how life changed in the single blink of an eye. "*Fintster iz mere* (darkness is upon me)," Shayna whispered softly to herself as she wondered what this delay will cost them. With the Soviets quickly devouring this country and its neighbors and the Germans gobbling up countries to the west, will Jonah be able to find another sponsor and complete the paperwork in time for them to get away? Shayna kissed her daughter on the head and stood up. She needed to store her fears in another compartment of her mind for now. Some friends were joining them for dinner and it was time to start cooking.

◆ ◆ ◆

The next day Shayna and Chaya-Sarah were, once again, in Kovno. After waiting on long lines, finding the man Regina told her about, filling out forms and answering many questions—Where are you from? What color are your eyes? Is this your daughter?—Shayna was finally handed their exit visa by a young male clerk. She studied the piece of paper.

On the top of the document was the seal of the Republic of Lithuania. Below the seal were the words *LEIDIMAS SAUF CONDUIT* (Authorization for Safe Conduct) in bold letters. Toward the middle, left side of the document was a picture of her and her daughter. When their images were captured, the bright flash blinded them momentarily. They were not smiling in the picture, but Shayna was thrilled at that moment. The document was a large sheet of crisp parchment-type paper, but it was worth so much more than the paper it was printed on. It was everything. Shayna graciously thanked the person who handed it to her, folded the document neatly and placed it into her handbag.

Shayna and Chaya-Sarah were soon on the train back to Vilna. *How many times have we made this trip?* Shayna wondered as they sat down. *How many more times will we make it?* She placed the handbag that held the precious piece of paper safely on her lap and gave it a few pats for good measure. She took a deep, deep breath and began to relax. Then she remembered what the Russian police supervisor told her. He indicated that she still needed to get a stamp that would allow them to travel safely through Soviet Russia. This was not something he was able to provide. She had to get that from the Soviet Office of Internal Affairs. Unfortunately, that office had moved. He was not sure where. Shayna stared back at him. *Was there no end to this madness?* she thought to herself. Shayna leaned her head back and closed her eyes as the train began to move. Her last thought before she dozed off was that she cleared one large hurdle, but now another one lay in their path. She silently prayed for God to help her find a way over it, around it or through it.

◆　◆　◆

As autumn wore on and the days grew shorter, there was still no news from Jonah about another sponsor. Shayna began working on her contacts to get her and her daughter the stamp they needed to travel across the Soviet Union. Once again, lines were long and people were difficult to get in touch with. Shayna fought to keep her hopes from falling to the ground along with the brown leaves that dropped from the trees outside her apartment window. She and all the refugees were feeling the pressure to leave, but at the same time found the potential doors of escape closing. It felt as though the Soviet authorities wanted them out of there, yet they were not going to make it easy for them to go. The Soviet presence was everywhere. Stories abounded of Russian soldiers knocking on doors or stopping people in the street and questioning them daily. Everyone knew someone or even entire families who were hustled away by the Russian police and not heard from again. Signs on Jewish businesses changed from Yiddish to Russian and more schools and synagogues were closed. In October, Chaya-Sarah's school closed. Although this was another frightening reminder that they were in the Soviet Union now, Shayna was relieved to keep her daughter at home with her.

By late October, Shayna made another trip to Kovno where there was money waiting for her from Jonah at the Thomas Cooke Travel Agency. She was also thrilled to find a message from him with the news that he found another sponsor for them. He told her that he was doing his best to complete the papers as soon as possible. By the end of November, a grateful Shayna received the sponsorship papers she would need for an American visa. It felt like a doorway to America was opening even though she still needed one more stamp to be able to get closer to that door. In December, she was finally able to get that Soviet travel stamp from the Soviet Office of Internal Affairs. Shayna studied the stamp that was placed in the upper left corner on the back of her visa. She understood most of the Russian words on it which made it clear that their business in the Soviet Union was just to pass through on their way to their final destination, the United States of America. Shayna marvelled at how beautiful that simple stamp looked to her. It was as precious to her as pure gold coins.

The next day, Shayna and Regina went together to book their passage on the train to Moscow. When they finally got their train tickets, the two women embraced. They were overcome with anticipation and hope. In just two days, they were to embark on an eastward journey that would take them 600 miles to Moscow, the capital of the Soviet Union.

"Now we will just need two more visas," Shayna said, thinking out loud. "One for Japan and one for America."

"Yes," Regina said taking a deep breath. "And, God-willing, we will be able to get those in Moscow."

"God-willing," Shayna repeated as the two women parted and left the train station. In her mind, Shayna was already packing for what she hoped would be a one-way trip for two to America.

❧ CHAPTER 20 ❧

December 1940
Soviet Russia

Life is a dream for the wise, a game for the fool,
a comedy for the rich, a tragedy for the poor.

~Sholem Aleichem (Solomon Rabinovich)

Two days later Shayna and Regina waited with their children on the crowded platform at the train station in Vilna. In the cold morning air, Chaya-Sarah pressed her face into the wool of her mother's coat like a lamb looking for succor. She was only just introduced to Regina's son and was feeling uncharacteristically shy. Even though their mothers had been friends for the better part of the last year, the children never met. At twelve, Gabriel, called Gaby, was several grades ahead of Chaya-Sarah which, in the grade school world, was the equivalent of residing on a distant planet. It was apparent that the two thought of each other as alien beings. After introductions were made, they eyed each other suspiciously and in children's body language seemed to say, "I'm not sure about you." The women laughed when they saw the reactions of their children to one another.

"Oy, boys and girls," Regina commented.

"Yes, look at them now. In a few short years we won't be able to keep them away from each other," Shayna observed.

When the doors of the train opened, the cars filled quickly with the anxious refugees. In addition to every variety and size of suitcase and bag, these people carried the full range of human emotions with them. Each of them experienced the fear and uncertainty of being thrust from the warmth and comfort of home into the cold and the unknown. Each was boarding a train that was to take them to a place they dreamed of, but at the same time it would be taking them away from someone or something they loved. Something familiar. The place they called home. In spite of the insecurity of their situation or maybe because of it, their faces were blank. They all just looked weary. Chaya-Sarah moved in front of her mother, eagerly navigating the throng of people. She found two seats by the window and plopped down in one of them, looking up to see that her mother was right behind her. "Is this good, mama?" she asked cheerfully.

"It's perfect," Shayna said, lifting their suitcase onto the metal rack above their seats. She laughed to herself. For the first time since fleeing her home over a year ago, she almost felt like a tourist instead of a home-less refugee. She always wanted to see the world, but this was not how she imagined it would be. She turned and helped Regina place her two suitcases above the seats directly behind Chaya-Sarah's and Shayna's seats. Regina was able to take more with her than Shayna and Chaya-Sarah who fled from Poland with just the clothes on their backs. Regina was also able to ship many family heirlooms and other valuables to America before the Russians took over.

The two women exchanged smiles, but their eyes were full of emotion. They were finally leaving Lithuania after a long and tumultuous year. Shayna thought about the train station in Warsaw where she last gazed into Jonah's warm, chestnut brown eyes. *Did that really happen only fifteen months ago?* To Shayna it felt like ten years. She sat down next to her daughter and looked out the window. A large block of bright sunlight seemed out of place on the dingy train tracks. *But it was not the tracks that mattered,* Shayna thought to herself, *it is where they lead.* She imagined the tracks laid out in a straight line to Jonah. The thought gave her a sudden thrill even as the horrible events of the past year held their grip on her heart. Shayna glanced down at her daughter and stroked her head. She felt an uncomfortable tightness in her chest. They were still not out of harm's way. Waiting outside the train, they moved under the watchful eyes of the Russian soldiers. They tried to appear inconspicuous as they spied the soldiers stopping people, asking to see their papers and occasionally taking them away. Even now a soldier boarded the train and looked around as if he misplaced something. Shayna held her breath as he walked down the aisle. He stopped momentarily in the middle of the packed car, looked in the faces of the passengers, then turned abruptly. He walked back to the door and climbed down out of the car. Shayna sighed audibly and turned again to her daughter. She licked her forefinger and used it to push back an errant curl that came loose and fell on her daughter's forehead.

Chaya-Sarah looked up at her mother and asked, "When will we get to Moscow, mama?" She knew exactly where they were going from hearing her mother talk about that strange city for the last several months. Shayna started to answer when Chaya-Sarah jumped in and they both said simultaneously, "We'll get there when we get there."

"Mama, will you ever tell me how long it takes to get anywhere?" Chaya-Sarah asked, laughing and not expecting an answer.

Shayna kissed the top of her daughter's head. "Why don't you put your head on my shoulder and take a little nap?" she suggested.

To Shayna's surprise, Chaya-Sarah did as she was asked. The child must be tired, Shayna thought, as she turned her attention to the other passengers, some still struggling to find seats and a place to stow their luggage. A young woman took the seat next to her and they nodded politely to one another. Then Shayna decided to follow her daughter's example. She leaned her head back against her seat and allowed her eyes to close. By the time the train began to move, Chaya-Sarah was asleep with her cheek resting on her mother's shoulder. Shayna's eyes remained closed so she did not notice the train moving them away from the bustling city and out into a land of fields and forests. She only felt the speed of the train and realized with a thrill that it was rushing her and her daughter away from the dark events of the past year and toward a brighter future. But the excitement did not last long. The train was also taking her farther away from her family. The sadness felt like a heaviness in her chest and her eyes filled with tears. She thought of her sisters and brothers and their children and wondered how they all were. What were they doing? Were they still in their homes? Were they well? Were they safe? She thought of her dear parents and Jonah's who mercifully were not here to see this war. Images of her family and moments she spent with them that now seemed so far away in time and distance filled her head as the motion of the train lulled her into a light slumber. Before she fell asleep, she said a silent prayer that the war will end soon and her family would be safe from harm.

◆　◆　◆

When the train stopped in Moscow six hours later, everyone stood up and stretched, gathered their belongings and slowly made their way onto the platform. As they walked through the train station in Moscow, Shayna and Chaya-Sarah looked out on a strange landscape that was unlike anything they had ever seen before. Surrounding them were grand stone structures that created a sweeping architecture with soaring archways that felt more like the museums Shayna had seen in pictures than a simple train station. Chaya-Sarah's eyes and mouth opened wide in wonder and she held on tightly to her mother's hand as she took in the splendor around her. Everything was larger than life. Even the ceiling of the train station seemed to reach as high as the sky and the main terminal they walked into was equally expansive. Shayna looked out at the massive sea of travelers scurrying purposefully in every direction. She picked up her daughter and held her tight for fear that the crowd might jostle them off their feet or separate them. Her knowledge of Russian helped her read the large signs posted everywhere and find their way to the exit they needed.

When they were finally outside, they braced themselves against the bitter cold of December in Moscow. A curtain of falling snow dimmed the light of the afternoon sun and filled the air with dancing snowflakes. They landed on Chaya-Sarah's delighted face and melted instantly into cold drops of water. She tried to catch a few, but they were elusive. Huge buildings, some with distinctive onion-shaped domes, towered over them like snow-capped mountains. Crowds of people hurried by in every direction, wearing every manner of dress. Some looked like they belonged on the cover of fashion magazines. The women were wrapped in warm coats with high fur collars and wore sleek, black boots. Others wore rags and looked like poor peasants. On the streets, a virtual parade of motorcars and busses passed before them, blaring their horns and spewing a foul-smelling exhaust. Chaya-Sarah had never seen anything like this before. She was amazed that the busses seemed as large as train cars and she wondered if they held as many people.

Shayna took her daughter's hand, but she did not have to. Chaya-Sarah was holding on to her mother's coat, staring at the scene before her with wonder and some fear. The child was too young to understand that the technological advancements of this part of the world were perhaps one hundred years ahead of those in the village where she grew up. Still, she was aware of the vast differences. The traffic noises sounded louder than thunderstorms and the vehicles moved at lightning speed. Even the people on the sidewalks and crossing the streets seemed to walk at a quicker pace than she ever saw before in other cities and towns.

Shayna began to pay close attention to her new surroundings, studying maps and questioning people on the streets. With the scattered bits of Russian she knew, she quickly determined how to get around in Moscow. It was clear that they were going to travel by bus now instead of on foot or horse-drawn wagon. Their first stop was the Thomas Cooke Travel Agency where Shayna was relieved to see that the line was not too long and it was moving quickly. Shayna also found money waiting for her from Jonah. The American dollars will easily cover their stay in Moscow. Shayna wired a short message back to Jonah to make sure he knew they arrived safely in Moscow and received his money.

With evening closing in, they needed to find a place to stay. Regina suggested the Savoy for its convenient location and because she and her husband stayed there when he was on one of his Yiddish speaking engagements. The Savoy was not the largest hotel in Moscow, but it was one of the oldest and most elegant. Holding her mother's hand, Chaya-Sarah's face lit up and her dark eyes glowed as she took in the opulence of the hotel lobby. The walls were decorated with what looked like sculpted rivers of gold, and the high windows were covered with silk brocade curtains. They sparkled with the reflected light of the crystal chandelier that hung from the center of the ceiling. It all felt like a dream to the girl whose closest experience with such grandeur and beauty came from gazing up at the stars and the moon, not from anything manmade.

To keep costs down, the women decided to share a room with two double beds. They would be delighted by the luxurious room decorated with silk and brocade fabrics that overlooked a square with a statue at its center. Before they reached the charming room, Chaya-Sarah discovered another distinctive feature of the Savoy that terrified her. After each getting the room key, Shayna and Regina were directed to use the staircase or the elevators toward the back of the hotel lobby to access their fourth-floor room. The children ran ahead to play on the wide, red-carpeted staircase with its impressive gold balustrade. When they reached the bottom of the stairs, something caused them to both stop abruptly and look up. Towering above them was a majestic, almost eight-foot tall Kamchatka brown bear in a menacing pose as if it were guarding the staircase. Its smooth, dark fur was hidden in the shadows of the lobby walls, but now they beheld the giant in its full glory, its bared claws and teeth gleaming like pearl daggers. The art of taxidermy was something Chaya-Sarah was aware of, but only in the form of small forest animals preserved in a shop window in Warsaw. She was charmed by their cute, lifelike positions and bright, glassy eyes. That mild introduction, however, did nothing to prepare her for this beast before her.

"Mama!" Chaya-Sarah cried as she scurried back to her mother. Gabriel just stood there looking up and gaping.

"Come this way, *maidel*," Shayna guided her daughter away from the sweeping staircase and its furry sentinel. "We're going to ride the elevator."

During their week-long stay in Moscow, Chaya-Sarah stayed far away from the staircase and its ursine guard. Luckily, she was enchanted by the elevator and preferred that mode of transportation. Even when they were not going anywhere, she begged her mother to ride the elevator with her. "Can we please go on it one more time?" She asked so sweetly that Shayna was unable to resist her cheeky girl. So Shayna found herself stepping into the elevator several times a day for rides to nowhere.

The second day in Moscow, Shayna and Chaya-Sarah made their way to the American Embassy where they got their United States visa. It was just a stamp on the document Shayna already received in Lithuania, but it was so much more. It was going to allow them both passage to and entry into America. They also needed to visit the Japanese Embassy to get the visa that will allow them to enter Japan. The Japanese visa was a long piece of paper with their pictures on it and delicate pen markings that looked so artistic, but were unreadable to Shayna. These documents meant the world to her. When she finally received them, she folded them carefully and placed them in her handbag, feeling closer to Jonah than she had in a year. With the security of being in possession of these documents, there were moments in Moscow when Shayna almost believed she was a tourist instead of a refugee. In addition to the luxurious feel of the hotel, they ate in restaurants where they were serenaded by strolling gypsies playing soulful violin music. They went to the Yiddish theater and enjoyed a stage production of *Tevye The Milchekeh* (Tevye the Dairyman). Based on the short stories of Sholem Alecheim, the show would later come to be known all over the world as "Fiddler On The Roof."

For the week they were there, the largest city of the Soviet Union was good to Shayna and Chaya-Sarah, but not everyone in Moscow was having a positive experience. One such man sat behind them on the bus ride to the theater. They did not notice him at first, but he was aware of the mother and her daughter speaking Yiddish to one another. In fact, he understood every word of their animated conversation.

"I wish *tati* was here to go to the show with us," Chaya-Sarah sighed.

"God-willing, we will go to plenty of shows with him in America," Shayna countered.

"How much longer until we get to America, mama? Chaya-Sarah asked. Shayna took this question seriously and considered her answer thoughtfully.

"Well, the train to Vladivostok takes a week, then the boat to Japan will take a day and a half," Shayna thought aloud. "I hope to be in Japan for a week or two at the most." She stopped and did some calculations in her head. "I hope we will be in America by the first of February."

"That's my birthday!" Chaya-Sarah shrieked with delight. "We'll be with *tati* for my ninth birthday!"

"God-willing," Shayna said, gripped by anxiety as she pondered the long journey still ahead of them.

The man behind them leaned forward and cleared his throat before speaking. "*Antshuldik mir* (excuse me)," he said, "*Bistu a Yidishe tokhter?* (Are you Jewish)?" When Shayna answered in the affirmative, the man got very excited. He heard her say that they were going to America. He told Shayna that he had family in America, but things were very bad in Russia and he was not able to communicate with them. He then politely asked Shayna if she would be so kind as to contact his family there for him and let them know that he and his wife are well. Of course, Shayna told him she was happy to. He wrote their contact information on a torn piece of paper and handed it to Shayna. She took it and tucked it safely into a zippered compartment in her handbag.

"*A shaynem dank* (thank you so much)!" the man cried profusely.

As they walked off the bus and toward the theater, Chaya-Sarah looked up at her mother and questioned her. "Mama, why doesn't that man go to America to be with his family like we're doing?"

"Not everyone has the means, *maidel*," she answered, her voice sounding sad and faraway. "Not everyone is able to go."

◆　◆　◆

In the winter of 1940, the Trans-Siberian Railway was the longest, single train excursion in the world. It departed Moscow twice a week and traveled eastward across Russia over 5,600 miles of an ever-changing panorama of mountains, flat plains and dense forests. The train made several stops a day in one of the many Russian cities, towns, and remote villages along its route until, approximately one week later, it reached Vladivostok, Russia's easternmost port city on the Sea of Japan. Even with the large distance and variety of terrain the train covered, the view out the window was of a snowy white landscape for the duration of Shayna and Chaya-Sarah's trip. They settled themselves into the cabin they shared with Regina and Gabriel. The women chose second-class accommodations and were pleased with their room that seated and slept four. There was a closet to stow their belongings and, at night, the two seats on either side of the cabin opened into beds. Hidden compartments above the seats opened into upper berths to sleep two more.

They boarded the train with a large and diverse group of people. Some were stylish, sweet-smelling women who leaned on well-dressed men carrying immaculate leather suitcases. They, Shayna presumed, were heading for their first-class cabins. Other people who were probably on their way to third-class seats did not look so privileged. They could very well have been refugees with their worn clothes and the tattered bags they carried. Shayna heard mostly Russian spoken in the snippets of conversations that reached her ear, but occasionally a Yiddish word floated by. *Thank God, we are among friends*, Shayna thought to herself. Still, she did not forget for a minute that she was traveling in a world that was often hostile to Jewish people, and she had many miles to go and more than one more border to cross before reaching the safety of America.

The women made themselves comfortable in their seats while they engaged in casual conversation about the layout of the train and the services it provided. Both women were watching their children as they spoke. Gabriel was paging through a superman comic book that a relative brought him from America before the war while Chaya-Sarah appeared to be searching the cabin for mischief to get into.

"It's going to be interesting keeping this one occupied for a week long ride on a train," Shayna said with a smile and a nod toward her daughter.

Their heads all turned suddenly when there was a knock at the cabin door. It opened slowly to reveal a smartly dressed, greying man in a dark blue, starched uniform with a white trim around the lapel and the pockets. He greeted them in Russian and asked to see their tickets. The women reached into their handbags as Chaya-Sarah walked over to him, fascinated by a gold chain that hung loosely from the hip pocket of his jacket.

He smiled when he noticed her staring at it and reached in to pull out a beautiful round watch with roman numerals that was attached to the chain and fit perfectly in his palm. He handed it to Chaya-Sarah. She smiled gratefully, took the watch and studied it while he checked their tickets and reviewed for the women the location of the showers and toilets as well as the dining and club cars. He told them that the club car was always open for drinks and snacks and explained the specific hours that the dining car was open for meals. Glancing at his watch in Chaya-Sarah's hands, he announced that the train will be departing in 30 minutes. The women thanked him as Chaya-Sarah returned the man's watch. He patted her on the head, wished them all a good trip, turned and left to attend to the people in the next cabin.

As a response to Shayna's comment before the conductor came in, Regina said, "Gabriel likes to read, but let's hope that there are some other children on the train that Chaya-Sarah can play with."

"Yes, let's hope," Shayna agreed, smiling wryly as she glanced at her daughter. "Otherwise, it's going to be a very long week."

◆　◆　◆

Later that day Shayna and Regina with their children trailing behind made their way to the dining car for dinner. They paused at the door to take in the scene before them. The elegant dining car was carpeted with a sea of tables adorned with white table linens, fine china and silverware. Wine was being poured at some of the tables by waiters dressed in white. The air in the car buzzed with the pleasant hum of spirited conversations punctuated by the clinking sounds of glass touching glass and silverware meeting plates. Shayna and Regina and their children found a table in the middle of the car just as a waiter was coming by and lighting silvery candelabras that stood at the center of each table. They took their seats at the table for four and noticed, as the sun went down, the darkening windows along the walls of the dining car began to sparkle with the reflection of the candlelight. The women sat across from one another near the windows and each child sat near the aisle. The children followed the example of their mothers and removed the carefully folded cloth napkins from the plates in front of them and set them gracefully on their laps.

Looking at the charming scene around her, it was easy for Shayna to forget that she and her daughter were refugees. Chaya-Sarah, too, got swept up by the finery, noticing with delight how the objects on the table vibrated with the motion of the train and created a symphony of sound. She moved her spoon nearer to the wine glass and laughed at the rat-tat-tat sound they made together. She looked over at her mother who was engrossed in a serious, adult conversation with Regina. Gabriel's nose was in his comic book. If Chaya-Sarah thought that no one noticed she was enjoying this amusement, she would have been wrong.

A young Russian soldier in a dark blue uniform winked at Chaya-Sarah as he took a seat, facing her, at the table on the other side of the narrow aisle. She gave him a shy smile, then continued to watch him as he moved his spoon nearer to his wine glass and gestured to her that he had an orchestra at his table, too. He winked, again, then he removed the cloth napkin and put it neatly on his lap. He ran his fingers through his thick, black hair, leaned forward on his elbows and began talking to his table companions. Apparently, the Russian soldier was more interesting than anything at her table, including the food, because during the meal Chaya-Sarah kept looking over at him. He was looking at her, too, and when their eyes met, he gave her another wink and a broad, warm smile that made him look quite handsome. The flirtation between Chaya-Sarah and her young Russian soldier continued throughout dinner that evening and contributed to the relaxed and convivial atmosphere in the dining car. By the time dessert arrived, the winks and smiles between the two blossomed into a fully formed friendship.

When the soldier finished his meal, he stood up and walked over to Chaya-Sarah's table. He bowed graciously, greeted the four of them in Russian and introduced himself as a captain in the Russian army. Shayna greeted him in Russian and introduced everyone at the table. Smiling at Chaya-Sarah, the soldier reached into his uniform's breast pocket and took out a square piece of paper. He said something in Russian, then handed it to her. She looked down at it and saw a picture of two adorable children, a boy and a girl with jet black hair like their father, smiling at the camera. The girl looked to be the same age as Chaya-Sarah and her brother was clearly younger.

"*Zayer shayn* (very beautiful)," she told him in Yiddish and passed it around the table.

He did not know what she said, but he knew it was something good. He shook his head proudly and began pointing to himself, nodding and raising his eyebrows, showing her that these youngsters belonged to him. Chaya-Sarah nodded and pointed to her mother to establish she understood the relationship he was trying to convey. Then she pointed to his pocket. *Were there more pictures in there?* she wondered. He took out another picture of an attractive young woman who must have been his wife. Chaya-Sarah smiled and nodded her approval. Continuing to address her mother in Russian, he invited them to join him in the club car tomorrow as he pantomimed the hand motions of playing cards. Chaya-Sarah immediately understood his gestures.

"Can I, mama?" Chaya-Sarah asked. "Can I play cards with the soldier?"

Shayna looked at the young man, then back at her daughter. "Yes, tomorrow," Shayna said to Chaya-Sarah as she smiled and nodded at the captain.

"Good, tomorrow then," he said and winked again at Chaya-Sarah.

Even though they had no common language, Chaya-Sarah and the young soldier played the next day for hours and the days that followed, filling what could have been a dreary, boring week with fun and games. He showed her magic tricks and taught her card games. When he saw how curious she was about his gun, he checked to ensure it was unloaded and then handed it to her. Other children stood by and watched with fascination as she studied it, but the soldier only let Chaya-Sarah handle it. She liked her soldier friend very much and he was charmed by the bright, effervescent girl who reminded him of his daughter. For Shayna's part, she was thrilled that her daughter was being so thoroughly entertained. She, of course, never let Chaya-Sarah out of her sight for a moment. Even during the many stops the train made that afforded everyone the opportunity to bundle up in their winter coats and step outside for some fresh, albeit very cold, air, Shayna made sure she was always able to see Chaya-Sarah's dark, dancing braids. At those stops all with unfamiliar sounding names like Novosibirsk and Tyumen, Shayna stood and chatted with Regina or some of the Yiddish-speaking friends she made aboard the train while her daughter played with her soldier friend in the mounds of white snow that surrounded the train stations.

It was five days into the Soviet journey when the train stopped in the city of Irkutsk. Many Russians knew this city to be the location of an important limestone quarry. Russia had been mining limestone since the nineteenth century and processing it into lime, the powdery substance used in building construction. It was a cold, but sunny morning with mounds of fresh snow piled high around the train yard, sparkling in the bright sunlight. A flurry of passengers left the train to stretch and enjoy the fresh air. Shayna and some friends stood and chatted near some large mounds of snow, their exhaled breaths instantly freezing into a white mist in the frigid air. Chaya-Sarah and her soldier friend were making snow-balls that they playfully tossed at one another. At one point, the soldier stopped to button his long, black coat against the cold wind. Chaya-Sarah saw this as a perfect opportunity for mischief. At the moment he was distracted, she ran at her friend with all her might, crashing into the side of his right leg. At eight-years-old, Chaya-Sarah was a slight twig of a girl, and certainly no match for the Russian soldier who, at six feet tall, was a formidable presence even to other soldiers. Balance, though, can be a strange thing for animals that walk on two legs. An unexpected shift in weight, especially when both feet are not firmly planted on the ground, can quickly change a vertical position to a horizontal one. Chaya-Sarah's playful attack did just that. It caught the soldier by surprise and toppled him right onto a large, white mound.

The soldier winced. To Chaya-Sarah's dismay, she saw that he was not laughing. Instead, the expression on his face made him appear to be angry or in pain. She wondered why he seemed so upset about falling into a mound of snow. Shayna had seen her daughter charge the soldier and cause him to lose his balance. She continued to watch carefully now, especially since the soldier did not seem to be responding with delight. Others noticed the fallen soldier, too, and a crowd began to gather around him and the girl who pushed him. Everyone watched as he picked himself up, frowning, and began to brush the powdery substance off his long, black coat. As he did, something unexpected began to happen. The snow he was trying to brush off was not disappearing from his coat. On the contrary, solid white streaks were being formed by the brushstrokes of his hands.

There were murmurs in the crowd as people tried to figure out what was happening. What many of them did not know was that the train station in Irkutsk was surrounded by large mounds of limestone. They were also unaware that unprocessed lime was as white as snow, but not nearly as soft. Packed into mounds, scattered around the train yard and waiting to be collected into burlap sacks, lime particles were a surprisingly hard surface. The particles also did not brush off a dark coat easily as would snowflakes. Even among the people who did not know he had fallen into a mound of lime, it was clear that the white substance on his coat was not snow.

The soldier looked down at his once spotless black coat now smeared with chalky, white streaks. He did not look happy. Chaya-Sarah stared at her friend in horror. Turning white as the lime, she held her breath as she waited for the repercussions. The soldier lifted his head slowly. His intense gaze fell upon the girl who did this to him. Shayna stood just a few feet away and was poised and ready to run over and rescue her child, if necessary. The soldier looked down, again, at his coat. Everyone was watching and it seemed like the whole crowd was holding its breath.

He looked back up at Chaya-Sarah who returned his gaze with unblinking, doe eyes. Suddenly, his mood seemed to change. He let out a hearty laugh that almost startled her. "My charming friend is also very strong!" he cried out. She did not understand his Russian words, but his laughter and the jovial tone in his voice told her everything she needed to know. Many in the crowd, especially Shayna and Chaya-Sarah, let out an audible sigh of relief. The soldier, still laughing, found a mound of real snow and began to use it to wash the lime off his coat. Chaya-Sarah smiled and ran over quickly to lend a hand. With some scrubbing, the wet snow easily removed the chalky lime residue from his coat. All was forgiven and the two were friends once more for the remaining days of the trip.

◆　◆　◆

On the afternoon of December 30, the train finally came to the end of its long journey across Russia in the city of Vladivostok. Shayna and Regina and their two children collected their belongings. Warm farewells were exchanged by all. Chaya-Sarah hugged her Russian soldier and from behind his back, he presented her with a doll with rosy cheeks and big, brown eyes. Chaya-Sarah beamed at him as she took the gift. Shayna tried to give it back to him, but he insisted so she thanked him graciously.

The four weary travelers walked away from the Trans-Siberian train station and into the Soviet port city. After traversing thousands of miles of desolate, unpopulated plains and remote farming villages, they were surprised to find themselves in a modern, bustling city. An advanced network of trams shared the streets with cars and taxicabs. The icy air barely lifted the mercury on the thermometer to ten degrees fahrenheit, so even though the sun shone bright in the clear, blue sky, its warmth was not felt. People rushed by in thick, winter coats and fur hats. The four of them walked out onto the sidewalk, bracing themselves against the unforgiving wind. Shayna bent down to ensure the knitted scarf she bought Chaya-Sarah in Moscow was wrapped snuggly around her daughter's neck. They made their way to the inn where they had a reservation and would, again, share a room for the night.

After dinner, they settled into their hotel room. When they finally got into bed, Chaya-Sarah snuggled close to her mother for warmth. "Can you sing a song, mama? she asked. Shayna sang to her daughter until she heard the soft, even breathing of her child as she fell into a deep sleep. Shayna laid her head back on her pillow. She thought of her husband a world away with still so many miles of land and sea between them. Tomorrow a boat would take them to Japan. From there, the plan was to board a ship bound for America. *America*, Shayna thought as she closed her eyes. The word sounded magical to her. She was exhausted, but anticipation kept her up most of the night. When she finally slept, she dreamed of a massive ocean liner and of Jonah's loving embrace.

CHAPTER 21

December 1940
Japan

Freedom is the oxygen of the soul.

~Moshe Dayan

From her comfortable seat on Shayna's lap, Chaya-Sarah turned around to see the glow of candlelight reflected on her mother's face. Even in her child's mind, she realized that for the first time in a long time, her mother looked relaxed, even happy. She was right. Shayna felt lighter and more hopeful than she had in a long, long time. It happened as soon as she stepped foot on the boat at the port of Vladivostok that would take them to Japan. It was a Japanese ship so they were officially not in the Soviet Union any longer. This brought Shayna and many of the refugees aboard this boat a great sense of relief. They felt relatively safer than they felt in the last year. At the same time, they harbored no illusions. They knew they were not home free yet and were very aware of the dangers they still potentially faced. Everyone aboard the ship knew that Japan entered the war, that the country had, in fact, signed an agreement with Germany and Italy just three months earlier. So, they felt sure that they needed to move quickly. These people also understood that, unlike the places they came from in Europe, the Empire of Japan bore no ill will to the Jewish people. They believed that in Japan they did not have to fear pogroms, economic sanctions, labor camps and other hostile actions. Most importantly, they hoped that their visas would enable them to safely enter Japan and board a ship bound for America.

The light mood of those bright thoughts was enhanced by this night of December 31 in 1940 being the last night of Chanukah. The Festival of Lights message of miracles was not lost on the Jewish refugees who boarded the ship that afternoon and gathered to celebrate just after sunset. Each of them felt that a miracle got them to this ship. Not that this was a fancy or even a large ship. In fact, the accommodations on the vessel did not compare at all to those on the Trans-Siberian journey that many of these passengers just recently enjoyed. Rather, this part of their travels was more on the rustic side. The ship was not a fancy one with its simple cots for beds, cramped cabins below deck and rough, wooden tables with benches in the main dining hall where they now gathered. They all bundled up in the drafty room and Shayna lifted Chaya-Sarah into her lap in an effort to warm her in the frigid sea air that bit sharply at ears and fingers and noses. No one complained, though, as they listened to a rabbi, who was among the refugees, recite the *bracha* (blessings) and watched him light the menorah candles. Many aboard the ship recognized Rabbi Isaac Rubinstein, the former Chief Rabbi of Vilna, and were honored and grateful for his presence. He and his wife were also on their way to America. They, along with Chaya-Sarah and Shayna, joined him in the blessings:

Baruch atah Adonai Elohaynu Melech Ha'Olam asher kideshanu bemitzvotav vetzeevanu leh-hadlik nayr Chanukah. (Blessed art Thou, Lord our God, King of the universe, who has sanctified us with His commandments, and commanded us to kindle the Chanukah light.)

Baruch atah Adonai Elohaynu Melech Ha'Olam shehahsah neesim lahahvotaynu bayamim hahaym bizman hazeh. (Blessed art Thou, Lord our God, King of the universe, who performed miracles for our forefathers in those days, at this time.)

After the candles were lit and the blessings recited, there was hugging, some dancing and many joyful shouts of "*A Freilachen* (Happy) Chanukah!" in the room. For the moment, everyone was grateful and felt happy. They were served a piping hot Japanese noodle soup for dinner. It was unlike anything any of them tasted before, but it was very much enjoyed and appreciated. "It's just like my mama's chicken soup," one man shouted. Everyone laughed and cheered in agreement. The good food, the glow of the lights and the warmth of the companionship helped everyone forget they were floating on a dark foreign sea far from any place familiar to them. For the rest of her life, Chaya-Sarah would remember that night on the ship and the hope she saw in her mother's beautiful, shining eyes.

After dinner, the weary travelers began to get up from the tables. They had been rocking on the open sea for almost six hours with at least fifteen more to go before they reached the shore of Japan. Everyone rose, steadied themselves on the boat and wished each other a safe journey. Celebrating Chanukah on the open sea was a first for all of them and they were tired and eager to get some rest. Shayna and Chaya-Sarah, along with Regina and Gabriel said good-night to their dinner companions and left the dining hall.

As they walked through the hallway on the way back to their cabin, they heard a door slam in the distance. That was immediately followed by the thunderous sound of feet, lots of them, pounding on the wooden deck. As the sound grew louder, the concerned women and children stopped and stared in the direction of the noise. Suddenly, they saw the reason for the commotion. Running toward them was a large group of young, Japanese men and they were naked! They were also soaking wet. Their bodies glistened with water droplets that flew off them in every direction. Each one looked down and mumbled something in Japanese as they raced by the shocked passengers. Shayna looked at her daughter whose eyes were as wide as saucers. Chaya-Sarah had never seen a naked man before. Within seconds, the men disappeared down a stairway and everyone began laughing.

"Oh my goodness," Regina cried out. "It looks like those young men just got out of the shower!"

"And," Shayna added, still watching Chaya-Sarah's reaction. "They forgot their towels!"

The group laughed all the way back to their cabin. Once there, the women helped their children change into their warmest night clothes. Regina commented that this room felt more like army barracks than tourist accommodations. Shayna agreed as she discreetly changed into a warm nightdress, put their clothes neatly back into the suitcase and placed their coats on several hooks in the wall. Chaya-Sarah jumped into bed, shivering in the cold air and waited for her mother to join her. With her position near the wall, she sang quietly to herself as she pulled a loose hair-pin out of her hair. Her hand naturally began scraping the hairpin against the wall. She did not notice that her action caught Regina's attention who watched with curiosity as the creative girl began to carve her initials into the wall beside the bed. Regina quietly snuck over to get a closer look just as Chaya-Sarah was putting the finishing touches on the letter *kaf* (k).

"So you're the one!" Regina exclaimed with a smile. Caught red-handed, Chaya-Sarah gave her a sheepish grin and slid under the covers.

That night on the sea was tough for the weary travelers. The ship pitched and tossed every which way in the choppy waters, and the icy wind found its way inside through cracks and crevices in doors and windows. In their flimsy cot, Shayna huddled with Chaya-Sarah under several blankets in an effort to keep her daughter warm and prevent her from falling out of bed as the ship rocked them back and forth. Then she tried to shut out the cries and moans of seasick people coming from other cabins so she could get some sleep. She did not get much, but as long as her daughter was comfortable, she was satisfied.

In the first morning light, Shayna was relieved to be able to get up to stretch and venture up on the ship's deck. She was thrilled to see the shoreline of Japan appear on the horizon. It was still far away, but there it was, the island country, the most distant and exotic place she and most of the other passengers ever ventured. As the ship got closer to land, Shayna was enchanted by the physical beauty of the island. Even in the harshness of winter, the bare, but ice-encrusted, maple and birch trees assumed a graceful shape. On the slender pine trees, mounds of pristine, white snow clung to outstretched branches like fluffy clouds floating in the air. As the ship docked, Shayna stood transfixed by the beauty of the scenery as well as the significance of their reaching the safety of Japan. She was still a long way from America, but she was so much farther from the war-torn countries they fled.

When the passengers slowly disembarked, they found a pleasant surprise awaiting them. Not only were the Japanese people friendly and kind, the authorities also sent representatives from the Jewish community of Kobe to meet the Jewish refugees at the dock. They graciously guided the travelers to the train station where they boarded the train for the two-hour ride to Kobe, the port city that they hoped would lead them to America. The envoy also provided the refugees with meticulously prepared pamphlets showing a map of Kobe and where to find hotels and eateries and other places they might need.

For Shayna, the first stop in Kobe was the Thomas Cooke Travel Agency where there was money from Jonah waiting for her. They booked passage on a ship that was to leave the port of Kobe on January 8. That was one week away. She wired a brief message back to let Jonah know that they arrived safely in Japan and when their ship was leaving. She wanted to tell him so much more, that the Japanese people were charming and she felt like a tourist here and not a refugee, and how she laughed when Chaya-Sarah pointed out the diminutive aspect of many of the Japanese people. *All that had to wait,* Shayna thought. *God-willing, it won't be long before I can tell Jonah everything in person.*

Japan was a fascinating experience for Shayna. The cuisine was strange, but delicious. She and the other Jewish refugees discovered that rice, which was plentiful at every meal, was just like kasha. Chaya-Sarah tried her first banana and loved it. The hotel where many of the Jewish refugees stayed was very comfortable and Shayna and Chaya-Sarah enjoyed their own spacious hotel room. At the center of the room was a large, shallow urn surrounded by cushioned pillows. Deep inside the urn were burning embers of coal that kept the room warm and cozy. The hotel also provided them with rubber hot water bottles that warmed their beds at night.

Shayna took advantage of the time they had before the ship left to do some siteseeing and enjoy the stores in and around Kobe. With no language in common with the people of Japan, Shayna and Chaya-Sarah did a lot of pantomiming and exaggerated gesturing to communicate. As they made their way around the city, Shayna always kept a piece of paper in her handbag with the name of the hotel on it just in case they ever got lost. For the first time since their escape from Poland, Shayna started to look forward to a brighter future. With some of her extra money, she bought a beautiful set of dishes that was packed carefully in a crate for the journey to America. While her mother was looking at dishes, Chaya-Sarah saw a delicate vase that she decided she must have. She told her mother she wanted it, but Shayna just shook her head from side to side.

"It's too expensive," Shayna told her. "And we don't need it."

Chaya-Sarah found her mother's response unacceptable. For some inexplicable reason, she needed to have that vase. She found a way, as only an eight-year-old can, to let her mother know that she was not leaving the store without that vase. It was only a few minutes into her daughter's tantrum that Shayna relented and the vase was purchased, wrapped carefully and placed with the set of dishes inside the crate.

Their hotel was a busy one with a steady flow of people coming and going in the lobby. Maybe because the country joined the war with Germany and Italy, Japanese soldiers seemed to be everywhere. Some proved to be helpful to the refugees staying at the hotel. One handsome young soldier seemed to take particular interest in Shayna, and she noticed him, too. It was hard not to. He seemed to always be there with a smile on his face and twinkle in his eye when Shayna needed help with something. The first time they saw him, they were getting out of their taxicab with the large crate of dishes. He quickly intervened even before the porter helped them and, lifting the crate, he joined them in the elevator, brought it to their room, and set it down carefully. He seemed to linger for a while, smiling at Shayna who offered him some tea.

Chaya-Sarah sat for a while with the two adults who were laughing and giggling over their tea. Not having any language in common, Chaya-Sarah could not imagine what they were talking about. They seemed so involved with each other, they did not even notice her. *Adults can be so strange sometimes*, she thought to herself. Looking for something to do, she went over to the urn and sat down on one of the velvety pillows. She lifted the large metal stick and began to stir the burning coals that filled the urn. The heat released by the moving coals warmed her cheeks and made her smile. She was amused by this activity for a while, until it got her mother's attention. Shayna jumped up and went over to scold her daughter and urge her to move away from the burning coals.

"Please stay away from this, *maidel*. It's not a toy for children," Shayna said as she took her daughter's hand and walked her to another part of the room. "You could, God-forbid, start a fire." Chaya-Sarah allowed herself to be led away from the coals, but her mother's comment did not end her fascination with the hot coals. In fact, it would only serve to make the coals even more irresistable to the young girl.

◆ ◆ ◆

Later that afternoon, Shayna and Chaya-Sarah went to bathe in the hotel's public bathhouse. Shayna learned that a public bath in Japan, called a *sento*, was a place where men and women bathed together, but in different parts of the pool. She was warned that it might seem like a swimming pool, but because it was a bath, no bathing suits were worn. Other Jewish refugees told her that it was like a *mikvah*, except there was one notable difference. The *mikvah* was a private bathing area while this was a shared experience.

When they arrived, they found the *sento* was empty with nobody in the water. Shayna looked around the room. Several vertical paper panels on a metal runner separated the pool into two halves, visually, if not physically. Shayna was somewhat confused by the set up. *Was it possible that the panels are there to separate the men's from the women's area of the pool?* Shayna thought to herself. She dismissed that thought when she tried to adjust the panels because, no matter which way she moved them, there was always an opening between the two sides. The panels did not seem to cover the area completely. *This whole area must be the woman's bath,"* Shayna thought because a woman at the entrance directed them into this room and these panels clearly did not provide very much privacy.

"Let's get undressed and get into the water," Shayna said. They started to unbutton their clothes when something stopped them cold. Two men with salt and pepper grey hair entered the *sento*. Shayna and Chaya-Sarah watched the two men come in, casually talking and laughing with one another. Suddenly the men noticed that they were not alone. They looked at Shayna and Chaya-Sarah, bowed deeply, then strolled to the other side of the room. Before Shayna could react, the men removed their clothes, acting as if being nude in front of a strange woman and girl was the most natural thing in the world. The naked men then walked at a relaxed pace into the pool. They submerged their bodies with only their heads and shoulders sticking out of the water. The two men looked up at Shayna and Chaya-Sarah, smiled warmly and waved.

Shayna was too shocked to do anything, but stare. *What do we have here?* Shayna asked herself. *This is no mikvah!* Then, to Shayna's complete surprise, they both began calling out something in Japanese and gesturing with their hands. It looked like they were motioning for her and her daughter to join them in the bath. Shayna was incredulous. It may have been a friendly gesture, but it had the opposite effect that the men intended. Shayna immediately took her daughter's hand and bolted out of the bathhouse.

◆　◆　◆

On Tuesday, January 7, the day before they were to leave for America, Shayna and Chaya-Sarah both arose early that morning unable to contain their excitement. They spent the day doing some last minute errands. Shayna needed to visit the Thomas Cooke Travel Agency one last time to collect money, pay for their passage on the ship to America and wire a message to Jonah. When they got back to the room, Chaya-Sarah felt sleepy. She cuddled with one of her dolls on the couch and immediately dozed off. When she awoke from the late afternoon nap, she rubbed her eyes and looked around the hotel room. Her mother was not there. She called out for her, but there was no answer. She was alone. She was not afraid to be alone nor was she concerned about her mother's whereabouts. She knew Shayna probably just stepped out for a minute to visit with a neighbor and would be back shortly. In the meantime, she tried to occupy herself with some wooden toys her mother bought for her, but she soon grew bored with them and felt restless. *What could she do*, she wondered, *while mama was out?* The room had grown cold and she shivered as she looked around.

Her eyes were immediately drawn to the red velvet, gold-tasseled cushions that were positioned comfortably around the coal-burning urn. The color and plush fabric made them look very inviting. She ran over and sat down on the plumpest looking pillow. She spied the large, iron stick for stirring the coals and suddenly remembered the delicious warmth emitted when the coals were stirred. She knew mama told her not to play with the coals, but the idea of the warmth was too irresistible. She reached for the stick. She just wanted to move the coals around to warm up the room. She began to poke carefully at the hot coals. Leaning in toward the urn, she felt its pleasant warmth reach her face and neck. The ambient air was still cold, though, and she remembered learning that the hotter coals were on the bottom, nearer the fire. Now, she tried in earnest to stir the coals, coaxing the hotter ones on the bottom up to the top. Focused as she was on stirring the coals and enjoying the heat, she did not notice the burning red ember that flew up and landed in the middle of one of the cushions on the other side of the pot. It was so tiny. And it lay quietly for a few seconds minding its own business. Then the burning ember began to feed on the delicious and combustible velvet pillow. As it fed, it grew—slowly at first—so Chaya-Sarah did not notice it.

She sat back on her pillow and was resting from her labors when she got the first whiff of an acrid odor in the air. It was different than the warm, burning smell that came from the coals in the urn. This smell was more intense, almost sour. The child shrugged and went back to tending the coals. The fire was growing on the pillow on the opposite side of the urn, so she did not see it. Nor did she notice the sinewy curl of black smoke that began to rise from the burning pillow and snake up into the air. It would take a few more minutes and a bright curl of yellow flame to lick the air above the pillow for Chaya-Sarah to realize that something other than coal was on fire. She jumped up and stared in shock and disbelief at the velvet pillow on the other side of the urn. It was on fire. The flames danced upward and seemed to be growing right in front of her frightened eyes. Her hands flew to her opened mouth as she gasped in horror and instinctively backed away from the fire. Fear and panic set in, but she knew exactly what to do.

"Mama!" she cried as she ran to the front door. She burst through it and immediately looked right and then left for her mother, but the halls were empty. She turned back around. The fire was getting bigger and she could see the curl of black smoke rising from the cushion that was now completely engulfed in flames. She turned back to the empty hallway and called out for her mother. When there was no response, she dashed up and down the empty halls, banging on doors and crying out, "Mama, where are you? Mama there's a fire!"

Suddenly, a door across the hall flew open and there was Shayna. She had not been gone long, maybe ten or fifteen minutes. *What on earth happened in that short time?* She ran over to her breathless child, "*Mayn kind, vos iz der mer* (My child, what is the matter)?"

Chaya-Sarah felt there was no time for words. She grabbed her mother's hand and pulled her back into their room. It did not take long before Shayna smelled the pungent odor of the fire, then saw the flames. Adrenalin filled her body. Her eyes frantically searched the room and fell on the pitcher of water on the dressing table. She grabbed the pitcher, ran to the cushions, and emptied the full contents of the pitcher over the flames. The flames immediately drowned in the cold water and were gone. Just the charred cushion remained along with the acrid smell of burned fabric.

Shayna frowned at the damage, but breathed a sigh of relief, then immediately turned to her daughter. She pulled her daughter in close and cried, "*Vey iz mir,* are you okay? How did this happen?"

"Yes, I'm okay, mama," Chaya-Sarah answered, looking guilty. "I was just trying to warm up the room." Before Shayna could respond, there were other voices in the room and both Shayna and Chaya-Sarah looked up to see their soldier friend coming in. Some other people were standing in the doorway as well. He walked over and seeing the doused fire in the burned pillow, realized what had happened. He looked at Shayna, questioningly, then at Chaya-Sarah.

"We're fine," Shayna said, shaking her head and looking at her daughter.

The soldier waved to the others at the door to signal that everything was fine. He then put an arm around Shayna and said some words in Japanese that sounded comforting. Shayna shook her head. She imagined he was saying that at least no one was hurt. Some of the others came in to check on them and a few more words were said between the adults. Shayna thanked everyone then sat down on the bed, exhausted. Everyone saw that they needed to leave the mother and daughter alone, muttered quietly to one another and left the room.

When the door closed behind the last person to leave, Shayna looked at her daughter. Chaya-Sarah looked back, but was not able to read her mother's eyes. They were open wide, but dark and impenetrable. A remorseful Chaya-Sarah slunk over to her mother, preparing herself for the punishment she knew she deserved. Yet Shayna remained quiet. Chaya-Sarah stood very still, holding her breath. After a few minutes, Shayna took her daughter's braided head gently into her hands, looked into her eyes, and asked, "*Vos vel ikh ton mit dir* (What am I going to do with you)?" Chaya-Sarah had heard this enough to know the question was rhetorical. They both looked at each other for a few minutes and Chaya-Sarah was shocked when the mother she thought would be so angry with her inexplicably pulled her close and hugged her.

"Let's go have dinner, then we'll come back and finish packing," Shayna said. "Thank God, we're leaving tomorrow."

Chaya-Sarah nodded. She was relieved that mama was going to let this one go. What she did not know was that her mama was too exhausted to reprimand her for misbehaving. In fact, all Shayna really wanted to do was get on that ship to America, right this minute. She did not even care about packing their things. She would even have been fine traveling steerage. It was not so much physical exhaustion. No, it was more an emotional weariness. Seeing that pillow engulfed in flames seemed emblematic of the events of the last year and four months. It made everything she had been through suddenly come crashing down on her at once. She felt the weight of it all—the fear for their lives, the uncertainty, the separation from loved ones, the distance between her and her husband. She had enough of all of it—enough running, enough war, enough being a single mother, enough living in a hostile world.

Shayna released her daughter, but kept her at arm's length while she looked at her. "I love you so much, *maidel*," she told her child. "You're my whole life."

"I love you, too, mama," Chaya-Sarah said as her mother pulled her into another hug.

"God-willing, we'll see your father soon," Shayna said, choking up. "I need your father." She had not meant those words to come out that way. She was surprised they had. Shayna gently moved her daughter away to look at her, again, her sweet girl with the bright, cocoa-brown eyes. Shayna smiled now to lighten the mood. "He has more patience than I do."

Shayna was ready to reach America and she was more than ready to find Jonah.

CHAPTER 22

January 1941
United States of America

Democracy . . . grows directly out of the Israelite vision
of individuals, subjects of value because they are images of
God, each with a unique and personal destiny. There is no
way that it could ever have been "self-evident that all men
are created equal" without the intervention of the Jews.

~Thomas Cahill, *Gifts of the Jews*

The sun was high in the sky that Wednesday in January when Shayna and Chaya-Sarah stood on line at the dock in Kobe, Japan, waiting to board the oceanliner that will take them to America. Regina and Gabriel, his nose planted firmly in a book, stood directly behind them. As they moved closer, Chaya-Sarah became aware of the ship towering majestically above them. Her breath caught in her throat as she lifted her head to observe the full height of the huge vessel. Her head then slowly swept from side to side as her eyes took in the full expanse of the ship from bow to stern. Even the round silver-framed portholes lined up in a neat row along the side of the ship seemed more like pin holes than windows relative to the size of the ship. She had never before seen a man-made conveyance whose size was on such a monumental scale. She was accustomed to being smaller than many around her, yet she never felt so tiny before. The ship, dubbed the S.S. *President Pierce,* was part of a fleet of ships owned by the American President Lines. The ship was originally named the Hawkeye State when it was built in 1921. At that time, it was the largest American combined passenger and cargo ship to sail the Pacific ocean.

"*Azoy groys* (it's so big)!" she remarked as she took her mother's hand and continued to stare at the steel mountain before her.

"Yes, *maidel*, it certainly is," Shayna responded smiling down at her daughter, then her eyes swept the floor to make sure that their suitcase and the crate of dishes were still by her side. She clicked open her handbag and took out their ticket. She could not read it, but that was no matter. She knew what it meant. Yesterday, Regina read her the words on the ticket and explained them to her to begin her English language education. "En route from Kobe to San Francisco" were the words that thrilled her. Next was the ship's name, and the sailing date of January 8, 1941. She shivered when she heard the words printed below the ship's name and sailing date:

THE SUM OF EIGHT ($8) DOLLARS, U.S. CURRENCY TO COVER TAX REQUIRED BY THE UNITED STATES FOR ALIENS IN ACCORDANCE WITH "AN ACT TO REGULATE THE IMMIGRATION OF ALIENS INTO THE UNITED STATES" AND ISLAND POSSESSIONS.

The shiver had nothing to do with the money. These words reminded her that it was a privilege to enter the United States of America, not a right. She also knew that it was, unfortunately, a privilege denied to many. She took a deep breath and slipped the ticket carefully back into her handbag and snapped it shut. Shayna kissed her daughter's head, then looked up at the ship. She felt the steady thrum of her heartbeat keeping time with the ship's engines as the line of people shuffled forward, bringing her closer to the ship that would carry them to a new world.

Finally, it was their turn to show their ticket and walk onto the ship. Boarding the S.S. *President Pierce* with her daughter by her side, she felt like she just stepped on American soil. Her heart soared. The *Goldene Medinah* (Golden Land)—that light in a long, dark, dusty tunnel of ignorance and oppression—was truly within reach. Since the day she was born, Shayna heard about this mysterious and far off place. A place of hope and salvation, and in the imaginations of many, it was the answer to all their questions and the solution to all their problems. Some spoke of it wistfully, like the man on the bus in Moscow who saw it as a distant, glowing star that would always be far away. For others, like Shayna, it was an attainable miracle, but only now did she allow herself the luxury of believing that. A small, secret part of her that had gone to sleep when she watched Jonah's train leave the station in Warsaw began to awaken and allow her to believe that he was truly within her reach.

As she busied herself getting acquainted with the ship and finding their cabin, she did not notice the lightness in her step and the cheerful animation in her conversation that had not been there for a long time. She laughed easily and found humor in everything. Even their third-class accommodations, less than perfect, were a source of merriment. She and Regina agreed to take what was left of the accommodations so that they could leave on an earlier ship. When they entered the room, they realized that it would be noisy in their cabin which was situated on the floor just above the engine room. Shayna just smiled. "No matter . . . At least the heat from the engines will keep us warm at night," she said cheerfully as she began unpacking some of their clothes and hanging them in a barely adequate, doorless closet.

A few hours later, Shayna and Chaya-Sarah were leaning against the railing of the ship, looking out over the ocean and toward their future. Other passengers waved down to friends who stood on the port, cheering and wishing them a safe trip. As the crowd grew more dense, Shayna got behind her daughter and embraced her as they both held onto the railing and waited for the last leg of their journey to begin. They were electrified by the excitement in the air and transfixed by the beauty of the Pacific waters. The sudden and deep bellow of the ship's horn, signalling its departure, made them both jump. "Mama, that's the loudest sound I ever heard!" she remarked as she put her hands over her ears. Shayna thought silently to herself, "Good, she's already forgotten the bombs in Poland." The horn sounded again. Almost immediately they could feel the ship begin to move. Shayna was elated even as thoughts of her siblings and their children weighed heavily on her mind. She prayed silently to God to keep them safe and let them survive the war.

The voyage across the sea was a calm and relaxing one. Shayna's charming and outgoing nature made her many new friends, and Chaya-Sarah loved being at sea. Walking on the outer deck of the ship with her mother, she marveled at the endless beauty of the shimmering water. It fascinated her that there was water as far as her eyes could see. She always had a sense that the world was a big place, but only now did she see how big. At night, she leaned on the railing as far out as her mother would let her and feasted her eyes on the sparkling tapestry of stars that blanketed the expanse of darkness around the ship. "Look mama, I saw those same stars in Poland!" she said as she pointed to the sky, recognizing the shapes of some of the constellations from stargazing with her father.

Chaya-Sarah made her share of new friends, too. One such group of friends were American soldiers who fell in love with the bright young girl with the sparkling eyes and long braids. She played card games with the young, handsome men who were far from home. They shared with her some of the toys they were bringing home for the children in their lives, and introduced her to citrus fruit. She eyed the bright orange ball with wonder as they showed her how to peel back the skin and separate the juicy sections. They all roared with delighted laughter when her eyes opened wide as she bit down on the fruit and the tangy sweet juice sprayed into her mouth for the first time.

A gathering of Greek diplomats who were aboard the ship could also be counted among Chaya-Sarah's admirers. One day she was playing below in the cabin when Gabriel came running in, excited and out of breath. He immediately sat down on his bed and began playing with not one, but two decks of cards.

"Where did you get those?" Chaya-Sarah wanted to know.

"The Greek guys gave these to me," Gabriel answered her, his eyes never leaving the cards.

"They gave you two decks?" Chaya-Sarah was suspicious now.

"Actually, they told me one was for you, but I need them both," Gaby confessed.

"One of those decks is supposed to be mine?" she questioned him, hands on her hips.

"Sorry," Gabriel said sheepishly. "But my brother and I play a game that uses two decks."

Chaya-Sarah glared at him, then she left their cabin and immediately began searching for the Greek diplomats. She looked in all the usual places, then finally found them sitting at a table and playing cards. She approached them and they greeted her warmly. Without having a language in common, she somehow managed to convey to them that Gaby would not give her the deck of cards they gave him for her. When they figured out what she was saying, they all looked at each other in dismay. One of the men reached into a briefcase and brought out another deck of cards for Chaya-Sarah who smiled and thanked him graciously. She played with them for a while, then ran to show her mother her new deck of cards and tell her the story of how she got them. Later that night as they ate dinner with other passengers at a large, round table, Shayna recounted the tale of her daughter confronting the Greek diplomats and securing the deck of cards that was originally meant for her.

"*Mayn kleyn maidel hot groyse chutzpah* (my little girl has a lot of nerve)," Shayna proclaimed proudly.

"*Azoy vi ir mama* (like her mother)," Regina added as she smiled and lifted her glass of wine.

After a pleasant week-long cruise on the waters of the Pacific ocean, they began to see the first signs of land. Their ship was approaching Waikiki, Hawaii on the island of Oahu where it would dock for one day. As the ship got closer to the port, Shayna and Chaya-Sarah stood on deck watching the tropical wonderland reveal its beauty. The two were struck by the beautiful blue of the sky and the sparkling, golden sand of the beach. They had seen palm trees in pictures, but never in real life and never an endless forest of them. Exotic birds some with bright yellow heads soared above the ship as if to welcome them. And the air was so fresh and sweet, Chaya-Sarah felt like she could taste it. She was enchanted.

After the ship docked, passengers were able to get off for several hours. For many, including Shayna and Chaya-Sarah, that time was spent exploring the island of Oahu. They visited Diamond Head, a popular tourist destination and one of the many volcanic cones in Hawaii. It was named by British soldiers one hundred years earlier who mistook the volcano's sparkling minerals, called calcite crystals, for diamonds. On the climb up to the crater, Chaya-Sarah sat down on a bench that was situated under the most amazing tree she had ever seen. It created a perfect canopy over the bench like a giant umbrella. Near the bench was a large rock. It called to her. She removed a hairpin from atop her braided head and carved her name, leaving her mark in this beautiful island world. Chaya-Sarah was here. Her mother watched her and just laughed.

When they returned to the ship that evening, they were tired but very happy. Spending the day amid such peaceful and natural beauty washed away any remaining tension they carried with them during their escape from war-torn Europe. To add to their joy, both Shayna and Regina had letters waiting for them from their husbands. They both opened their letters with great excitement.

"Max says that he has a lovely apartment waiting for us when we get to New York and it is completely furnished," Regina announced with a smile, looking over at her son.

In Shayna's letter, Jonah told her that someone from Thomas Cooke will meet them when they arrive in San Francisco the next day. He will have money and their train tickets to New York. That was wonderful, but there was no news of an apartment. Shayna and Chaya-Sarah were happy for Regina and thrilled that they were getting closer to Jonah, but hearing about her apartment made them feel somewhat sorry for themselves. It also got Shayna thinking and worrying. Where would they live in New York City? She knew there was only one bedroom in Esther's apartment. Jonah had been sleeping on a couch in the living room. There was certainly no room for her and her daughter.

"Don't worry," Shayna said, reassuring her daughter and herself, "*Tati* has something for us, too."

◆ ◆ ◆

The next day, on January 22, 1940, the ship docked at the port in San Francisco. Shayna took a deep breath as she stepped onto the soil of the contiguous United States, the same soil on which Jonah stood. Shayna felt a flutter of excitement in her chest. There was a nip in the air, but it was nothing like the freezing cold they experienced in Europe and Russia. They found the Thomas Cooke agent waiting for them just as Jonah wrote. He presented them with their tickets for the five-day train ride to New York City and more than enough money for food and anything else they needed along the way. The train was leaving the next morning so they would be staying in a hotel overnight.

Later that night, Shayna was in bed, ready to turn out the lights, while Chaya-Sarah stood by the window, gazing out at the night sky. "Come to bed, *maidel*," Shayna urged. "We have to get up early tomorrow morning to get the train." But Chaya-Sarah did not move. She was transfixed. Atop the building just across the street was a most amazing sight. She looked up in wonder at a giant winged horse that seemed to be ready to fly off into the dark night. The horse was a brilliant red and the light emanating from the image was even brighter than the sun. Just below the horse were the strange looking symbols **MOBIL** which were similar to symbols she saw on the ship and on signs in the ports. She knew from Shayna that they were American letters that she will soon be learning in school. She squinted her eyes to accommodate the intensity of the light from her first neon sign.

The next morning Shayna and Chaya-Sarah bid farewell to Regina and Gabriel Weinreich who wanted to stay in San Francisco and do some siteseeing before going to New York. The women embraced and wished each other well. They both expressed gratitude about having one another's company for the journey from Lithuania. They talked about getting together at some future time and the different challenges that lay ahead of them. Regina and her husband who had both travelled to New York many times, planned to continue the work that was started in Lithuania—writing, researching and helping to build the YIVO Institute For Jewish Research—in New York City. Shayna, along with her husband, planned to build new lives for themselves and their daughter from the ground up, learning English, securing jobs, and creating a home in this foreign land.

Shayna and Chaya-Sarah boarded the train for the five-day journey to New York City without their former traveling companions. Regina's knowledge of English had been helpful both on the ship and at the American ports. Now, Shayna was somewhat at a loss. The people she encountered on the train were all English-speaking. The mother and daughter were happy to keep mostly to themselves, staying in their cozy berth with Shayna sleeping or enjoying the scenery that passed by the window as Chaya-Sarah played with the toys that the soldiers on the ship gave her. They were both getting more and more anxious to reach Jonah and, after the calamitous events of the last year and a half, were happy to just relax and enjoy the steady thrumming of the train's wheels on the tracks. They ventured out into other areas of the train when they got hungry and needed to stretch or use the facilities.

The train stopped at many stations along the way, some humble and some quite large. As the train approached each stop, she heard, from an overhead speaker, a fuzzy voice making a static-filled announcement in English that was impossible for Shayna to understand. This was followed by some people leaving the train and others boarding. Shayna noticed that the train stopped at the smallest stations for only five or ten minutes and the larger stations for a few minutes longer, but it never stopped for more than fifteen or twenty minutes. She was familiar with trains so she became accustomed to this rhythm and was not concerned that she did not understand the words over the loudspeaker. She knew that New York City was the last stop where everyone will be getting off and, most importantly, Jonah would be waiting.

On the third day, the train stopped in a very large train station in a city called Chicago. Shayna practiced the foreign word to herself as she had been doing with other English words she was beginning to learn. She listened for the word 'Chicago' over the loudspeaker and noticed, too, that this announcement was longer than usual. And when it was over, something odd happened. Every single person on the train got up and one by one filed out the door. *Well, this is strange*, Shayna thought. Not only was everyone leaving, but no one was getting on the train. She grabbed her handbag and she and Chaya-Sarah followed the people leaving the train. As they walked, she approached different people in an effort to get information about what was going on.

"*Antshuldik mir* (excuse me)," Shayna said in her native tongue. "*Far vos geyen ale mentshn aroys fun der ban* (Why is everyone leaving the train)?"

Unfortunately, everyone responded with blank stares and shoulder shrugs. Shayna was starting to wonder how she was going to find anyone who could help her when a young man with sandy hair and a briefcase approached her. He looked at her, then began pointing to the watch on his left wrist. He slowly made two circles around the watch face. He then pointed in the direction that everyone was walking and looked at Shayna questioningly. She responded by repeating the circular motion twice, holding up two fingers, then motioning they needed to follow everyone out of the train station. From what Shayna could gather, the train would be stopped at this station for two hours. The man shook his head vigorously in agreement. Shayna nodded and thanked him as he smiled and turned to leave. She looked at her watch and made a mental note of the time they needed to return to the train, then they followed the crowd out of the train station.

Shayna and Chaya-Sarah braced themselves against the frigid winter wind that assaulted them outside. Holding hands, they walked up and down the sidewalks of downtown Chicago, enjoying the variety of items in the shop windows and taking care not to venture too far from the station. They found a busy diner with silver chairs and bright blue seat cushions. The place was so crowded, they were not able to get a table, so they sat at the counter on round seats that had the same blue seat cushions. Chaya-Sarah was thrilled when she discovered she could spin around and around in her chair. She continued to do so until her mother complained of getting dizzy and asked her to stop. They both ordered egg salad sandwiches on rye bread. It was the most familiar item on the menu. Shayna ordered a cup of coffee to drink and a glass of milk for Chaya-Sarah. As soon as the milk was served to her, she thanked the waitress. As her fingers encircled the glass, she paused. She noticed two strange things. One was that the glass was cold. The other was that there was no froth at the top of the white liquid. She hesitated and eyed the drink suspiciously.

"Mama, this milk doesn't seem right," she announced.

"The milk is different in America," Shayna responded. "Try it," she urged. Chaya-Sarah was thirsty so she took a sip and instantly recoiled and pushed the drink away.

"This can't be milk, mama, it's awful!" she cried out with an expression of disgust on her face. "It tastes like cold water!"

Shayna tasted it and had to agree. It looked like milk, but it smelled and tasted completely unlike the milk she and her daughter grew up with. Chaya-Sarah was accustomed to drinking milk that came directly from the mother cow. It was warm and rich, and tasted almost like what Americans called cream. This cold, pasteurized American milk was something very different. From that moment on, Chaya-Sarah decided she would never again drink milk.

After they finished their sandwiches, Shayna looked at her watch. "Let's order dessert. We have plenty of time before we need to go back to the train. What do you want?"

Chaya-Sarah watched a waitress go by with a plate that held a shiny, red square topped with white swirls of what looked like cream. It looked delicious. "*Vos iz dos* (what is that), mama?" she asked as she pointed to the table where it went. Shayna got the attention of their waitress who was, along with the other waitresses, wearing a white dress with pink trim on the sleeves and a pink belt. Shayna pointed with raised eyebrows to the interesting looking dessert.

"That's jello," said the waitress exposing a large wad of chewing gum in her mouth. "We have it in lime, cherry, or orange and it's served with whipped cream."

Shayna and Chaya-Sarah looked at each other. They did not understand what she just said, but whatever it was, Chaya-Sarah wanted what was on that other customer's plate. She pointed to it and the waitress shook her head that she understood and wrote something on her pad, then she looked at Shayna. Shayna pointed to a piece of bobka that was on display on the counter on a raised plate with a glass cover. "Coming right up," the waitress said cheerfully, still chewing her gum.

Chaya-Sarah was delighted when the plate of delicious looking dessert was placed in front of her. She did not eat it right away, though. She was having too much fun playing with it. She discovered that when she touched the red substance, it moved in a funny way. She prodded it harder and laughed when it shuddered and swayed then snapped back into its original position. The only food she ever saw move that way was *shmaltz* (chicken fat) when a big glob of it had fallen on the floor. It was so slimy and elusive, it was almost impossible for her mother to clean up. She gingerly scooped a piece of the jello and watched it dance on her spoon as she moved it in front of her face.

"Are you going to play with your food or eat it?" Shayna asked with a smile.

Chaya-Sarah opened her mouth to let in the smooth, jelly-like substance. Her eyes grew wide as she removed the spoon from her mouth and let the strange food dissolve on her tongue. She thought about it for several seconds then cried out, "Mmmmm, *karsh* (cherry)!" Then she gave the next spoonful to her mother who tasted the sweet confection and nodded her head in approval. They each enjoyed their desserts, then Shayna looked at her watch. An hour and a quarter passed since they left the train. Although they had plenty of time, she did not want to risk missing their train, so she told her daughter it was time to go.

Chaya-Sarah took her last bite of jello and whipped cream as Shayna opened her handbag and took out the right amount of American dollars to cover their lunches and the tip. Then they bundled themselves into their coats with Shayna making sure that her daughter's was buttoned all the way up. After being in the warmth of the diner, the cold air hit their faces and lungs like a spray of snow and ice. It was a bright, blue-sky kind of day, but the sun was unable to raise the temperature of the frigid air. Shayna looked around, got her bearings and took her daughter's hand as they began to hurry toward the train station.

Once at the station, they went directly to the original track where their train stood when they left it. But when they arrived, Shayna was shocked. There was no train on the track. Nor were any people there. Shayna gasped audibly. She knew the train had been here. That was exactly where it was when they got off. She looked around and started to panic. *Where was the train? Did it leave already?* She looked at her watch again. It was not two hours yet. What will she do if they missed their train? Did she have enough money to pay for another pair of train tickets? What about their suitcase and all their things? Shayna immediately began to look for people with whom she could communicate to find out what happened to their train. The first two people she encountered spoke only English. The second two people also spoke only English. The fifth person spoke Spanish. Shayna was able to communicate with her due to the Spanish she picked up the years she lived in Uraguay. Apparently, their train had been taken away to be cleaned. That was what happened in Chicago and why everyone was able to leave for a few hours. After cleaning, it would be on a different track. Shayna thanked the woman profusely. She was so relieved, but felt even better when they got to the right track and found their train waiting for them.

Fifteen minutes later, they were sitting comfortably in their seats, but the remnants of the panic she just experienced were still with her. Shayna looked down at her daughter who sat beside her. Chaya-Sarah held some dolls on her lap, but she was tired and rested her head on her mother's shoulder. Shayna could still feel the pounding of her heart as the train came to life and began its journey to New York City. She sat back and took a deep breath to calm her jangled nerves. They were less than a day and a half from Jonah, and she vowed silently to herself that they would not step off this train until she saw his face.

◆　◆　◆

On the morning of January 27, 1941, Jonah paced back and forth along the platform in front of Track 9 at Pennsylvania Station. Built in 1910 by the Pennsylvania Railroad company, the station was a marvel of neoclassical architecture with marble columns, pink granite and tall arching windows that reached skyward. But Jonah did not notice these grand design elements. His mind was only on his wife and daughter, as it had been since he left them at the train station in Warsaw. Since that painful moment, not a second passed that he did not think about them and long for them. Now that they were almost here, he could not contain his excitement. He looked at his watch. The train was due in fifteen minutes.

"*Yonaleh*, sit down," Abe urged him. "You'll wear out your shoes." Abe took the day off work to be with his younger brother as did their sister Esther and her husband, Izzy.

"Come sit next to me," Esther coaxed as she made room on the bench where she sat with Izzy and patted the space next to her. Jonah sat, but not for long. An announcement of a train's arrival was made over the loud speaker. It was not his wife and daughter's train, nevertheless, Jonah jumped up and looked at his watch. What was it now, ten minutes? He was so nervous, he began pacing again and wondered to himself, *how can ten minutes take so long?*

When the train from Chicago pulled into the station and finally came to rest on the tracks, Jonah could not wait another minute. He pushed opened the doors and rushed onto the train and began running through the aisle in search of his family. As he ran, he searched the faces, hungry for those of his wife and daughter. They were not in the first car, so he ran on. They were not in the second car. As he stepped into the third car and looked up, his heart leapt. There they were, his two beautiful girls just a stone's throw from him, gathering their things. He called out to them. They both heard a voice they had not heard in a long time, but they knew it as surely as they knew their own voices. They looked in Jonah's direction, saw him and screamed.

"Yonah!"

"*Tati!*"

The next few minutes would be remembered by all involved as a blur of arms and embraces, kisses and tears. Jonah swept his daughter up into one arm and embraced his wife with the other. Just before he did, he noticed, through salt-water soaked eyes, that Chaya-Sarah looked taller, a painful reminder of the time that passed when he was not with her. Her growth spurt notwithstanding, at fifty-nine pounds, his slight girl still felt as light as a feather. She kissed her father's cheek too many times to count. She did not realize how much she missed the warm, spicy smell of her father's aftershave lotion. She put her arms around him and buried her face in his neck. They all held on as if they would never let go. In this moment, time seemed to stop. The longed-for reunion finally and miraculously arrived. For all three of them, it was as real as anything ever felt, but they still could not believe it was happening.

Shayna and Jonah laughed and cried as they released each other to be able to get off the train. With his free hand, Jonah grabbed the crate of dishware and Shayna the suitcase. They inched their way off the train and met up with the others on the platform. Jonah did not take his eyes off his wife who returned his loving gaze as she hugged her sister- and brothers-in-law. Greetings were exchanged and everyone began talking at once as the tears flowed freely and handkerchiefs were removed from pockets to dot eyes and blow noses. Abe sniffed as he stuffed his handkerchief back into his pant's pocket. "Ok, let's go," he said. "My niece and sister-in-law must be very tired and very hungry." The group all murmured in agreement.

Still tethered to one another, they moved en masse to the station's Thirty-third Street exit. Out on the sidewalk, they stopped for a minute as Izzy pointed out the direction of the nearest subway entrance. Chaya-Sarah lifted her head from its nest in Jonah's neck, and squinted in the bright morning light. They all began moving toward the subway, but she noticed that her mother did not. Shayna stood in place as if she were frozen to the spot on the sidewalk.

"Oy, the dishes," Shayna cried out, her right hand involuntarily flying to the right side of her face. "We forgot the dishes!"

In a flash, they all joined Shayna in the realization that in the excitement of the moment, they left the crate on the platform beside the train. Without another word or a moment's hesitation, they all turned and rushed back into the train station. They quickly made their way back to

Track 9 to retrieve the goods. When they arrived at the area, the train was still there and only a few people were milling about. They went to the spot where they last saw the crate beside the third car. The space was empty. There was no crate with the beautiful dishware that Shayna bought for her new home in America. They all stood for a few minutes, staring at the concrete floor as if the crate might magically appear. Not surprisingly, it did not. Jonah began running down the length of the train in search of the crate among items left on the platform. When he found no crate, the family watched as he exchanged words they could not hear with a train station employee. When the conversation ended, Jonah turned and walked back to his family. No one needed to ask what he found out. The answer was on his face. Their crate must have been stolen. Shayna immediately broke the silence.

"A *ganof* (thief) took my dishes," Shayna said bitterly, "Let's go."

The group walked somewhat dejectedly out of the train station, and found their way to the subway entrance. Chaya-Sarah was hesitant as they walked down a stairway that took them underneath the sidewalk. She did not understand how it was possible for a train to travel underground. After a ten-minute wait in the subterranean world, the train appeared before them. Chaya-Sarah was delighted and amazed. They boarded the nearest subway car and were whisked into a dark tunnel.

◆　◆　◆

An hour later, they arrived at Esther's apartment in Brooklyn. Abe's wife, Rose, was waiting there with two of their children, Harvey and Melvin, who were a few years younger than Chaya-Sara. They were afraid to meet their strange relatives from Poland, so they hid under the kitchen table. The rest of the family sat around the table, listening to Shayna's stories of their escape. Aunt Esther served eggs, bulls-eye style, and French fries with Heinz ketchup to the weary travelers. Chaya-Sarah thought she never tasted anything so good. After they ate and rested for a while, Jonah took them to visit his aunt Chava-Shayna, his father's sister, who lived in the building next door and was eager to see them.

On the way there, Shayna's thoughts turned to where they were going to live. She did not want to bring it up yet, but Jonah still had not said anything and the suspense was too much for her. "Where will we be staying?" Shayna asked Jonah.

"We'll stay with Esther and Izzy for a little while," Jonah responded.

"Esther and Izzy only have a one bedroom apartment," Shayna said.

"Yes, they do, but we'll be fine," Jonah said dismissively. "You'll rest up, then we'll find an apartment to rent." Jonah glanced over at Shayna. She did not look happy.

When they returned to Esther's building after visiting Jonah's aunt, they began to climb the stairs to Esther's second floor apartment. Shayna and Chaya-Sarah were tired, too tired to notice that Jonah passed the floor where Esther lived and continued walking up the stairs to the third floor. Still oblivious to that fact, they exited the stairwell and followed him down the third-floor hallway. When Jonah stopped in front of a door, they waited patiently while he removed a set of keys from his pocket. He unlocked the door and held it open for them. Dutifully, mother and daughter entered. Before them was a large, beautifully furnished apartment that did not look at all like Esther and Izzy's. It was more spacious and had completely different furniture. Both mother and daughter studied the strange surroundings with confusion, then looked questioningly back at Jonah.

"Whose apartment is this?" Shayna asked.

Jonah did not have to answer. His broad smile and sparkling eyes told them everything. Chaya-Sarah ran over to her father and looked up at him adoringly. "*Tati*, is this ours?" Chaya-Sarah asked.

"It's all yours, *maidel*, and your mama's," he said beaming at his daughter. She hugged her father, then raced off to investigate the new apartment.

"But you said . . . ," Shayna began, then stopped immediately.

"I wanted to surprise you," Jonah answered. "Esther helped me pick out the furniture. Of course, it still needs . . ." He was interrupted by Chaya-Sarah who came running back to her parents.

"Our apartment has three bedrooms!" she cried out joyfully. "Come and see, mama!"

Shayna was speechless. Tears of joy filled her eyes and slid silently down her cheeks as she gazed at her husband. Jonah's warm, brown eyes looked back at his wife with so much love. He put his arm around her shoulders and she reached around his waist. They both turned their heads to watch Chaya-Sarah explore every nook and cranny of her new home—sliding drawers open, peaking into closets and bouncing on beds and couches.

Shayna took a deep breath as the corners of her mouth inched upward slowly and started to create a smile. Before that could happen, her mind began to race with thoughts about what she needed to do to ensure her family's comfort and well-being in their new home. The list was a long one. She wanted to get started right away. For now, though, she would stand this way with Jonah just a little while longer.

Epilogue

I know not with what weapons World War III will be fought,
but World War IV will be fought with sticks and stones.

~Albert Einstein

In June 1941, six months after Shayna and Chaya-Sarah reached American soil, Nazi Germany broke the Molotov-Ribbentrop Pact and began the invasion of Russia. They used the same moment in time to begin their relentless assault on the Jewish citizens of Eastern Europe. Historians and eye witnesses have recorded the horrific details of the Holocaust. It is not necessary to repeat them here, but the evidence is clear. Had Shayna and Chaya-Sarah remained in Poland or Lithuania in June of 1941, they would have likely not survived. They missed the Holocaust by six months.

In September 1942, the ship that brought Shayna and Chaya-Sarah to America, the S.S. *President Pierce,* was converted to a warship and its name was changed to the U.S.S. *Hugh L. Scott.* In November of that same year, the ship was among several that were torpedoed by two German submarines, the *U-130* and the *U-173.* The ship caught fire and sank off the coast of Morocco. The *U-173* was later sunk by U.S. destroyers. The *U-130* escaped.

When the war was finally over in 1945, Shayna and Jonah searched high and low for surviving family members. They hoped and prayed that their loved ones and friends escaped the horrors that the world, at that time, was only beginning to understand. Shayna and Jonah placed many ads in the Classified section of newspapers and included their address and phone number. They combed phone books and contacted family and friends all over the world to find out if anyone heard from the family members they left behind. They were grateful to discover that Shayna's eldest brother, Yehuda (Yudke) Ozdoba escaped to Israel along with his wife, Rivka, and two sons, Shmuel and Itzak. One daughter remained in Russia.

Over time, Shayna and Jonah began to discover relatives, friends and acquaintances who managed to survive. Some of these people had, during the course of the war, encountered a family member and reported where the relative was last seen. Finally, a grim picture emerged. Of Shayna and Jonah's siblings and their spouses and children, only those who left Poland before 1941 survived. Everyone else was either murdered in the Holocaust or died fighting in the war.

In Memoriam

Edke Ozdoba, her husband, Meerche, and their children were murdered in the Holocaust. Edke was last seen in Baronowicze, Poland.

Mirzsa Ozdoba, her husband, Chaim Ladowicz, and their children Volf and Dvora (Dvairie) were murdered in the Holocaust.

Rachel Kaufman, her husband, Mayer Nissky, and their children were murdered in the Holocaust in 1942.

Rivka Kaufman, her husband, Nachman, and their children were murdered in the Holocaust. A family friend, Chaim-Beryl, reported they were last seen in either the Treblinka or Sobibor Extermination Camps.

Shmulke Ozdoba served in the Polish army. It is presumed that he died fighting and his wife and children were murdered in the Holocaust.

Sholem Ozdoba served in the Polish army. He, his wife, Etta, and their three children were murdered in the Holocaust in 1943.

These children of Yehuda (Yudke) Ozdoba were murdered in the Holocaust: Dovid Ozdoba; Mordecai Ozdoba; Jakob Ozdoba and his wife, Elka; Rachel Ozdoba, her husband, Yisrael Chmiel, and their son Avraham.

May their memories be a blessing.

Postscript

In 1946, Jonah received a phone call from a Polish man he did not know. The man said he wanted to buy the house in Zbojna that Jonah and Shayna built. Apparently, the man and his brother were fighting over it. The man thought he could outsmart his brother by locating the owner and purchasing the house. Once he became the rightful owner, he could kick his brother out. The only problem was that Jonah refused to sell it to him. "Let them fight over the house," he told his family, "I don't want his money."

Sixty years later, Helen (Chaya-Sarah) and her husband, Bob, visited Poland. They hired a Polish translator and toured the areas where Helen's ancestors had lived for centuries and where she spent the first seven years of her life. Amazingly, they encountered an elderly couple in Zbojna who remembered Shayna and Jonah Kaufman and always wondered what happened to them. The couple knew the story of the two Polish brothers who fought over the Kaufman's abandoned house after the war. The woman did not know that one of the brothers had contacted Jonah decades earlier. She only knew that the argument went on for several years until eventually the house burned down. Everyone assumed that one of the brothers finally settled the dispute with a match. The couple showed them the property where the house had been. Helen stood on the spot where her life began. It was a modest plot of land and there was no house on it, but it was not empty. It was abloom with the soft purple sprays of wild lilac bushes.

Sylvia (Shayna), Helen (Chaya-Sarah) and Jonah Kaufman
in Catskill Mountains, New York, 1947

Helen (Chaya-Sarah) Kaufman with I. Robert (Bob) Twersky
on their wedding day, March 19, 1950

A Note from the Author

This book is an account of a true story that was told to me by my grandmother, Sylvia Kaufman (born Shayna Ozdoba), and my mother, Helen Twersky (born Chaya-Sarah Kaufman) who both experienced it first-hand. I heard the events of this story throughout my childhood, but as an adult, I sat with them, together and separately, in a series of interviews, to collect the details and answer my questions. Some of these interviews were recorded on audiotape and others were written by me in the form of copious notes. My grandfather, Jonah Kaufman, had sadly passed away when I was twelve-years-old so, although I knew him very well, many of his experiences were told to me by my mother and grandmother. Following the interviews, and to inform my telling of the story, I studied maps of their route. I also did years of research on the historical facts of the two world wars and the Holocaust, genealogical records, America's stance in WWII and on immigration, Jewish life in Poland prior to 1939, and the Jewish immigrant experience in America in the 1930s.

Please note that I created the following people, names, or events to support the flow of the narrative:

- I made up the name *Aaron* to refer to the husband of Shayna's cousin Mindel (Mindy) Lipkovich Berkowitz. He was a real person as were any details provided about him; however, neither my mother nor grandmother remembered his first name. Apologies to any of his living relatives. Corrections are welcome.

- I made up the name *Raisa* to refer to the wife of Shayna's brother Shmulke Ozdoba. She was a real person as were any details provided about her; however, my mother and grandmother did not remember her name. Apologies to any of her living relatives. Corrections are welcome.

- I made up the names *Gittel* and *Meryl* to refer to the two women Shayna met at the Lithuanian border. They were real people as were any details provided about them; however, my mother and grandmother did not remember their names. Apologies to any of their living relatives. Corrections are welcome.

- The woman (with all the packages) and man (reading the paper) on the wagon Shayna rode when first leaving Zbojna are fictitious and based on the many people I imagine my grandmother encountered on her journey.

- With a few exceptions, dialogues in this story are dramatizations based on my imagination. They are there to propel the story forward and to help the reader understand the characters, their motives, and their actions. The tone and content of all dialogues in the story, however, are firmly rooted in actual facts given to me by my mother and grandmother as well as based on my knowledge of the characters, their relationships with one another and the outcome of events in the story.

All other names, people and events in this story are true and presented, to the best of my ability, in a narrative that captures the story as it was reported to me by my mother and grandmother.

Acknowledgments

To my immediate family: Andrew, Brian, Ehud, Ethan, Fran, Jacob, Jennifer, Jessica, Jordan, Kimberly, Robert, Shayna, Steve, Suzanne, and Zev. You are the descendants, by blood or marriage, of Sylvia (Shayna) Ozdoba and Jonah Kaufman and their daughter Helen (Chaya-Sarah) Kaufman Twersky. I thank each of you for helping make this project a labor of love and I am grateful for your constant and loving support that gave me the courage and drive to complete this project. This book is truly for you. May it serve to help you and your descendants gain a richer understanding not only of the people who came before you, but also of your place in the grand parade of human history.

To my editors: I am eternally grateful to Judith J. Slater and Harriet L. Amato without whom this book, in its present form, could not exist. They poured over the manuscript for this book more than once, looking for errors and discrepancies as well as making suggestions to improve the flow of the story. Only through their efforts—the careful scrutiny and fine-tuning of my words—has this book come as close as I believe it has to being worthy of my family's remarkable story. They also both helped turn a career writer of instructional manuals into a one-time literary non-fiction writer as was my dream. There is no way I can imagine having the pride and confidence in my telling of this story without the magnificent contributions of their time and effort, judgment and guidance.

To my alpha readers: Fran King Twersky, Jessica Twersky, Judith J. Slater, Suzanne Twersky Nevo and Wendy Bratter. It is not an exaggeration to say that I could not have done this without you. The emotional rollercoaster ride of writing a book whose subject is so near and dear to one's heart requires a lot of support. You were there for every word—encouraging me, asking pertinent questions, and providing the feedback that helped me believe in this project and carry on. Sometimes just knowing that you were eagerly awaiting the next chapter was all the motivation I needed to get in front of my computer and forge ahead. I cannot thank you all enough.

To my genealogy consultants and foreign language translators: Many thanks to Rosa Bondar Pinsky who was my stalwart and intrepid navigator through the complexities and vagaries of post-war Jewish genealogy. She helped me find information about my family members who perished that I would not have otherwise found. I am also very grateful to Moishele Mario Alfonso who provided expertise in the Yiddish words and expressions used in the book. (Apologies for not always using the standard YIVO spelling of some words.) Many thanks to my other translators—Annetta Borukovich (Lithuanian), Kenneth Ivor Jeffries and Akilco Tanaka (Japanese), and Roman Pinsky (Russian)—for their time and effort in helping me uncover the meaning of historic documents written in unfamiliar languages.

To other family and friends: Donna and Tom Rubenoff, Joan Finkelstein, Karen Weiss, Kathy Stein, Karmit Pilossof, Marcia Friedman, Miriam Hoffman, Nancy Wyman, and Sandra Jeffries. Over the many years I have worked on this project, each of you, in your own special way, has helped create an everflowing fountain of encouragement, inspiration and support. Thank you all for many excellent ideas and, most importantly, for your interest in this story and enthusiasm for the book!

To my dear readers: Many thanks to you for reading this book and for being a part of carrying the memories of my family and the lessons of their story into the future.

To my references: This list would not be complete without mentioning the many fine books and their authors who were an important part of my research. They helped me confirm the facts of my family's story as well as frame it in the proper historical context. They also served to deepen my knowledge and understanding of the world of Eastern European Jewry prior to World War II. They are too numerous to mention, but here is a small sampling of the most meaningful:

- *Flight and Rescue,* United States Holocaust Memorial Museum

- *Memories of My Life in a Polish Village,* 1930–1949, by Toby Fluek

- *On the Edge of Destruction: Jews of Poland Between Two Wars,* by Celia S. Heller

- *Paper Walls: America and the Refugee Crisis, 1938–1941,* by David Wyman

- *Poland Virtual Jewish History Tour,* by Rebecca Weiner and Mitchell Bard

- *Yiddish: A Nation of Words,* by Miriam Weinstein